NEW TESTAMENT COMMENTARY

By

WILLIAM HENDRIKSEN

Exposition
of
Philippians

BAKER BOOK HOUSE

GRAND RAPIDS, MICHIGAN

ISBN: 0-8010-4029-9

First printing, July 1962
Second printing, September 1968
Third printing, November 1971
Fourth printing, April 1974
Fifth printing, September 1975
Sixth printing, September 1977

PRINTED IN THE UNITED STATES OF AMERICA

TABLE OF CONTENTS

LIST OF ABBREVIATIONS

The letters in book-abbreviations are followed by periods. Those in periodical-abbreviations omit the periods and are in italics. Thus one can see at a glance whether the abbreviation refers to a book or to a periodical.

A. *Book Abbreviations*

A.R.V.	American Standard Revised Version
A.V.	Authorized Version (King James)
Gram.N.T.	A. T. Robertson, *Grammar of the Greek New Testament in the Light of Historical Research*
H.B.A.	Hurlbut, *Bible Atlas* (most recent edition)
I.S.B.E.	*International Standard Bible Encyclopedia*
L.N.T. (Th.)	Thayer's *Greek-English Lexicon of the New Testament*
L.N.T. (A. and G.)	W. F. Arndt and F. W. Gingrich, *A Greek-English Lexicon of the New Testament and Other Early Christian Literature*
M.M.	*The Vocabulary of the Greek New Testament Illustrated from the Papyri and Other Non-Literary Sources,* by James Hope Moulton and George Milligan (edition Grand Rapids, 1952)
N.N.	*Novum Testamentum Graece,* edited by D. Eberhard Nestle and D. Erwin Nestle (most recent edition)
N.T.C.	W. Hendriksen, *New Testament Commentary*
R.S.V.	Revised Standard Version
Th.W.N.T.	*Theologisches Wörterbuch zum Neuen Testament* (edited by G. Kittel)
W.D.B.	*Westminster Dictionary of the Bible*
W.H.A.B.	*Westminster Historical Atlas to the Bible*

B. *Periodical Abbreviations*

AThR	*Anglican Theological Review*
Bib Sac	*Bibliotheca Sacra*
Coll Mech	*Collectanea Mechliniensia*
ExT	*Expository Times*
JBL	*Journal of Biblical Literature*
JThS	*Journal of Theological Studies*
NTS	*New Testament Studies*

Please Note

In order to differentiate between the second person singular (see Phil. 4:3) and the second person plural (see Phil. 1:3), we have indicated the former as follows: "you"; and the latter as follows: "y o u."

Introduction
to
The Epistle to the Philippians

I. Reasons for Studying Philippians

The search for "tranquility" is on, and in a big way! In order to attain peace of mind Americans are swallowing tons of tranquilizers. In addition to the *drugs* there are the tranquilizing *books*. These have become best-sellers overnight, single editions running into the hundreds of thousands. Those who read them are urged to wind themselves like clocks, and to begin the day by saying to themselves:

"What a wonderful morning this is! And what an exceptionally fine wife (or husband) I have! And what lovely children! What a wholesome and delicious breakfast awaits me! And what a congenial boss I have at my job!"

But such "peacefulizers" may do more harm than good. They provoke the following objections:

First, whenever the soothing thought fails to comport with reality, the ease of mind which results will fail to be of an enduring character.

Secondly, the most stubborn fact of all is *sin*. No amount of mental push-ups or "positive thinking" can brush it aside.

Thirdly, the only peace that is worthy of the name is peace with God. This cannot be self-manufactured.

Fourthly, those *trusting in* tranquilizers, whether books or pills, could be proceeding from the false assumption that spiritual unrest or soul-struggle is an evil in itself. But it is often far better to *face* reality than to try to *escape* it. Evasion leads to spiritual torpor. Confronting the facts about oneself is the only course which can lead to "the peace of God that surpasses all understanding."

Now if one wishes to know how this *real* peace or tranquility of heart and mind can be obtained, he should turn to that epistle which contains the very expression which was just quoted (Phil. 4:7). This little gem of four sparkling chapters pictures a man who has actually found it. He has unearthed life's most cherished treasure. He is "the happiest man in the world." Listen to him, as he says in this epistle:

"Rejoice in the Lord always; again I will say, Rejoice."

"I have learned in whatever circumstances I am to be content. I know what it means to live in straitened circumstances, and I also know what it means to have plenty. In any and all circumstances I have learned the secret, both to be filled and to be hungry, both to have plenty and to be in want. I can do all things in him who infuses strength into me . . . I am amply supplied."

3

And this man who had learned life's greatest secret was a prisoner in Rome, facing possible death by execution!

So, the reasons for studying the epistle to the Philippians are the following:

1. It reveals *the secret* of true happiness. How this happiness can be obtained is clearly disclosed in this letter.

2. It reveals *the man* who had learned the secret. Philippians is one of the most personal of all of Paul's epistles. It shares this characteristic with II Corinthians, I Thessalonians, and Philemon. Nowhere are we brought closer to the real Paul, pouring out his heart to those whom he deeply loves.

3. It reveals *the Christ* who taught him the secret. Christ as our Pattern and Enabler is portrayed here in the greatness of his condescending love (Phil. 2:5-11; 4:13).

II. The City of Philippi

Without a knowledge of the history and geography of Philippi it is impossible to derive the most benefit from a study of Philippians.

A man of restless energy, determination, and organizing talent was Philip II, the father of Alexander the Great. When he seized the throne in 359 B. C., the "Macedonia" over which he began to reign was about the size of the state of Vermont or of Maryland. Consult a map of Northern Greece. (It was a small segment of that vast region which originally was called *Thrace.*) To the East it did not even touch the Strimon River. To the South it left the three-fingered Chalcidice Peninsula outside its boundary. To the West it hardly touched what is now Albania. And to the North it pushed up for a distance of perhaps nowhere more than forty miles into what is now Jugoslavia.[1] Philip set about at once to "modernize" his army. He gave it longer spears, charging cavalry, better organization, etc. With this new tool he began to extend his domain.

Armies and expeditions, however, are expensive. So Philip annexed the gold-region [2] in the neighborhood of a place which because of its numerous springs was called Krenides, meaning "The Little Fountains." He enlarged this town, naming it after himself, "Philippi." With such eagerness did he work the gold-mines that he secured from them more than one thousand talents a year, using some of the revenue to maintain his army and some to enlarge his kingdom by means of bribes. He is reported to have made the statement, "No fortress is impregnable to whose walls an ass laden

[1] See the map on p. 313 of H. G. Wells, *The Outline of History*, Garden City, New York, Star-edition, 1930; cf. this with the map "Lands of the Bible Today" in the December, 1956 issue of *The National Geographic Magazine*.
[2] Cf. Strabo VII, 34.

with gold can be driven." And so, "This gold of Krenides spread itself over Greece, preceding the phalanx like an advance guard and opening more gates than the battering rams and catapults" (Heuzey). And the territorial expansion begun by Philip was continued on an even larger scale by his son, Alexander.

Inestimable consequences flowed from this conquest. It has been truly said that if Philip and Alexander had not gone East, Paul and the gospel which he proclaimed could not have come to the West. For, these conquerors brought about the *one* world of Hellenistic speech that made possible the spread of the gospel to many regions.

The city founded by Philip was situated fully ten miles inland from the Gulf of Neapolis (now Kolpos Kavallas), northwest of the island of Thasos in the Aegean Sea. By Paul it must have been regarded as a city in the North, for while the place of his birth, Tarsus, was situated 37° N. lat. (like Springfield, Missouri), and Jerusalem where he received his training 32° N. lat. (like Montgomery, Alabama), Philippi was located 41° N. lat. (like the city of New York). To reach Philippi from the sea a person would have to enter a port which, in common with many other places, bore the name Neapolis (cf. "Naples"), that is, "new city." Probably because this was the place where Paul landed, bringing the gospel of Christ, it was subsequently called Christopolis. It still exists under the name of Kavalla, and is today the heart of the Greek tobacco industry.[3]

Proceeding from Kavalla a person crosses the Pangaeus Range through a narrow depression. A stretch of the old Roman highway, the Via Egnatia, connects the port with the ruins of Philippi. From the crest of the hill between the thriving port and these ruins one has a marvelous view. Looking *back*, one beholds the Aegean Sea with its islands: Thasos to the southeast and Samothrace much farther away, to the east. One can even discern to the south the towering summit of Athos. Looking *ahead* one sees the plain of Drama, skirted by mountains and watered by the Gangites. This plain can be lovely. It can also be a terrible marsh. The contrast depends on the season of the year when one happens to view it. On a hill which dominates this plain lay Philippi. An air-view reveals the ruins of two churches and the remains of the Roman forum.[4]

---

[3] See the article "Jerusalem to Rome in the Path of St. Paul," in *The National Geographic Magazine*, December 1956, p. 747; also the photograph on p. 179 of *Everyday Life in Ancient Times*, 1953, published by the National Geographic Society, Washington, D.C.; and the air-views in connection with the text of Acts 16 and of Philippians 1 on pp. 18 and G11 of *The Good News, The New Testament with over 500 Illustrations and Maps*, published by The American Bible Society.

[4] Cf. W. J. Conybeare and J. S. Howson, *The Life and Epistles of St. Paul*, reprint 1949, Grand Rapids, pp. 219-226; Herodotus vi. 46, 47; vii. 113; Strabo VII. 34, 35; 41-43; W. Keller, *The Bible As History*, New York, 1957, p. 384; E. G. Kraeling, *Rand McNally Bible Atlas*, New York, 1956, pp. 438–440; and G. Ernest Wright, *Biblical Archaeology*, London, 1957, pp. 255-257.

Two centuries after the founding of Philippi Rome conquered Macedonia, and divided it into four political districts. To the famous Roman general Aemilius Paulus belongs the credit for the decisive victory at Pydna (near Mt. Olympus) on the western shore of the gulf of Salonica (168 B. C.).[5] By this time, however, the gold mines having become nearly exhausted, the city of Philippi had been reduced to "a small settlement" (Strabo VII. 41). In the year 146 B. C., Macedonia became one of the six provinces governed by Rome.

The subsequent enlargement of the city resulted from the important event which occurred here in 42 B. C. It was then that the historic battle of Philippi took place between Brutus and Cassius, defenders of the Roman republic, on one side, and Antony and Octavian, avengers of Caesar's death, on the other. After two engagements Antony and Octavian were victorious, Brutus and Cassius were dead.[6]

Soon afterward Philippi was made a Roman *colony* and was called *Colonia Julia Philippensis*. Antony settled some of his disbanded veterans there. There followed (31 B. C.) the naval battle of Actium, an ancient Grecian promontory in Epirus off the Ionian Sea (see N.T.C. on Titus 3:12). It was here that Octavian won the victory over Antony, who had become hopelessly infatuated with the woman who was his undoing, namely, Cleopatra, the romantic Egyptian queen who previously had been the mistress of Julius Caesar. Realizing the hopelessness of their cause both Antony and Cleopatra committed suicide.[7]

Octavian had now become sole head of the Roman Empire. His new name was *Caesar Augustus:* in 29 B. C. he was declared *Imperator;* in 27 *Augustus*. When he dispossessed the partisans of Antony of their estates in Italy, these people were now given the privilege of joining earlier Latin-speaking settlers in Philippi. The name of this city now became

COLONIA JULIA AUGUSTA VICTRIX PHILIPPENSIUM

Philippi, then, was a Roman *colony*. As such it was a Rome in miniature, a reproduction on a small scale of the imperial city. Its inhabitants were predominantly Romans, though the natives lived alongside of them and gradually coalesced with them. The Roman citizens naturally took great pride in being Romans. Moreover, they enjoyed all the rights of Roman citizens everywhere, such as freedom from scourging, from arrest except in

---

[5] Plutarch's *Aemilius Paulus* is unforgettable; especially the manner in which he contrasts the Roman general with the Macedonian king, Perseus.

[6] Cf. Plutarch, *Brutus* XXXVI–LIII and (same author) *Caesar* LV–LXIX (Shakespeare's *Julius Caesar* is based on Plutarch); also F. B. Marsh, *A History of the Roman World From 146 to 30 B. C.*, London, second edition 1953, pp. 281-284.

[7] Cf. Plutarch, *Antony;* see especially XXV–LXXXVII; Shakespeare, *Antony and Cleopatra* (based on Plutarch); Dryden, *All For Love* (a reworking of Shakespeare); G. B. Shaw, *Caesar and Cleopatra* (dealing with Cleopatra's earlier years); F. B. Marsh, *op. cit.*, pp. 295-311.

extreme cases, and the right to appeal to the emperor. Their names remained upon the rolls of the Roman tribes. Their language was Latin. They loved to dress according to Roman style. The coins of Philippi bore Latin inscriptions. Each veteran received from the emperor a grant of land. Upon the entire community, moreover, the *Jus Italicum* was conferred, so that the inhabitants of this city enjoyed not only economic privileges, such as exemption from tribute and the right to acquire, hold, and transfer property, but also political advantages, such as freedom from interference by the provincial governor, and the right and responsibility to regulate their own civic affairs.

In control of the government of the city was a pair of officials who were fond of calling themselves *praetores duumviri*, that is, *the two civic commanders*, freely translated στρατηγοί in Greek. And as in Rome, these *civic commanders* or *magistrates* had their fasces-carrying *lictores*, that is, *policemen* or *constables* (ῥαβδοῦχοι).

In creating here and there such *colonies* Rome knew what it was doing. The advantages were mutual: not only did *the colonists* receive many privileges, as has been shown, but also *Rome* profited by this arrangement, for thus its frontiers were being safeguarded against the enemy and its veterans were being rewarded.

We are now in a better position to understand (a) Luke's account in Acts 16 with reference to the establishment of the church in Philippi, and (b) Paul's epistle to the Philippians. As to the former, see the next section: The Church at Philippi. As to the latter, note the following:

(1) Paul, writing from a prison in Rome, mentions the progress of the gospel among the members of *the praetorian guard* (1:13). He refers to this guard because he knows that his readers, many of whom belonged no doubt to the families of veterans, would have a lively interest in it. In no other epistle does the apostle mention this guard.

(2) He says, "Only continue to exercise y o u r citizenship in a manner worthy of the gospel of Christ" (1:27).[8] In the light of the facts which have been enumerated it is probable that the earthly (Roman) citizenship of which the Philippians were proud is *the underlying idea* of the heavenly citizenship to which the apostle refers. Spiritual realities, however, always transcend earthly symbols. Thus, though many citizens of Philippi probably felt perfectly at home in their city, so that they would not have exchanged Philippi for Rome to take up residence there, believers, on the contrary, can never feel at home here on earth. They realize that their homeland, the country to which they as citizens belong, is in heaven, and that they are sojourners and pilgrims here below (Phil. 3:20).

---

[8] Cf. W. J. Conybeare and J. S. Howson, *op. cit.*, pp. 223-226; Raymond R. Brewer, "The Meaning of POLITEUESTHE in Philippians 1:27," *JBL* LXXIII, Part II (June, 1954), pp. 76-83.

(3) He speaks about the grievous suffering which the readers have to endure and the bitter conflict in which they are engaged (1:27-30). Philippi, being Roman to the core, had its imperial cult. It can be assumed that the non-Christian community — especially the *Augustales* who deified the emperor — exerted heavy pressure upon the Christians to join in this emperor-worship. Resistance to this pressure resulted in reproach and persecution. This, no doubt, was *part of* their suffering. It was not the *whole* of it. See comments on the passage.

(4) Here in a Roman colony, more than almost anywhere else, there was a tendency to flatter Nero with divine titles and honors. Hence, it is in such an epistle as this that the glory of Christ, his full deity, is set forth (2:5-10), in order that the readers may remain unswervingly loyal to *him* as to their *only* God and Savior.

(5) Greetings from members of *Caesar's household* (4:22) are mentioned *in this letter only*. See on 4:22.

III. The Church at Philippi

In the course of his second missionary journey (A. D. 50/51-53/54) Paul, accompanied by Silas and Timothy, reached Troas, located to the south of what is considered the site of ancient Troy. Although Troas is today a deserted ruin, in the time of the apostle it was one of Asia's chief ports. Here the vision of "the man of Macedonia" summoned the missionaries to Europe. Here also they were joined by Luke (Acts 16:9, 10). The ship on which they sailed must have passed the Aegean outlet of the Hellespont, for it made a straight course to the island of Samothrace, where Demetrius had set up the world-famous statue of Victory. On the next day the party reached Neapolis, Philippi's port. Here the boat-trip ended. It had been a speedy one, having taken only *two* days. The winds must have been favorable; contrast the trip in the opposite direction — Neapolis to Troas — toward the close of the third missionary journey, which was going to take *five* days (Acts 20:6). From Neapolis the missionaries proceeded at once on foot to Philippi. In obedience to the direction of the Spirit Paul performed most of his labors in important centers; such as Pisidian Antioch, Philippi, Corinth, Ephesus, Rome. It has long been held that this was a policy which he followed in the firm belief that from the more strategic centers the gospel-message would fan outward,[9] as it actually did. At any rate, Philippi was an important center. Luke says, "and from there to Philippi, since it is

---

[9] In *Paul and the Salvation of Mankind*, Richmond, Va., 1959, J. Mund rejects this idea.

INTRODUCTION

a leading city of the district of Macedonia, a colony" (Acts 16:12). In addition to *political*, Philippi also had *geographical* and *commercial* significance. From Philippi on the Egnatian Way the traffic moved via Dyrrachium, Brundisium and the Appian Way, to Rome (and vice versa).

This city of Philippi was so unlike any which the travelers had visited thus far that they had to spend a few days here to get their bearings. Then came their first Sabbath in Europe. At the western exit of the city a great colonial arch-way spanned the Via Egnatia, which about a mile farther crossed the swift and narrow Gangites River that empties into the Strymon. Somewhere along the bank of the Gangites the men found "a place of prayer." The word used in the original occurs at times as a synonym for "synagogue." Here, however, there seems not to have been a synagogue: no *men* were present; there was no formal worship, and no reading of law and prophets. There were probably few Jews in Philippi. Is it possible that also in showing a hostile spirit toward the Jews this *Roman colony* had followed the mother-city? These were the days of Emperor Claudius (A. D. 41-54) who, though at first friendly to the Jews, had subsequently ordered them to leave Rome (A. D. 50 or shortly afterward). At any rate, Paul and his companions spoke to *the women* that were gatherered at this place of prayer for their Jewish religious devotions.

In the little group assembled here was a woman named Lydia. Her home-town was Thyatira (now Akhisar, Turkey), on the way from Pergamum to Sardis (Rev. 2:12, 18; 3:1), in the province of Lydia, in what today is called Western Asia Minor. Though a born pagan, she had become acquainted — in her native town? — with the religion of the Jews and had accepted it as her own, having become a proselyte of the gate. Hers surely was a far superior way of worshipping God than any pagan cult with it foolish idolatry and gross immorality. Yet, somehow it had failed to give her complete satisfaction, the peace which her soul craved.

She was a business-woman, and may have been a widow who was continuing the pursuit of her late husband. We may think of her as an importer. She was a seller of purple. That should cause no surprise, for the place of her birth was located in the heart of the region of the purple-garment industry. Such garments were expensive, for the purple dye was derived from the shellfish in the waters of Thyatira, and the throat of each shellfish produced only *one* drop of the dye! (A cheaper grade was obtained by simply crushing the shellfish.) Now since Philippi was a Roman colony it was naturally an excellent market for purple garments. Romans loved the royal color! With it they trimmed togas and tunics. They wove it into their rugs and tapestries. Philippians were eager to copy Rome and its customs. To handle such an expensive product Lydia must have been a woman of means. The account in Acts supports this conclusion, for it implies that she

9

had a spacious mansion in Philippi, perhaps a typical Roman town-house of the better class, one that had ample room to accommodate several guests.[10]

As has often been remarked, Lydia had come from Asia with her earthly treasures, and was about to discover spiritual treasures in Europe. Though she probably had to walk a considerable distance to get to the place of prayer on the river-bank outside the city, and though she did not expect, perhaps, that the scheduled meeting would be of any great significance, *she went!* And here she met the missionaries, who spoke with great conviction, proving that the Old Testament prophecies, with which she was acquainted, had been fulfilled in Jesus Christ. The chief speaker was Paul. Whether Lydia was converted at that first meeting or subsequently is not clear from the text and is unimportant. The main fact is that by means of the preaching of Paul this woman, whose heart the Lord had opened, was led to accept Christ. So was her "household" subsequently. Then she and all the members of her family were baptized.

At once Lydia gave evidence of the genuine character of the great change in her life. Her eager generosity reminds one of Mary of Bethany (see N.T.C. on John 12:1-8). With rare tact she extended an invitation which the missionaries could not refuse, for rejecting it would have amounted to an insult. She said, "If y o u have judged me to be faithful to the Lord, come into my house and stay." Her wish, so urgently expressed, prevailed (Acts 16:15).

It is clear from Acts 16:40 that Lydia was by no means the only convert in Philippi. Moreover, men as well as women were translated from the kingdom of darkness into that of light. But while matters were proceeding favorably something occurred which at the time must have been considered an unpleasant interruption. One day, as the missionaries were going to the place of prayer, a female fortune-teller met them. She was a slave owned by masters who were making money out of her gift. Her lot was indeed a sorry one. She had "a spirit, a Python" (thus literally, Acts 16:16).

In Greek mythology the word *Python* refers, first of all, to a serpent or dragon that dwelt in the region of Pytho at the foot of Parnassus in Phocis, north of the Gulf of Corinth. It was believed that this dragon used to guard the oracle of Delphi with its oracular sanctuary. He was, however, slain by the god Apollo, as Ovid describes most interestingly.[11]

---

[10] Cf. N.T.C. on John, Vol. II, p. 392. For the general plan of a Roman house of the well-to-do see T. G. Tucker, *Life in the Roman World of Nero and St. Paul*, New York, 1922, ch. 9; also *Everyday Life in Ancient Times*, pp. 322, 323.

[11] "Accordingly, when the earth, mud-covered by reason of the recent deluge, became heated up by the hot and genial rays of the sun, she brought forth innumerable species of life; in part she restored the ancient shapes; and in part she created new monsters.

"She, indeed, would have wished not to do so, but she then also bore *you*, enormous Python, you hitherto unknown snake. You were a terror to the new population, so vast a space of mountainside did you occupy.

By an easy transition this word Python began to be applied to divination or fortune-telling in general, so that "a spirit, a Python" indicated "a spirit of divination."

Plutarch, Greek essayist and biographer (about A. D. 46-120), tells us that in his day ventriloquists were called Pythons. But though it is possible that the slave-girl referred to in Acts 16:16 was a ventriloquist, this cannot be proved. The meaning here seems to be simply that she had "a spirit of divination." [12] She was a demon-possessed girl who was regarded by the superstitious people of this region as being able to predict future events. And they were willing to pay for her predictions.

Now one day as she was going *into* or *toward* the city, she *met* the missionaries who were on their way to the prayer-meeting *outside* the city's gates. But having met them she first walked past them and then turned around and followed them. She began to cry out, "These men are servants of the Most High God who proclaim to y o u a way (or "the way") of salvation." [13]

It is understandable that Paul did not cherish the idea of being advertised by a demon-possessed girl (cf. Luke 8:28, 29), as if there were some connection between the kingdom of light and that of darkness, between the servants of the Most High God and . . . Beelzebub! So at last, after the girl had behaved in this fashion for several days, the apostle, worn out through and through by the unwelcome notoriety he was receiving, suddenly turned around and said to the spirit, "I order you in the name of Jesus Christ to get out of her." And it came out that very hour.

But now the real trouble started. The masters of the slave-girl, men who had been making money out of her, became very bitter, and having grabbed Paul and Silas (as the most important of the four?) dragged them to the Agora, the public square or forum. Brought before the *praetors,* the two bringers of good tidings were denounced as *Jewish* trouble-makers. How shrewd this charge and also how inconsistent! The *accusers* were proud of being *Romans, not Jews!* But they forgot that they were never more like wicked Jews than they were right now! Note the similarity:

"This monster the god of the glittering bow destroyed with arms never before used except against does and wild she-goats, well-nigh emptying his quiver, crushing him with countless darts till his poisonous blood flowed from black wounds.

"And in order that the fame of his deed might not perish through lapse of time he instituted sacred games whose contests throngs beheld. These were called Pythian from the name of the serpent he had overthrown" (Metamorphoses I. 434-447. See also T. Bulfinch, *The Age of Fable,* New York, edition 1942, pp. 21, 159, 297.

[12] Cf. M.M., p. 559.

[13] Was she hinting that there were several ways of salvation, and that what Paul and his companions proclaimed was only *one* way out of many? Note that the original lacks the definite article, and *can* therefore be translated *a* way, instead of *the* way. But over against this stands the fact that in Greek the article is not always necessary to make a word definite.

The charge of the Jewish leaders against Jesus:

"We found this man perverting our nation, and forbidding (us) to give tribute to Caesar, and saying that he himself is Christ, a king" (Luke 23:2). *It was a lie and a piece of hypocrisy.* The *real* reason for their agitation is stated in Matt. 27:18: "*Out of envy* they had delivered him up."

The charge of these Romans against Jesus' messengers: Paul and Silas:

"These men, being Jews are exceedingly disturbing our city, and are advocating customs which it is not lawful for us to accept or to practise, since we are Romans." *This, too, was a lie and a piece of hypocrisy.* The real reason for their agitation is stated in Acts 16:19: "Her masters saw that the hope of their gain was gone."

The charge was of an inflammatory character, for Roman colonists were very jealous of their rights and customs as Romans. Besides (as was stated earlier), had not the emperor Claudius recently ordered all Jews from Rome? And now here were these two Jewish vagrants making trouble in Miniature-Rome! Roused by the infuriated, wailing rabble, the praetors caused the two men to be stripped and beaten with rods. Such a flogging was exceedingly painful. Moreover, among the Romans there was no fixed number of lashings, no rule limiting them to "forty stripes less one." To make matters even worse, when the lictors had inflicted many blows, Paul and Silas were thrown into prison, and the jailer was charged to guard them securely. That individual, having received the order, threw them into the inner dungeon, a musty hole, where their feet were locked wide apart in gruesome stocks. Were their wrists also manacled in irons, attached to chains which were bolted into the walls, as was the case with other prisoners? Truly horrible was their condition. Yet this, too, was providential, for it meant that deliverance from such profound agony, from such seemingly unbreakable bonds, would stand out all the more clearly as an act of God and not of man!

As happens so often, "man's extremity was God's opportunity." At midnight Paul and Silas were praying and singing hymns to God. Were any of the following among these hymns: Psalm 2, 16, 20, 23, 27, 42, 43, 46, 68, 69, 71, 130? Such singing surely required a very special measure of God's grace. And then suddenly there was a great earthquake, so that the foundations of the prison were shaken. At one stroke all the prison-doors were opened, the bolts in the tottering walls loosened, and the locks in the stocks sprung. Naturally the jailer, asleep in the house which adjoined the prison, woke up, and came rushing out to the prison-court. It being night he could not see much. Yet, through the semi-darkness he discerned that the prison-doors were open! Filled with terror, he quickly concluded that this could

12

mean one thing only, namely, that the prisoners had escaped. This, he was sure, meant *shameful* death for him (cf. Acts 12:19). Rather than suffer such a disgrace, he would take his own life. Was not this in effect what Cassius and Brutus had done in this very vicinity? Had not Antony and Cleopatra also committed suicide? Was not Seneca constantly defending suicide as a right and privilege? Though the jailer may not have been acquainted with the opinions of the philosophers, it is at least certain that, being a pagan, he cannot have evaluated life as highly as did the Jew (King Saul, Ahithophel, Zimri, and Judas Iscariot were *exceptions*) and especially the Christian. So, in despair he quickly drew his sword and would have killed himself had not Paul, having by this time perhaps stationed himself before the main entrance where he saw what was about to happen, called out loudly, "Do not harm yourself, for we are all here." The astonished jailer then called for lights. Trembling with fear the man fell down before Paul and Silas, brought them outside to the prison-court, and asked, "Sirs, what must I do to be saved?" What did he mean? Merely this, "How can I escape from my present predicament, and hold on to my job?" In the light of the entire situation and also of the answer which he received it is hard to believe that this was all he meant. The following items must not be overlooked:

a. The demon-possessed girl had been telling the people, "These men are servants of the Most High God who proclaim to y o u a way (or "the way") of salvation." It is very well possible that the jailer had heard about this.

b. It is also not improbable that the man had been for some time worried about the condition of his soul.

c. He must have noticed that the behavior of Paul and Silas under the terrible lashings which they received and subsequently in the dungeon was entirely different from anything he had ever seen or heard.

d. It is wholly probable that he knew that at Paul's word the slave-girl had experienced a remarkable change. News, especially of this character, travels fast. And did he perhaps see a connection between these men and the occurrence of the earthquake? Had he become convinced, therefore, that the slave-girl might not have been entirely wrong, that there was indeed a close relation between these two men and divinity, and that they would be in a position to answer the deepest question of his soul?

All these considerations lead me to conclude that the explanation which the man in the pew generally ascribes to the jailer's question is probably the right one. And on this basis the answer which he received was very fitting: "Believe on the Lord Jesus, and you will be saved, you and your household." Of course, this advice needed amplification. So Paul and Silas, having entered the jailer's house, spoke the word of the Lord to the jailer and to all that were there. Moreover, those who heard the message accepted it. And their faith revealed its genuine character in loving deeds. Having taken the missionaries back to the courtyard, where there must have been a cistern or tank with water, or perhaps a spring, the jailer now tenderly washed their wounds. Then immediately he himself was baptized and all those of his household. In the house once more, the jailer set the table for the missionaries. General rejoicing followed.

At break of day the praetors sent the lictors, saying to the jailer, "Release those men." What may have been the motivation of the praetors' change of mind? Can it be that Codex Bezae is correct when it suggests that the authorities had seen a connection between the earthquake and the missionaries, and that in their fear they had arrived at the conclusion: Paul and Silas are actually what they claim to be? Or had thorough investigation convinced the praetors that the strangers had been falsely accused? Whatever may have been the reason for the sudden turnabout, one fact is definitely stated, namely, that, informed by the jailer that he had been officially instructed to release the prisoners, the latter, who meanwhile had re-entered their dungeon, refused to heed the command: "Now therefore come out and go in peace." Instead of leaving the prison, Paul said, "They have beaten us publicly, without trial, men that are Romans, and have thrown us into prison, and do they now throw us out secretly? No indeed! But let them come themselves and lead us out!"

Gross injustice had been done, and Roman law had been violated on more than one count: Roman citizens had been scourged, publicly disgraced, and imprisoned; all this without a trial! Moreover, justice had been trampled by its would-be defenders! The honor of the missionaries, the rights of every Christian in Philippi, the cause of the gospel, and even the good reputation of Roman jurisprudence demanded that the men who had been "shamefully treated" (cf. II Thess. 2:2) be officially vindicated. Hence, Paul acted with sound judgment when he insisted on an honorable discharge for himself and his companion. In fact, that was *the least* he could have demanded!

When the lictors reported to their superiors the true state of affairs regarding these prisoners, particularly that they were *Romans,* the praetors were frightened. They realized that not only their position but their very life was in danger because of the crimes which they had committed. Hence, they readily complied with Paul's request. It must have been quite a scene: purple-robed praetors descending into the dungeon and then "eating crow," offering humble apologies as they politely led Paul and Silas to liberty! And when they had brought them out, they begged them to leave the city. The colonists of Philippi must not get to know that the two strangers who had come into town and had been so deeply humiliated were *Roman citizens!* Surely, these colonists would not have spared the praetors. So, the sooner the strangers leave the city the better!

The latter, in turn, were willing enough to comply with the urgent request. The work in Philippi had met with a considerable measure of success. Lydia and the jailer were by no means the only converts. This appears from the fact that when the missionaries have departed from the prison and have re-entered Lydia's hospitable mansion, they find a number of "brothers" there. To this assembled congregation, the first church in Europe, they speak words of encouragement. Then Paul and Silas wend their way to Thessalonica. Timothy accompanies them or follows a little later. For the present Luke remains in Philippi.

Glancing back at this account of the establishment of the church at Philippi we see that among those who undoubtedly continued for some time to exert a wholesome influence upon it there were especially two that were alike in their unselfish devotion to the cause of Christ and in their big-heartedness, namely, Lydia and Luke. In Lydia's home believers were always more than welcome. And as to Luke, in his Gospel he reveals not only the love of God in Christ but also his own personality. Hence, as we read it we are not surprised to see how mercy is bestowed upon the penitent prodigal, how the sick are healed, the weary strengthened, women (especially widows) and children honored. Moreover, if to these two (Lydia and Luke) a third must be added, the converted jailer certainly deserves consideration (in view of Acts 16:33, 34).

Now the church of Philippi seems to have drawn its character from that of its leading members. Accordingly we are not surprised to learn that when on this second missionary journey Paul was proclaiming the gospel in the next place after Philippi, namely, Thessalonica, he was cheered once and again by a gift from the church of Lydia and Luke (Phil. 4:16). The same thing happened a little later, making possible the work in Athens and Corinth (Phil. 4:15; and see also II Cor. 11:9). Paul's second visit to Philippi and vicinity occurred during his third missionary journey, outward bound. Writing to the Corinthians he praises the eager generosity of the churches of Macedonia (among them, of course, Philippi), in contributing toward the relief of the Jerusalem saints (II Cor. 8:1-5). The third visit to Philippi occurred on this same third missionary journey, but now homeward bound. Paul had planned to set sail directly from Corinth to Syria, when a plot was discovered which caused him to change his plans. So he reversed his course and proceeded toward Jerusalem by way of Macedonia. At this time, however, his contact with the church of Philippi seems to have been very brief. One event of some significance is clearly implied, however: at Philippi Luke rejoined him (Acts 20:5, note "us"). (Some add that Paul attended a Passover at Philippi, but that is not necessarily implied in Acts 20:6.)

For the purpose of understanding the epistle to the Philippians the next contact, though it was not a visit of Paul to the church, is the most important of all. This contact, so characteristic of the church at Philippi, occurred during the apostle's first imprisonment in Rome. See the next section: Paul's Purpose in Writing Philippians.

During this imprisonment Paul wrote that he hoped to send Timothy to visit the church, and he added, "But I trust in the Lord that I myself shall also come soon" (Phil. 2:19, 24). It is certainly within the realm of probability that the apostle actually carried out this plan, and that upon his release he journeyed from Rome by way of Crete and Asia Minor to Philippi. The latter may have been his headquarters when he wrote the epistles known to us as I Timothy and Titus (see N.T.C. on The Pastoral Epistles, pp. 39-42). As far as we know this was Paul's last visit to the church at Philippi.

Fully a half century afterward Polycarp wrote his *Letter to the Philippians*.[14] The occasion was as follows: Ignatius, on his way to Rome and martyrdom, had passed through Philippi. The Philippians had written to Polycarp concerning Ignatius and had expressed a desire that the former make a collection of the latter's letters. Perhaps they had also asked for advice concerning a matter of discipline. Polycarp now answers them, praising them for having followed the pattern of true love and having shown sympathy to those who were bound in chains. He tells them that he rejoices about the fact that the firm root of their faith, famous in times past, is still flourishing and bearing fruit for Christ. He remarks about the incomparable wisdom of the glorious and blessed Paul who had been among them, and he reminds them of the fact that Paul had boasted about them to all the churches. He warns them, however, against avarice. In this connection he states that he feels deeply grieved for Valens and his wife (called by Lightfoot "the Ananias and Sapphira of the Philippian community"), and offers advice with respect to the treatment which such offenders should receive. This writing of Polycarp is at the same time a covering letter, for in the same package Polycarp includes the letters of Ignatius for which the Philippians had asked.

All in all it appears, therefore, that two generations after Paul's death the church at Philippi was still standing firm. The information which has come down to us concerning the state of the church in the immediately succeeding centuries is too scanty to furnish a basis for generalization. A not too encouraging glimpse into the situation that obtained there about the fifth

---

[14] Perhaps there were two letters. The one-letter theory does not fully explain the final sentence in Chapter 13, which seems to imply that when it was written Ignatius was still alive (or at least that Polycarp had not yet been informed about Ignatius' death), while according to Chapters 1-12 (see especially Chapter 9) Ignatius is considered dead. Hence, there are those who think that what the manuscripts have handed down as a single letter of Polycarp to the Philippians is in reality two letters, and that the earlier of these two letters comprises Chapters 13 and 14 of the traditional text. See P. N. Harrison, *Polycarp's Two Letters to the Philippians*, London, 1936.

century is afforded by the inscription in marble which was attached to the city gate on the Egnatian Way (toward Neapolis). This inscription contains the wholly spurious correspondence which king Abgar V is alleged to have had with Jesus! By the Philippians of that later day the inscription was regarded as a charm against enemies and catastrophies! But the charm was wholly ineffective. During the Middle Ages the city was repeatedly attacked by hostile forces and ravaged by earthquakes and fires. The last inhabitants finally left the swampy place.

There are, however, a few records of bishops of Philippi whose names are appended to the decisions of various councils (held in the years 344, 431, 451). We also know that in the year 1212 Philippi must still have been a town of some importance, for in that year Pope Innocent III made it a see. Its last archbishop died in the year 1721. However, it would seem that the see outlived the city itself.

An arched enclosure built by the Romans is held by many to have been the prison where Paul and Silas sang their songs and the jailer was converted. This belief receives some support from the fact that in a day when presumably the memory of these things had not yet faded away the enclosure was covered with a chapel. In the vicinity of Philippi evidences — such as grotto-shrines and chiseled reliefs — of several different pagan religions have been found. One shrine was devoted to the Egyptian gods Isis and Serapis.

From 1914–1938 a French archaeological expedition excavated this region. It found what remained of paved streets and squares, the forum, temples, public buildings, and pillared arcades. However, many of the discoveries concern the post-apostolic history of the city. Except for a few inscriptions — for example, a monument which a presbyter set up in honor of his parents and his wife — and the remains of Byzantine churches, especially the huge piers of the Derekler basilica, there remains today little evidence of the Christianity which once flourished here to such an extent that Paul called this church "my joy and crown." But the apostle's letter to the Philippians makes up for the loss.[15]

IV. Paul's Purpose in Writing Philippians

One day, while Paul was in prison, he received a welcome visitor. His name was Epaphroditus. He was a leader in the church at Philippi. He had been sent to Paul as a delegate from that church. He carried with him a

---

[15] For archaeological sources see General Bibliography at the end of this book; also I.S.B.E., art. "Philippi" (note "Literature" at the close of the article) ; and article "Archaeology, Christian" (and Bibliography at the end of that article) in *The New Schaff-Herzog Encyclopaedia*, Volume I of *The Twentieth Century* augmentation.

generous gift from the Philippians. If he took the land-route, his journey was comparable to that from New York to Chicago. In both cases it would be a journey of a little more than eight hundred miles of actual travel, from east to west, and from 41 N. lat. (for Philippi and for New York) to 42 N. lat. (for Rome and for Chicago). However, due to the radical difference in modes of travel, ancient versus modern, it took Philippi's messenger much longer than it would take us to travel the comparable distance. He was probably on the way about a month.[16] Moreover, the journey by land from Philippi to Rome would have taken even longer had it not been for those good Roman roads, the products of excellent highway engineering. They were usually about fourteen feet wide, of sturdy construction (large blocks of carefully fitted hard stone laid on concrete which capped a well-prepared base), well maintained, relatively safe, pointing straight ahead in spite of obstacles, and marked by milestones.[17] From Philippi to Dyrrachium on the Adriatic one would take the Egnatian Way; then, after crossing the Adriatic to Brundisium (this crossing would take about a day), one would continue on the Appian Way to Rome. It is possible, however, that Epaphroditus made his journey by the sea-route, either through the Gulf of Corinth or around the promontory of Malea. Under favorable circumstances one could save some time by doing this.

The background of the epistle may now be summarized as follows:

(1) Between the delegate's arrival in Rome and the writing of Philippians there had been a time-interval of at least two months, probably more. (See the next section: The Time and the Place of Writing.) The gift which Epaphroditus had brought was deeply appreciated by Paul. It was, indeed, a meaningful *Remembrance,* and in a sense the messenger who had brought it was also himself a gift from the church which he represented, for the intention probably was that he should be the apostle's constant attendant and assistant. Grateful *written* acknowledgment was surely in order.

(2) Epaphroditus must also have brought a *Report* about conditions that prevailed in the Christian community which he had left. Moreover, it is entirely possible that, in the weeks which followed, others had added to this report. It must be borne in mind that, due to Philippi's strategic location on the Egnatian Way and also because of blood-relationships and political ties between the inhabitants of the two cities, travel between Philippi and Rome was heavy and constant. It is at any rate clearly evident that, although by now several weeks had elapsed since Epaphroditus had arrived in Rome,

---

[16] For proof see J. B. Lightfoot, *Saint Paul's Epistle to the Philippians,* reprint, Grand Rapids, Mich., 1953, p. 38, footnote 1.
[17] See the pictures and description in W.H.A.B., p. 77; *Everyday Life in Ancient Times,* pp. 304, 305; G. E. Wright, *Biblical Archaeology,* Philadelphia, 1957, p. 265; T. G. Tucker, *Life in the Roman World of Nero and St. Paul,* New York, 1922, pp. 16-29; and L. H. Grollenberg, *Atlas of the Bible* (tr. of *Atlas Van De Bijbel*), New York (Thomas Nelson and Sons), 1956, p. 134.

the apostle's knowledge about conditions in the church at Philippi continued to be rather up-to-date (Phil. 1:5; 1:27-29). He had heard that although the Philippians were certainly adorning their confession with a life to God's honor, were willing even to suffer in behalf of Christ, were ever ready to do more than their share in contributing toward the need of others, were, in fact, setting a wonderful example for others to follow, nevertheless their church was *not entirely* free from personal friction (Syntyche and Euodia, for example, were not of the same mind, Phil. 4:2) and from *every* danger of giving heed to "those dogs," "those evil workers," namely, "the *concision*" (Judaistic teachers). See Phil. 3:1-3. There were those, moreover, "whose god is the belly, and whose glory is in their shame, who set their mind on earthly things" (Phil. 3:19).

(3) Epaphroditus (and others too, perhaps) had also told Paul, we may well assume, that the church at Philippi was deeply concerned about the apostle, and that it wanted to know more about his present condition. Did Paul think that he would soon be set at liberty? What was his own spiritual reaction to the bonds which he had to endure? If he regained his liberty, would he favor them with an early visit? Questions such as these amounted to a *Request* for detailed information about Paul. See Phil. 1:12-26; 4:18, 19.

(4) Finally, Epaphroditus, having been exposed to considerable danger, having suffered and recovered from grave illness, and having become deeply concerned about the effect of all this upon the church which had delegated him, was anxious to wend his way homeward to Philippi. This expressed desire met with the apostle's full approval, so that the latter not only *allowed* him to go back but actually *sent* him back (Phil. 2:25). But surely those by whom he had been delegated (the church at Philippi, especially its officers) had never intended that he would return to them so soon. What kind of *Reception* would be accorded him upon his return? Would it be critical or friendly?

In view of this background — and linked with it point by point — *the purpose* of Paul's letter can now be stated. *The immediate occasion* for dispatching a letter at this time was undoubtedly the return of Epaphroditus to Philippi. In all probability he carried with him the apostle's letter and delivered it to the church.[18] *Paul's purpose*, then, was as follows:

(1) To give *written* expression to his *Gratitude*.

In all probability, when the apostle received the gift he had acknowledged it as soon as possible, either by mouth of those who presumably had accompanied Epaphroditus on his journey to Rome and had immediately returned or through others who a few days or weeks later had traveled from Rome to Philippi. But, some time having now elapsed, the apostle also wishes to

---

[18] For a different view see one of the two suggestions offered by S. Greydanus, *Bizondere Canoniek,* Kampen, 1949, Vol. II, p. 159.

express his appreciation in *writing*. (It is possible that Paul's letter was delayed by the illness of Epaphroditus.) That the Epistle to the Philippians is indeed the first *written* acknowledgment seems to be clearly implied in Phil. 4:10, 18. However, not only does Paul thank the Philippians for their gift; he also thanks God for the Philippians! See Phil. 4:10-20; then 1:3-11.

(2) To provide the spiritual *Guidance* which the congregation needed.

Let the Philippians continue to exercise their citizenship in a manner that is worthy of the gospel of Christ (Phil. 1:27-30). Let them remain united in mind and purpose (Phil. 2:2). Let the attitude of Christ who humbled himself and became obedient unto death, even death on a cross, be descriptive also *of them* (Phil. 2:1-11). In the midst of a crooked and perverse generation let them be light-bearers, holding forth the word of life (Phil. 2:14-16). Let them beware of *the Judaizers* (Phil. 3:1-3). Let them not think that spiritually they have already "arrived." On the contrary, imitating Paul, let them "press on toward the goal" (Phil. 3:4-16). Their homeland being in heaven, let them beware of *sensualists,* the enemies of the cross, whose god is the belly (Phil. 3:17-21). Let them, in brief, strive after *courage* (Phil. 1:27, 28), *oneness* (Phil. 2:2; 4:2, 3), *lowliness* (2:3), *helpfulness* (2:4), *obedience* (2:12), *perfection* (3:12-16), *holiness* (3:17, 20), *steadfastness* (4:1), *joy and trust in the Lord* (4:1-7). In reaching out toward this ideal let them fix their attention on "whatever things are true, honorable, just, pure," etc. Then the God of peace will be with them (Phil. 4:8, 9).

(3) To fill the minds and hearts of the Philippians with the spirit of *Gladness*.

Do the Philippians request information about Paul? "Do not be unduly disturbed about me," he says, as it were: "The things that have happened to me have fallen out to the advantage of the gospel (Phil. 1:12-17). . . . In every way, whether in pretense or in truth, Christ is being proclaimed, and in this *I rejoice. Yes, and I shall continue to rejoice,* for I know that . . . this will turn out to my salvation . . . Now as always Christ will be magnified in my person, whether by life or by death . . . For the rest, my brothers, *rejoice in the Lord . . . Rejoice* in the Lord always. Again I will say *Rejoice . . .* Now *I rejoice* in the Lord greatly." From beginning to end the letter is bathed in this sunshine of joy. We can understand Bengel when he said: *Summa epistolae: Gaudeo, gaudete* (The sum of the epistle is: I rejoice; y o u must rejoice), even though we would not put it quite that strongly. Not less than sixteen times do the words *joy, rejoice* occur in this letter: Phil. 1:4; 1:18 (twice); 1:25; 2:2; 2:17 (twice); 2:18 (twice); 2:28; 2:29; 3:1; 4:1; 4:4 (twice); and 4:10. Yet, it is hardly correct to say that joy is *the summary or theme* of the letter.

Now the joy of which Paul makes repeated mention is the joy unspeakable and full of glory. It is the *great* joy which, far from being dependent upon outward circumstances, wells up from the heart of this prisoner who faces possible death and is chained night and day to a soldier, with few friends to comfort him and several enemies who are ever ready to raise up affliction to him in his bonds (Phil. 2:20, 21; 1:15-17). The apostle writes this letter in order that the readers, by fully sharing in this joy, may make full his own joy. Paul's case is in process before the imperial court. There had been a trial (Phil. 1:7), and the final verdict cannot be long delayed. Is he going to be set free? Deep down in his heart he believes that this is exactly what is going to happen. Yet, he does not exclude the opposite possibility. But, come what may, he is ready. See Phil. 1:22-26. As soon as the verdict has been made known, he will send Timothy to Philippi with the news. He adds, "But I trust in the Lord that I myself shall also soon come" (Phil. 2:19-24).

(4) To prevail upon the Philippians' Spirit-wrought *Goodness* of heart to extend to Epaphroditus a most cordial "Welcome Home."

A wonderful person, this Epaphroditus! The apostle calls him "my brother and fellow-worker and fellow-soldier," as well as "y o u r messenger and minister to my need." In the course of his labors for Christ the King he had suffered much. He had, in fact, risked his life, and had experienced days of illness so grievous that he had lain at death's very door. But God had shown mercy to this hero and had healed him. Meanwhile Epaphroditus had been informed that the members of the home-church, having heard about his illness, were worried about him. Epaphroditus naturally wants to remove that anxiety and so does Paul. Hence, the apostle decides to send him back to Philippi, and in his letter he states the purpose, namely, "Accordingly, I am sending him back the more eagerly in order that when y o u see him again y o u may rejoice and I may be less sorrowful. So extend to him a most joyful welcome in the Lord, and hold such men in honor" (Phil. 2:28-29). Thus the apostle provides a hearty reception for Epaphroditus, upon his probably unexpectedly early return.

V. The Place and the Time of Writing

Philippians belongs to a group of four letters — Colossians, Philemon, Ephesians, and Philippians — that are commonly designated the Prison Epistles. Here for the first time Paul writes as *a prisoner* (Col. 4:3, 18; Philem. 10, 13, 22, 23; Eph. 3:1; 4:1; 6:20; Phil. 1:7, 13; 2:17).[19] In reading

---

[19] It is true that at a later time also II Timothy was written from prison, but that epistle is in an altogether different category. Like I Timothy and Titus it was written to one of the apostles' official representatives, comparable, but only *to a certain extent,* to "pastors." Hence, these three form a group. See N.T.C. on The Pastoral Epistles.

these letters one notices how deeply the writer is affected by his imprison-ment. Nevertheless, he does not lose heart. Is he not the prisoner *of Christ Jesus?* The greatness of Christ Jesus is described in Colossians, Ephesians, and Philippians. Tychicus seems to be the bearer of the letter to the Colos-sians and the one to Philemon. The fugitive slave Onesimus accompanies him and must be returned to his master in Colossae; not as a slave, however, but as a brother. See Col. 4:7-9; Philem. 10-12, 16. It is not at all surpris-ing that Tychicus also has a letter for the church at Ephesus (Eph. 6:21, 22), located near Colossae. It is clear, therefore, that Colossians, Philemon, and Ephesians belong together. They are in all likelihood delivered to their re-spective addresses by the same person, Tychicus. And though Philippians seems to have been brought to its destination by someone else, namely, Epaphroditus (Phil. 2:25-29; 4:18), and therefore, in a way stands outside the group of three, nevertheless, all four have this in common, as already noted, that they are Prison Epistles, which by most interpreters are regarded as having been written during the same imprisonment.

Now the question arises: Where was this prison? According to the book of Acts Paul was in prison in Philippi (Acts 16:23-40), in Jerusalem (Acts 21:33–23:30), in Caesarea (Acts 23:35–26:32), and in Rome (Acts 28:16–31). However, Philippi and Jerusalem can be ruled out at once, for the apostle did not have the time to write from these prisons. (Besides, as far as Philippians is concerned, the prison in Philippi would be ruled out any-way: one does not write to the Philippians from Philippi!) There remain Caesarea and Rome, to which (because of what Paul writes in I Cor. 15:32; II Cor. 1:8-11; 6:5; and II Cor. 11:23) some would add Ephesus.

As a result we now have four theories with respect to the place from which these letters may have been written: (a) the traditional position, according to which they were written from Rome; (b) the view that they were com-posed in Caesarea; (c) the theory which supports Ephesus as the place of their origin; and (d) the "mixed" hypothesis, according to which a distinc-tion is made of one kind or another; for example, Colossians, Philemon, and Ephesians were written from Caesarea, but Philippians was written from Rome (or, according to others, from Ephesus); or the three were written from Ephesus, Philippians from Rome.[20]

---

[20] For the various views consult J. Schmid, *Zeit und Ort der Paulinischen Gefangen-schaftsbriefe,* 1931. For the view that all were written from Rome see J. B. Light-foot, *St. Paul's Epistle to the Philippians,* reprint Grand Rapids, Mich., 1953, p. 30; R. C. H. Lenski, *Interpretation of Galatians, Ephesians, Philippians,* Columbus, Ohio, pp. 325-329, 699, 700; M. R. Vincent, *The Epistles to the Philippians and to Philemon* (in I.C.C.), New York, 1906, pp. xxii-xxv and 160-162; S. Greydanus, *Bizondere Canoniek,* Kampen, 1949, Vol. II, pp. 127–140. The influence of the Caesarean and of the Ephesian theories is gradually beginning to "wear off," and in most recent works the traditional Rome-view, which was the view either expressed or assumed by all the earlier exegetes, is beginning to be endorsed more strongly

INTRODUCTION

In harmony with most interpreters, ancient and modern, I accept the Rome-view for all four Prison Epistles. It is true that the distance between Rome and Philippi was greater than, for example, that between Ephesus and Philippi. But since there was an excellent and much-traveled "highway" between Rome and Philippi, this matter of greater distance has very little value as an argument against the view that the apostle was at Rome when he wrote the four Prison Epistles. In fact, it is so weak that it can be disregarded.

The following points may be adduced in refutation of the Caesarean and Ephesian hypotheses and in favor of the Rome-view. Instead of enumerating them in haphazard fashion, I have tried to arrange them in such a manner that the grouping is both *logical* and *memorizable*. It will be seen that the first three points concern *the general situation* pertaining to Paul's imprisonment: he was *under guard;* which, as we know from the book of Acts, was true *in Rome;* he was experiencing *a lengthy imprisonment;* and he was in a city where there was *a multitude of preachers*. The fourth point has to do with *the contents* of the Prison Epistles. Points five and six pertain to *the verdict* which Paul was awaiting: he more or less expected it to be *favorable;* he knew that it would be *decisive*. Points seven, eight, and nine fix the attention on: a faithful church, few faithful friends, and the ever-faithful Christ.

So far, *Philippians* has been the starting-point for much of the argumentation, though wherever possible the other three Prison Epistles have also furnished material for arriving at a conclusion. Points ten and eleven, however, are derived not from Philippians but from *Colossians, Philemon, and Ephesians*. Point twelve is a tradition-summary touching all four letters. We now consider these twelve points.

---

than ever. As far as Philippians is concerned, the Rome-theory has never been eclipsed. In *The Interpreter's Bible* E. F. Scott favors Rome for Philippians, and F. W. Beare likewise favors Rome for Colossians; but John Knox seems to incline toward Ephesus for Philemon. F. W. Grosheide supports the traditional Rome-view (*Openbaring Gods In Het Nieuwe Testament*, Kampen, 1953, pp. 204, 208) .

The Caesarean theory was proposed by H. E. G. Paulus, *Philologisch-kritischer Kommentar über das Neue Testament* (Lübeck, 1800-1804) . It has had many defendants since his day. (See especially E. Lohmeyer, *Die Briefe an die Philipper, an die Kolosser und an Philemon*, Göttingen, 1930; Meyer's *Kommentar*.) Among others who favor this view are J. Macpherson, F. Spitta, and O. Holtzmann.

The Ephesian theory was advanced by H. Lisco (*Vincula Sanctorum*, Berlin, 1900) . However, three years earlier A. Deissmann, while lecturing at the Theological Seminary at Herborn, had already introduced it with application to Colossians, Philemon, and Ephesians (see *Light From the Ancient East*, tr. from the German by L. R. M. Strachan, New York, 1927, pp. 237, 238, in which book he endorses this theory for all four Prison Epistles) . What is, perhaps, the best defense of the Ephesian theory is found in G. S. Duncan's book, *St. Paul's Ephesian Ministry*, New York, 1930. Cf. D. Rowlingson's article "Paul's Ephesian Imprisonment, An Evaluation of the Evidence," *AThR*, XXXII (1950) , pp. 1-7. Among others the following favor this theory: Bowen, Appel, and Michaelis.

(1) *"Throughout the whole praetorian guard," and "Caesar's household."*
It has been argued that the expression "throughout the whole praetorian guard" (Phil. 1:13) should be rendered "in the whole praetorium," and that since a praetorium is simply a government house or provincial governor's residence (see N.T.C. on John 18:28) it may have been located at Caesarea (cf. Acts 23:35), or even at Ephesus; but not at Rome.

However, in the present instance the phrase is immediately followed by "and to all the rest," and refers, therefore, to *people*, not to a building. According to the most natural interpretation it indicates the imperial guard, nine thousand in number, which was instituted by Augustus.[21] It is exactly at Rome that the apostle would be constantly guarded by a soldier from this guard and because it rotated, the reason why this remarkable man was imprisoned would gradually become known "throughout the whole praetorian guard and to all the rest."

In the same category is the expression, "All the saints greet y o u, especially those of Caesar's household" (Phil. 4:22). Here again *the most natural interpretation* would refer the expression to that large number of slaves and freemen who served in the emperor's palace at Rome. They were household servants, cooks, gardeners, porters, doorkeepers, etc. See also on Phil. 4:22.

(2) *Established Facts versus Questionable Inferences. A Lengthy Imprisonment as a New Way of Life.*
In order to prove the Ephesian theory an appeal is made to four passages in Paul's Corinthian correspondence: I Cor. 15:32 ("If after the manner of men I fought with beasts *at Ephesus*"), II Cor. 1:8-11 (". . . the affliction which befell us *in Asia* . . ."), II Cor. 6:5 ("in imprisonments"), and II Cor. 11:23 ("in far more imprisonments"). The argument is as follows: since these passages antedate both the Caesarean and Roman imprisonments, they show that Paul must have been in prison during his stay at Ephesus, while he was on his third missionary journey.

However, when examined carefully, in the light of their contexts, these passages do not compel one to accept that conclusion. As to I Cor. 15:32, this can hardly be taken literally. It is not easy to believe that Paul, *the Roman citizen*, would have been *literally* cast before beasts at Ephesus. As to II Cor. 1:8-11, the "affliction in Asia" was not necessarily an imprisonment. As the context clearly indicates, it was of a kind that is still continuing, now that the apostle has reached Macedonia. The other two passages *may*, but do not necessarily, refer to an imprisonment *in Ephesus*. But even if they refer to an Ephesian imprisonment, it is very doubtful whether the latter would be of the nature implied in the Prison Epistles. These letters imply a lengthy period of imprisonment, imprisonment as *a new way of life*

---

[21] See J. B. Lightfoot, *op. cit.*, pp. 99-104; M.M., pp. 532, 533.

and not as a brief experience. Paul's ministry of less than three years at Ephesus, a ministry filled with kingdom-activity (see Acts 19:8, 10), leaves no room for such a protracted incarceration. Moreover, in his detailed account of Paul's activity in Ephesus Luke has not a word to say about it.

On the other hand, from the book of Acts (Chapter 28; cf. 23:11) *we know* that Paul was a prisoner in Rome. It is *possible* that when he wrote Philippians he had been transferred from his "rented house" (Acts 28:30) to the soldiers' barracks or that in some other way he had been placed under stricter custody (*custodia militaris instead of custodia libera*). But it is hard to prove this. One thing, however, is clear: *in general,* the conditions of Paul's imprisonment as described in Acts were the same as those which are implied in the Prison Epistles: for example, soldiers guarded Paul (cf. Acts 28:16 with Phil. 1:13, 14); he enjoyed freedom to receive visitors (cf. Acts 28:30 with Phil. 4:18); and he had the opportunity to bear testimony concerning his faith (cf. Acts 28:31 with Phil. 1:12-18; Col. 4:2-4; Eph. 6:18-20). As to this last item, it would seem that *at Caesarea* the apostle's opportunities to reach others with the gospel were far more limited (see Acts 23:35 and 24:27).

Hence, the view that Paul wrote these four epistles while he was a prisoner in Rome rests on *the established facts* with reference to his Roman imprisonment, while other theories are based on *questionable inferences.*

(3) *The Multitude of Preachers.*

From Phil. 1:14-18 it appears that in the city of his imprisonment there were *many* heralds of the gospel. Some were motivated by envy and rivalry, others by love. This multitude of preachers suits the large city of Rome far better than the far smaller Caesarea. (Cf. also Col. 4:2-4; Eph. 6:18-20.)

(4) *Arguments Based on Contents.*

It is urged that in material contents Philippians approaches the earlier epistles (especially Romans and Galatians; but see also I and II Corinthians; e.g., II Cor. 11), and that for this reason it cannot belong to the period A. D. 61-63 when Paul was imprisoned in Rome, but must be earlier, dating back to Ephesus and in general to the third missionary journey (A. D. 53/54-57/58). Reference is made, for example, to the scathing denunciation of what the apostle contemptuously calls *the concision* and to the immediately following emphatic affirmation of the doctrine of justification by faith alone (Phil. 3:2-16). This is then compared with similar emotion-filled utterances on the same subject in Romans (2:25-29; 9:30-33; 10:3); and Galatians (3:1-14; 4:12-20; 5:1-12; 6:12-16).

But even if it be granted that the subject-matter here in Phil. 3:2-16 is the same as that in Galatians (which is true except that Paul *rebukes* the Galatians, but *warns* the Philippians), similarity in subject-matter by no means proves identity in the place from which one is writing. *The apostle wrote as the concrete situation in any given case demanded!* And the warmth with which he was able to write on the theme of salvation not by law-works but solely by grace through faith never left him. We find touches of it even in the Pastoral Epistles (see I Tim. 1:12-17 and Titus 3:4-7). Moreover, if a change in subject-matter indicates a change in the author's whereabouts, then, considered by and large, the Prison Epistles (so largely Christological) and the Earlier Epistles (largely Soteriological) must come from *different* places!

Some, favoring the Caesarean theory, link the denunciation of the *concision* (Phil. 3:2-16) with the hostility which *the Jews* showed to Paul during the latter's Caesarean imprisonment (Acts 24:1; 25:7). But Phil. 3 is clearly not directed against Christ-hating Jews but against Judaizers, so-called "converted" (nominally Christian) Jews who were still clinging to the Mosaic ritual. See on Phil. 3:2-16.

It is exactly the contents of the Prison Epistles that point away from Ephesus and Caesarea. For, if written from Ephesus, during the third missionary journey, when Paul had on his mind *the collection* for the needy saints at Jerusalem, they would in all probability have contained references to this subject. Moreover, had Paul been in Ephesus, Epaphroditus, his friend and prison-attendant, could have made a quick visit to Philippi. All this discussion about "sending (back)" Epaphroditus (Phil. 2:25-30) would not have been necessary.

And if these epistles had been written from Caesarea, they would most likely have contained a kind word about Philip the evangelist who lived there and who a moment before had so generously entertained the apostle (Acts 21:8). In none of the Prison Epistles is anything said about this man or about his four remarkable daughters. The entire situation is clearly different. Paul is now in Rome, not in Ephesus or Caesarea.

(5) *Expectation of a Favorable Verdict.*

There are passages in these Prison Epistles which show that Paul *hopes* and, to a certain extent, *expects* to be acquitted (Phil. 1:25; 2:24). Upon his release he plans to go to Colossae and asks that a guest-room be kept ready for him there (Philem. 22). Now his plan *had been* to visit Spain (Rom. 15:28). The question is asked, accordingly, "If it were true that Paul was writing from Rome, with plans to proceed farther West, to Spain, would he have asked that a guest-room be kept ready for him at a place located not at all on the way from Rome to Spain but in the very opposite direction?"

The answer is that the plan to visit Spain had been announced when the apostle was still a free man, writing Romans from Corinth on his third missionary journey. At that time he intended to go to Rome and then to Spain. From there he probably planned to return to the churches in Asia Minor, Macedonia, etc. But God willed differently. Paul did indeed go to Rome after his third missionary journey, but as a prisoner! In all, his Caesarean and Roman imprisonments probably lasted about five years (cf. Acts 24:27; 25:1; Chap. 27; 28:30). It is altogether natural that when now at last he expects to be released, he announces a revision in his plan: he will first see the familiar faces in the East — moreover, in Asia Minor a dangerous heresy is threatening! — , and then visit strangers in the far West. In all probability the apostle carried out this revised plan.

Besides, the very expectation of *a favorable verdict* fits *Rome* far better than, for example, Caesarea. For Paul to be released while at Caesarea would have meant either bribing Felix (Acts 24:26) or consenting to the wish of Festus, namely, to be tried by the Jews at Jerusalem (Acts 25:9). Paul will have nothing to do with either suggestion. When the second one is made, he immediately appeals to Caesar in Rome (Acts 25:10). — On the other hand the closing chapters of Acts point toward *release from Roman imprisonment*. See N.T.C. on Pastoral Epistles, pp. 25-27; 39-40.

(6) *The Decisive Character of the Verdict.*

Though Paul rather expected to be released, he did not exclude from his mind the thought that he might, after all, be sentenced to death. One thing he knew for sure: *the verdict, whatever it was, would be decisive:* it would mean either life or death, with no possibility of further appeal (Phil. 1:20-23; 2:17, 23). Hence, he must have been *at Rome* when he wrote these letters, for at Ephesus or at Caesarea he, as a Roman citizen, would have been able to appeal to Caesar. In neither of these two places would the verdict have been decisive.

(7) *A Faithful Church Established Long Ago.*

In Phil. 4:15 Paul gratefully recalls what the Philippians had done for him "in the early days [literally, "in the beginning"] of the gospel." And they had remained faithful *ever since*. This sounds as if those early days were "long ago." But when the apostle was in Ephesus on his third missionary journey, the church at Philippi, established on the second missionary journey, was only a few years old. The solution: Philippians was written from Rome, as were the other Prison Epistles.

(8) *Few Faithful Friends, Timothy a Notable Exception.*

Often Timothy is enlisted in the cause of the Ephesian theory. The argument runs as follows: We know that Timothy was with Paul *in Ephesus,* but there is no source that informs us that he was with the apostle in Rome, though he *may* have been. We also know definitely that Paul sent Timothy *from Ephesus* (I Cor. 4:17; 16:10) to Macedonia, in which Philippi was located (Acts 19:22). And this exactly harmonizes with Paul's intention as expressed in Phil. 2:19-23. Hence, Paul must have been *at Ephesus* when he wrote Philippians. See, for example, J. H. Michael, *The Epistle of Paul to the Philippians* (in The Moffatt New Testament Commentary), New York, 1929, pp. xvi, xvii.

This argument impresses me as being rather superficial. There is nothing to prove that I Cor. 4:17 (cf. 16:10) and Phil. 2:19-23 refer to *the same errand.* The context, in fact, argues strongly against this identification. For in Phil. 2:21 the apostle states, that, with the exception of Timothy, all those who are with him "look after their own affairs, not those of Jesus Christ." But surely this expression even when interpreted in a qualified sense (see on 2:21) would not have suited Ephesus where the apostle had very many warm friends (cf. Acts 20:36-38), among them Priscilla and Aquila, his helpers in Christ Jesus who were ever ready to sacrifice their very lives for him (Rom. 16:3, 4; cf. Acts 18:18, 19, 26).

An expression such as this (Phil. 2:21) suits the last days of the first Roman imprisonment. It does not suit any other place or time, least of all Ephesus and the third missionary journey

Moreover, as to Timothy's having been (or *not* having been) with Paul in Rome, *we know* from the book of Acts that both Timothy and Aristarchus accompanied Paul to Jerusalem where Paul was arrested (Acts 20:4-6); also, that Aristarchus was with the apostle aboard the ship, when the apostle departed from Caesarea to go to Rome (Acts 27:2). (For the idea of Lightfoot, namely, that Aristarchus disembarked at Myra, there is no evidence whatever.) It must certainly be considered very probable that ever-faithful Timothy, if he was not actually with Paul on that ship, followed his master soon afterward. Any other course would have been unlike Timothy. See N.T.C. on the Pastoral Epistles, pp. 33-36.

(9) *The Faithful Christ, Not the Roman Emperor, Is God.*

As has been pointed out in Section II (The City of Philippi), the Roman citizen Paul and the inhabitants of the Roman colony of Philippi had much in common. In *Rome* emperor-worship reached its climax. Of course, it was also found elsewhere, in fact throughout the Roman empire, but elsewhere particularly in *the Roman colonies,* such as Philippi. If Paul is writing from *a prison in Rome* it is even easier to understand his words to the effect that writer and readers are "engaged in *the same* conflict" (Phil. 1:30, note especially the context, Phil. 1:27) than if he is writing from any other place. If he is writing from Rome his reason for placing added stress on the fact that the faithful Christ, and he alone, is God, becomes doubly clear (Col. 1:15; 2:9; Phil. 2:6).

(10) *The Flight of Onesimus*

The purpose of one of the Prison Epistles was to secure a kind reception for the fugitive slave Onesimus upon his return to his master, Philemon, who lived in Colossae. See the epistle addressed to the latter (cf. Col. 4:9). The slave had found his way to the city of Paul's imprisonment, had been brought into contact with the apostle, through whose instrumentality he had been converted. It is argued, accordingly, that it is easier to imagine that from Colossae Onesimus had fled to Ephesus, only about a hundred miles away, or even to Caesarea, about five hundred miles, than *all the way* to Rome, about a thousand miles of actual travel.

Now this reasoning may be correct when it pertains to a certain class of fugitives in any age. In the case of others, however, it is faulty. Understandably they love *distance,* and they love to boast about it ("I took my flight and ran away, *All the way* to Canaday!"). They also long to hide behind *the curtain of anonymity* which the large city with its teeming multitudes provides. Rome has been called "a haven for runaways"!

(11) *The Return of Onesimus.*

In this same connection some say that had the three epistles — Colossians, Philemon, and Ephesians — been written from Rome, Onesimus, who was returning to his master in the company of Tychicus, would have reached Ephesus before reaching Colossae, and, therefore, would have been commended to the Ephesian as well as to the Colossian church. They argue that the omission of his name from Ephesians (contrast Col. 4:9) indicates that Tychicus, traveling from Paul's prison in *Caesarea,* had already left Onesimus at Philemon's home in Colossae. Alone he traveled on to Ephesus.

But this argument, too, is very unrealistic. To have commended the fugitive slave to the church at Ephesus, so that this church would have been urged to accept him with open arms even before his own master at Colossae had had the opportunity to act in the case would have been a breach of etiquette, to say the least.

(12) *The Voice of Tradition.*

According to the tradition of the early church it was from Rome that Paul wrote the four Prison Epistles. Not until about the year 1800 did the Caesarea theory arise, and not until 1900 the Ephesus theory. In the absence of any cogent reasons to depart from the traditional position it is certainly wise to cling to it.

As has been indicated, in all probability Colossians, Philemon, and Ephesians were despatched at the same time and were carried to their respective destinations by the same messenger, namely, Tychicus. The only remaining question, then, is this: Did these three letters precede or did they follow Philippians? Some defend the latter position [22] but on grounds that have failed to impress most commentators. Lightfoot, arguing for the priority of Philippians, says that in this letter we have "the spent wave" of the Judaistic controversy which was brought so prominently to the fore in earlier epistles, especially in Romans (cf. Phil. 3:3 with Rom. 2:28; Phil. 3:9 with Rom. 9:30-33; 10:3), while in Colossians and Ephesians we are beginning to deal with incipent Gnosticism which subject is continued in the Pastorals. But about four years must have elapsed between Romans and Philippians, while, on the other hand, the time-interval between Philippians and the other

---

[22] J. B. Lightfoot, *op. cit.,* pp. 30–46. Thus also Bleek, Sanday, Hort, and Beet.

Prison Epistles cannot have been much more than a year (perhaps less; cf. Philem. 22 with Phil. 2:23, 24). It is hard to believe that in this very brief interval there can have been any great change either in the character of the heresy by which the church, as a whole, was threatened, or in the system of thought which (as some assume) was gradually being developed in the apostle's mind. Whatever difference in emphasis there be between Philippians, on the one hand, and Colossians, Philemon, and Ephesians, on the other, is mainly due to difference in situations and needs of the respective readers.

Although the question which letter was first or last cannot be answered with certainty, yet, if any choice must be made, placing *Philippians last,* as is done by most interpreters, seems to have by far the better of the argument. Among the many reasons that have been advanced for this position the following are, perhaps, the most convincing:

(1) Luke and Aristarchus, who accompanied Paul on his perilous journey to Rome (Acts 27:2), and were still with him when he wrote Colossians (4:10, 14) and Philemon (23), are no longer with him when he writes Philippians.

(2) Between Paul's arrival in Rome and the despatch of Philippians much time has elapsed. See Phil. 2:25-30; 4:10, 18. The distance between Philippi and Rome had probably been covered no less than four times:

a. Someone travels from Rome to Philippi with the news of Paul's arrival and imprisonment in Rome.

b. The Philippians collect a gift for Paul and send it to him by the hand of Epaphroditus.

c. Epaphroditus becomes gravely ill, and someone conveys this information to the Philippians.

d. Someone from Philippi reaches Rome and tells Epaphroditus (who in the meantime has fully recovered) about the deep concern of the Philippians for his health and safety.[23]

(3) The reaction of the praetorian guard and that of two categories of gospel-heralds to the presence and preaching of Paul (Phil. 1:12-18) indicates that when Philippians was written the apostle had been in Rome for some time.

(4) The apostle is expecting a verdict *any moment* (Phil. 2:23, 24; cf. 1:7). Yet, though there surely is a difference between Philemon 22 and Phil. 2:23, 24, inasmuch as in the former passage the apostle expresses *the hope* that release from imprisonment *will take place,* whereas in the latter he expresses

---

[23] Lightfoot's attempt to reduce these four journeys to two (*op. cit.,* pp. 35-37) has left most exegetes (myself included) unconvinced. But a criticism of this point belongs to a Commentary on the Book of Acts (27:2).

the confidence that such a release *is about to take place*, the implied differ·
ence in the time of writing was probably rather brief. If we place all four
Prison Epistles in the period A. D. 61–63,[24] with Colossians, Philemon, and
Ephesians followed shortly afterward (and toward the close of the first
Roman imprisonment) by Philippians, we are probably about as near to
the truth as we can get.

VI. Authorship and Unity

The question, "Who wrote Philippians?" is readily answered. It was the
apostle Paul. Timothy, to be sure, was associated with him, so that we read,
"Paul and Timothy, servants of Christ Jesus, to all the saints in Christ Jesus
who are in Philippi," but from the fact that Paul is throughout writing in
the first person singular it is clear that it is Paul with whom the main responsibility rests. Not Timothy but Paul was the author.

It was Ferdinand Christian Baur who, conducting a siege against the
fortresses of traditional Christian doctrine, assailed the Pauline authorship
of all the letters passing under the apostle's name, except Galatians, I and II
Corinthians, and Romans. See his *Paulus,* Stuttgart, 1845. His arguments
against Philippians were in the main as follows:

(1) The mention of "overseers and deacons" (Phil. 1:1) points to a post-
Pauline stage of church government.

Answer: A study of Acts 6:1-6; 11:30; 14:23; 30:27, 28; and I Thess. 5:12,
13 indicates that these offices existed long before Philippians was written.
See on Phil. 1:1.

(2) The epistle shows no originality. It is full of imitations of Paul's
genuine epistles.

Answer: If Paul wrote Philippians as well as Romans, etc., similar expressions would be entirely natural.

(3) The epistle shows traces of Gnosticism, especially in 2:5-8, where the
writer was thinking of the last of the aeons, namely, Sophia, who, attempting
to comprehend the Absolute, falls from *fulness* into *emptiness.*

Answer: This weird interpretation contradicts the context. See on Phil.
2:5-8; also II Cor. 8:9.

(4) The epistle is a post-Paulinic attempt to reconcile the Jewish-Christian
and Gentile-Christian parties, typified respectively by Euodia and Syntyche
(Phil. 4:2).

Answers: The context (see especially Phil. 4:3) clearly indicates that these

---

[24] For a discussion of this date and of the entire Pauline chronology see my *Bible
Survey,* pp. 62-64, 70.

names belong to women in the church at Philippi, and that neither of them had ever been the leader of any party that opposed Paul. On the contrary both had been "laboring *with* Paul" in the gospel. Baur's interpretation must be considered a very fanciful application of his Hegelian principle, a notion hardly worthy of consideration.

At first Baur's arguments were accepted by several of his Tübingen school disciples. But soon some began to disagree. Among those who regarded most of Baur's arguments as irrelevant or worse it was especially Karl Christian Johann Holstein who, nevertheless, revived the attack against the genuineness of the letter. He accepted in modified form *one* of the arguments of Baur that has not yet been mentioned, namely, that the doctrine of justification which Philippians sets forth is not that of Paul. He added other arguments. His reasoning, then, was as follows:

(1) Paul's doctrine of forensic, imputed righteousness is here in Philippians replaced by that of infused righteousness (see Phil. 3:9-11).

Answer: The author of Philippians clearly speaks of imputed righteousness in Phil. 3:9: "not having a righteousness of my own, which (is) of the law, but that (which is) through faith in Christ, the righteousness (which is) from God (and rests) on faith" (cf. Rom. 3:21-24; even Titus 3:4-8 is no different). It is true, of course, that by means of an infinitive of purpose the passage in Philippians links this imputed righteousness with subjective righteousness: "that I may know him," etc. (Phil. 3:10, 11).

(2) According to Paul the pre-incarnate Christ was *a heavenly man* (I Cor. 15:47-49), but according to Philippians (2:6: "existing in the form of God") this pre-incarnate Christ belongs to an order of beings *higher than heavenly humanity.*

Answer: The Corinthian passage refers not to the preincarnate but to the risen and ascended Christ, as is evident from the context (see I Cor. 15:49).

(3) The same people who are denounced by Paul (Gal. 1:6, 7) are more than tolerated by the author of Philippians (1:15-18). While Paul says that they are accursed individuals who *pervert* the gospel of Christ, Philippians says that they are *proclaiming* the Christ, a fact in which he rejoices though they preach Christ from envy and rivalry.

Answer: These are not the same persons. Those to whom Phil. 1:15-18 refers are not preaching a different doctrine. They are proclaiming the true Christ, but their motives are not pure. As to the people who are condemned in Gal. 1:6, 7, these are probably referred to in Phil. 3:2, where the denunciation is similarly sharp.

(4) The real Paul is no boaster. He says, "When I would do good, evil is present" (Rom. 7:21). But the author of Philippians says that he was *blameless* when measured by the standard of the law (Phil. 3:6).

Answer: There is no contradiction. A person can be blameless, indeed, with respect to the law considered as an external commandment, but he may still be very guilty with respect to the law viewed in its deeply spiritual meaning.

It will have become evident that the arguments against the Pauline authorship of Philippians are very superficial. They have been called frivolous. Scholarship in general, throughout the centuries, has always considered this letter to be a genuine product of the mind and pen of Paul. Weizsäcker was right when he said that the reasons for attributing the epistle to Paul are "overwhelming." And so was McGiffert when he declared: "It is simply inconceivable that anyone else would or could have produced in his name a letter in which the personal element so largely predominates and the character of the man and the apostle is revealed with so great vividness and fidelity" (*The Apostolic Age*, p. 393).

Not only does the letter claim to have been written by Paul, and not only do the conditions reflected in it harmonize, on the whole, with those described in Acts 28, as has already been indicated, but the character of Paul, as revealed in his other letters, is also clearly expressed in Philippians. Here, too, we find a person who is deeply interested in those whom he addresses (cf. Phil. 1:3-11, 25, 26; 2:25-30 with Rom. 1:8, 9; I Thess. 1:2 ff.; II Thess. 1:3, 11, 12); is anxious to see them (cf. Phil. 2:24 with Rom. 1:11; I Thess. 2:17, 18); and loves to encourage and praise them (cf. Phil. 4:15-17 with II Cor. 8:7; I Thess. 1:3, 6-10). Nevertheless, here, as well as in the other epistles, his praise never ends in man but always in God (cf. Phil. 1:6 with Rom. 8:28-30; Gal. 5:22-25; I Thess. 1:4, 5; II Thess. 2:13). Here, too, as elsewhere, he likes to review his past relations with the church (cf. Phil. 2:12; 4:15, 16 with I Cor. 2:1-5; 3:1, 2; I Thess. 2:1-12). He shows great tact in admonishing (cf. Phil. 4:2, 3 with II Cor. 8:7; I Thess. 4:9, 10; Philem. 8-22). Nevertheless, he is never afraid to assert his authority (cf. Phil. 2:12-18; 4:1-9 with I Cor. 16:1; I Thess. 5:27). He is a very humble man who is filled to overflowing with gratitude for the mercies which God showed to one so unworthy (cf. Phil. 3:4-14 with I Cor. 15:9; II Cor. 11:16-12:10; Eph. 3:8).

The testimony of the early church is in harmony with the conclusion which has been derived from the epistle itself.

Thus Eusebius, having made a thorough investigation of the oral and written judgment of the church, writes: "But clearly evident and plain are the fourteen (letters) of Paul; yet it is not right to ignore that some dispute the (letter) to the Hebrews" (*Ecclesiastical History* III.iii). Obviously Eusebius, writing at the beginning of the fourth century, knew that the entire orthodox church accepted Philippians as being among "the true, genuine, and recognized" epistles of Paul (*op. cit.*, III.xxv).

From Eusebius we go back to Origen (fl. 210-250). His works are full of quotations from Philippians; for example, "For we do not hesitate to affirm that the goodness of Christ appears in a greater and more divine light because . . . he humbled himself, and became obedient to death, even death on a cross, than if he had judged existence in a manner equal to God something to keep in his grasp, and had shrunk from becoming a servant for the salvation of the world" *(Commentary on John* I.xxxvii), clearly a reference to Phil. 2:6-8. He considered Paul to be the author of Philippians (same book I.xvii, a comment on Phil. 1:23).

Hippolytus, said to have been a bishop of Portus near Rome, was martyred somewhere about A. D. 235–239. He was a disciple of Irenaeus, who was a disciple of Polycarp, who was a disciple of the apostle John. Hippolytus quotes from Philippians again and again. Among the passages from this epistle which he uses frequently is the very one of which Origen was also fond, namely, Philippians 2:6-8. And he ascribes Philippians to "the blessed Paul" *(Fragment from Commentaries,* on Gen. 49:21-26).

From Origen we can go back to his teacher, Clement of Alexandria (fl. 190–200), and from Hippolytus we can go back to his teacher, Irenaeus. But before doing so, it is necessary to point out that also Tertullian who in his famous work against Marcion (begun A. D. 207) combats the notion that such expressions as "form of a servant" and "fashion as a man" prove that Christ did not truly become man, thereby definitely indicates that he was well acquainted with Philippians *(Against Marcion* V.xx). Moreover, references to that epistle abound in his various writings. He considers Paul the author (see, for example, *Antidote to the Scorpion's Sting,* Chapter XIII).

This brings us then to Clement of Alexandria and to Irenaeus. So frequently does the former refer to Philippians, which he regards to be the work of "the apostle," that in his *Stromata* or *Miscellanies* he quotes more than once from each of its four chapters.

What Irenaeus says about the authorship of Philippians must be considered of great significance, and this because of his many travels and intimate acquaintance with almost the entire church of his day. His voice in a matter as important as this may be considered the voice of the church. Now in his work *Against Heresies* (written about A. D. 182-188) he refers to passages from every chapter of Philippians. Particularly instructive is his explanation of the phrase "obedient unto death" (V.xvi.3, on Phil. 2:8), and the one with reference to Christ's subsequent exaltation (I.x.1, on Phil. 2:10, 11). Without the least hesitation he ascribes Philippians to Paul (III.xii.9) that is, to "the one who received the apostolate to the Gentiles" (IV.xxiv.2).

The Muratorian Fragment, an incomplete list of New Testament books, written in poor Latin and deriving its name from Cardinal L. A. Muratori (1672–1750) who discovered it in the Ambrosian Library at Milan, may be assigned to the period 180-200. It contains the following: "Now the epistles of Paul, what they are, whence or for what reason they were sent, they themselves make clear to him who will understand. First of all he wrote at length to the Corinthians to prohibit the schism of heresy, then to the Galatians against circumcision, and to the Romans on the order of the Scriptures, intimating also that Christ is the chief matter in them — each of which it is necessary for us to discuss, seeing that the blessed apostle Paul himself, following the example of his predecessor John, writes to no more than seven churches by name in the following order: to the Corinthians (first), to the Ephesians (second), to the Philippians (third), to the Colossians (fourth), to the Galatians (fifth), to the Thessalonians (sixth), to the Romans (seventh)." Philippians is also included in Marcion's Canon and in the Old Latin and Old Syriac Versions.

How gloriously did the Christians of Lyons and Vienna, many of whom were subjected to indescribable torture for the sake of their faith and to the cruelest forms of death, make use of Phil. 2:5-8! They became imitators of their Lord's humility and refused even to be called "martyrs." See their unforgettable *Letter to the Brothers in Asia and Phrygia.* This letter was written A. D. 177, and is found in Eusebius, *op. cit.,* V.i, ii.

But it is possible to go back even farther. Polycarp's beautiful Letter (or *Letters*) to the Philippians has (or *have*) already been described (see Section III, The Church At Philippi). Those who accept the two letter theory give the dates as A. D. 135 and 115. He definitely states that the blessed and glorious Paul had written to the Philippians. In his day, therefore, that fact was well-known.

Ignatius, on his journey to Rome, where he was going to be killed by beasts in the amphitheatre (about A. D. 108), wrote several letters. He clearly shows that he is well acquainted with Philippians. It is true that a few of the references are rather vague, but surely when he describes people who are "enemies of the cross of Christ . . . whose god is the belly" (*To the Magnesians* IX; *To the Trallians* XI), he is quoting Phil. 3:18, 19.

Finally, Clement of Rome, writing to the Corinthians probably about the last decade of the first century, uses a few expressions which remind one immediately of Paul's letter to the Philippians. This resemblance is seen especially when both are read in the original or in a translation that adheres closely to the original:

Philippians	*I Clement*
"Only continue to exercise y o u r citizenship in a manner worthy of the gospel of Christ" (1:27).	"(This will be so) if we are not exercising our citizenship in a manner worthy of him" (i.e., worthy of Christ, XXI).
"in (the) beginning of the gospel" (4:15).	"in (the) beginning of the gospel" (XLVII).

The conclusion of the entire matter is this: All the evidence, external and internal, points to Philippians as a genuine, authentic epistle, recognized as such already in the earliest written sources that have been preserved, and, whenever ascribed to anyone, always ascribed to *Paul*.

Closely connected with the authorship of Philippians is its unity. It is well at the very outset to define the exact question that is of importance in this connection. That question is *not*, "Did Paul write more than one letter to the Philippians?" The possibility that he did can be readily granted. Did he not also write a letter to the Corinthians which has not come down to us? See the reference to it in I Cor. 5:9. There are scholars who believe that the proposition, "Paul wrote more than one letter to the Philippians," can be defended on the basis of Polycarp's statement, "For neither am I, nor is any other like me, able to follow the wisdom of the blessed and glorious Paul, who . . . when he was absent wrote *epistolas* to y o u" (*To the Philippians* III.2). Others, for various reasons, dispute this conclusion. The real question, however, is *this*, "Does the existing, canonical letter of Paul to the Philippians consist of more than one letter?" Among those who deny the unity of Philippians are the following: Beare, Goodspeed, Hausrath, Lake, McNeile, Rahtjen, J. Weiss. Their reasons (with individual variations) are as follows:

(1) The *tone* of the letter suddenly changes from that of tender address to that of harshness, as the apostle begins to use terms like *dogs, evil workers, the concision*. Cf., 3:1 with 3:2 ff.

(2) The *content* also changes. There is a sudden attack on Judaizers, out of keeping with the contents of the rest of the letter. This is followed by a warning against sensualists. Clearly, the section 3:2-4:1 is an interpolation, which must have belonged to another letter. Then there is also the note of thanks for the gift that had been brought to the apostle by Epaphroditus (4:10-20). This, too, stands by itself, must be viewed as a separate letter. Perhaps this was written first of all.

This shows that what we actually have here is three letters (complete or incomplete): *a.* 4:10-20; *b.* 1:1-3:1; 4:2-9, 21-23; and *c.* 3:2-4:1. (It must be added immediately, however, that the critics are by no means united on the extent of each of the letters that supposedly entered into the combination which we now call Philippians.)

(3) The word *finally* (3:1) also indicates that the letter is about to end at this point, but in the canonical epistle it introduces two entire chapters, and stands nowhere near the end of the letter.

Reasons for rejecting this view and maintaining the unity of Paul's Epistle to the Philippians:

(1) The change of tone (if it is correct to call it that) can be easily explained. See my comments on 3:1, 2.

36

(2) It is not true that the section 3:2-4:1 comes as a complete surprise. Paul has already spoken about *the adversaries* (1:28) and about *a crooked and perverse generation* (2:14). Besides, the change from one subject to another when writing to friends is altogether natural. Must we assume, for example, that when Paul in a thrilling manner climaxes his glorious paragraph on the Resurrection and the Second Coming with the exclamation, "O death, where is thy victory," etc., and adds a very fitting and moving admonition, "Wherefore, my beloved brothers, be steadfast," etc. (I Cor. 15), and then suddenly changes to "Now concerning the collection" (I Cor. 16:1), he must have made use of two letters to convey these sentiments?

The unity of Philippians stands out very strikingly. The same ideas recur again and again; such as: the note of rejoicing, the oscillation between expectation of acquittal and leaving room for the possibility of being sentenced to death, eschatological references, the evil of disharmony. The thank-y o u note (4:10-20) also has been anticipated (see 1:5-7; 2:25).

(3) It is not true that the words used in the original and translated "Finally" necessarily indicate that the letter will end almost immediately. See my comments on 3:1, footnote 124.

(4) Philippians appears, as a letter of Paul, in all the Canons of Scripture during the second century. In them all the reference is to *one* letter, never to two or three letters. No valid evidence has been presented to upset that well-established tradition. A fine and very recent article confirming the unity of the epistle is that by B. S. Mackay, "Further Thoughts on Philippians," *NTS*, Vol. 7, Number 2, (Jan. 1961) pp. 161-170.

VII. General Contents

Attempts have been made repeatedly to construct a formal outline for Philippians, a central theme with its subdivisions. Several themes have been tried; for example, *Christ-mindedness* (suggested by Phil. 2:5), *Paul's Joy in Christ,* etc. But such themes either lack distinctiveness (is not Christ-mindedness in action in all the epistles?) or comprehensiveness (though joy is certainly a very prominent characteristic of this letter, it is not an all-inclusive theme: faith, hope, and love are also in evidence). What we have here is a genuine letter from Paul to his beloved church at Philippi. The writer passes from one subject to another just as we do today in writing to friends. (The difference is that Paul's letter is inspired; ours are not.) What holds these subjects together is not this or that central theme but the Spirit of God, mirrored forth, by means of a multitude of spiritual graces and virtues, in the heart of the apostle, proclaiming throughout that between God, the apostle, and the believers at Philippi there exists a blessed bond of glorious *fellowship*.[25]

And what a marvelous heart, what a rich and many-sided personality, was that of Paul! We see the apostle first of all as *a joyful servant of Christ Jesus:* "Paul and Timothy, servants of Christ Jesus. . . . I thank my God every time I remember y o u, always in every supplication of mine in behalf of y o u all making my supplication with joy . . ." (Phil. 1:1, 3).

Presently we see him as *an optimistic prisoner* (prisoner *of the Lord,* that is!) : "Now I want y o u to know, brothers, that the things that have happened to me have in reality turned out to the advantage of the gospel . . . and most of the brothers have been heartened in the Lord through my bonds" (Phil. 1:12, 14).

Again we see him as *a humble cross-bearer:* ". . . in humblemindedness each counting the other better than himself. In y o u r inner being continue to set y o u r mind on *this,* namely, on that which (was) also in Christ Jesus, who . . . humbled himself. . . . In fact, even if I am to be poured out as a libation upon the sacrificial offering of y o u r faith, I rejoice, and I rejoice with y o u all" (Phil. 2:3, 5, 7, 17).

Anon we see him as *a thoughtful administrator:* "But I hope in the Lord Jesus to send Timothy to y o u soon so that I also may be heartened by knowing y o u r affairs. For I have no one likeminded who will be genuinely interested in y o u r welfare. . . . But I consider it necessary to send (back) to y o u Epaphroditus, my brother and fellow-worker and fellow-soldier, and y o u r messenger and minister to my need" (Phil. 2:19, 25).

Then we see him as *an indefatigable idealist* (and in *that* sense, *perfectionist*) : "Not that I have already gotten hold or have already been made perfect, but I am pressing on (to see) if I can also take hold of that . . . for which I was laid hold on . . . forgetting what lies behind (me) and eagerly straining forward to what lies ahead, I am pressing on toward the goal for the prize of the upward call of God in Christ Jesus" (Phil. 3:12-14).

Next we see him as *a tactful pastor:* "I entreat Euodia and I entreat Syntyche to be of the same mind in the Lord. . . . Lend these women a hand, for they strove side by side with me in the gospel" (Phil. 4:2, 3).

And finally we see him as *a grateful recipient:* Nevertheless, y o u did nobly in sharing my affliction. . . . I am amply supplied, having received from Epaphroditus the gifts (that came) from y o u, a fragrant odor, a sacrifice acceptable, well-pleasing to God" (Phil. 4:14, 18).

Two further items must be stressed, in this connection. First, that the various facets of Paul's rich personality, the multiple categories in which he functions, *overlap.* Not a single one of them can be separated from any of

[25] In his excellent book, *Philippians, The Gospel at Work,* M. C. Tenney has a fine chapter on "The Fellowship of the Gospel," pp. 35-50. And see also my comments on Phil. 1:5.

the others. The same man who writes as a joyful servant of Christ Jesus is also writing as an optimistic prisoner, humble crossbearer, etc. Hence, in the following arrangement of the contents the name by which Paul is characterized in any given section is a matter *not of rigid classification but merely of emphasis.*

Secondly, throughout our attention is riveted not alone on Paul himself, but *on him in relation to his dearly beloved Philippians.* Remember the *fellowship!*

Thus understood, the contents of this genuine letter may be summarized as follows:

The Apostle Paul Pours Out His Heart to the Philippians, Whom He Prizes Highly and Loves Profoundly.

Chapter I

Verses 1-11

The Joyful Servant of Christ Jesus,

by means of
   salutation,
   thanksgiving,
   and prayer,
revealing his warm affection for the Philippians with whom he is united in a blessed fellowship.

Verses 12-30

The Optimistic Prisoner,

rejoicing in his imprisonment for the advantage of the gospel, and in the fact that Christ will be magnified in his person whether by life or by death; and exhorting the Philippians to remain steadfast, united, and unafraid.

Chapter II

Verses 1-18

The Humble Cross-bearer,

by an appeal to a fourfold incentive exhorting the Philippians to live the life of oneness, lowliness, and helpfulness, after the example of Christ Jesus, and to shine as lights in the midst of a wicked world, thereby filling the hearts of Paul and of themselves with joy.

Verses 19-30

The Thoughtful Administrator,

promising to send Timothy to the Philippians as soon as his (Paul's) own case has been decided,
and even now sending Epaphroditus back to them.

Chapter III

(the entire chapter)

The Indefatigable Idealist,

warning against evil workers (the *con*cision) who by placing confidence in flesh seek to establish *their own* righteousness and perfection; as contrasted with God's true servants (the *circum*cision) ;

for example, with Paul, who could boast of many prerogatives, but has rejected them all, and relies completely on the righteousness of Christ, in whom he is pressing on to perfection;

exhorting the Philippians to imitate him, to honor the friends and beware of "the enemies of the cross," sensualists, who set their minds on things of earth, while believers know that *their* homeland is in heaven.

Chapter IV

Verses 1-9

The Tactful Pastor,

in general, exhorting the brothers at Philippi to remain firm; and in particular, entreating Euodia and Syntyche to be of the same mind, and Syzygus to help these gospel-women;

urging the Philippians to rejoice in the Lord, to be big-hearted to all, and instead of worrying to bring everything to God in prayer that brings peace;

finally, admonishing the addressees to meditate only on praiseworthy things, practising these in imitation of Paul and with promise of rich reward.

Verses 10-23

The Grateful Recipient,

rejoicing in the generosity of the Philippians, and testifying that he has learned the secret of contentment and of readiness for every task;

resuming and completing his expression of appreciation for the generosity which the Philippians have shown both in the more recent and in the more distant past;

confessing his faith in God who will supply every need, and ascribing glory to him; and

concluding his letter with words of greeting and benediction.

Commentary
on
The Epistle to the Philippians

Summary of Chapter 1

Verses 1-11

Paul, the Joyful Servant of Christ Jesus

by means of salutation, thanksgiving and prayer, revealing his warm affection for the Philippians with whom he is united in a blessed fellowship.

1:1, 2 The Salutation.
1:3-11 The Thanksgiving and Prayer.

CHAPTER I

1 1 Paul and Timothy, servants of Christ Jesus, to all the saints in Christ Jesus who are in Philippi, together with overseers and deacons; 2 grace to y o u and peace from God our Father and the Lord Jesus Christ.

1:1, 2

I. *The Salutation*

1. In structure the letters which we find in the New Testament differ from those written today. Our letters *end* with the name of the sender. In Paul's day that name was mentioned first. Then came the name of the person(s) addressed and the rest of the opening salutation. There followed, generally in the order given: the thanksgiving and/or prayer (often both), the body of the letter, and finally the concluding items; such as greetings, word of farewell or even a benediction. It should be emphasized that this was the letter-plan as it existed in the polite society of Paul's day. The apostle simply took it as it was and poured a definitely Christian content into the customary form.[26] A glance at Philippians shows that Paul is following the then-prevailing letter-plan.

The sender's name is **Paul,** with whom *Timothy* is associated.

In a world held together politically by Rome and culturally by Greece it was natural that the writer should use his Greek-Roman name *Paul* instead of his Jewish name *Saul.* (For details on the meaning and use of these names see N.T.C. on I and II Thessalonians, p. 38.) It is also natural that he writes his own name first, for it was he himself who was the author of the letter, as is evident from the fact that in its entire contents, with the exception of the salutation, he uses the first person singular ("I" and "my" instead of "we" and "our"), while he refers to Timothy in the third person ("his," "him"). Examples:

"*I* thank *my* God in all *my* remembrance of y o u. . . . God is *my* witness

---

[26] See examples in A. Deissmann, *Light From the Ancient East* (translated from the German by L. R. M. Strachan), New York, fourth edition, 1922, p. 179 ff.; and in C. M. Cobern, *The New Archaeological Discoveries and Their Bearing upon the New Testament,* New York and London, seventh edition, 1924, pp. 582-590; and see also Acts 15:23-29; 23:25-30.

how *I* am yearning for y o u. . . . *I* hope in the Lord to send Timothy to y o u. . . . Y o u know *his* proved worth. . . . *Him*, then, *I* hope to send at once."

To the mention of his own name Paul adds **and Timothy**, as he also does in two other epistles written during the same imprisonment: Col. 1:1; Philem. 1:1; and as he had done in three earlier letters: II Cor. 1:1; I Thess. 1:1; II Thess. 1:1. The reasons for the addition of Timothy's name here in Philippians were probably the following: Timothy, though *not* co-author, was in full agreement with the message of the letter. Moreover, he was deeply interested in the Philippians, for he had been associated with Paul in bringing the gospel to them (Acts 16:11-40; I Thess. 2:2); had in all probability revisited them on more than one occasion (Acts 19:21, 22; 20:3-6; Phil. 2:22); and was destined soon to be᾽ sent to them again (Phil. 2:19-23). Moreover, Timothy was in Paul's vicinity when this letter was dictated, in a position to visit him. He may even have been the actual *writer* (not *author*) of the letter, Paul's secretary. That Paul dictated his letters appears clearly from Rom. 16:22; and may be inferred from I Cor. 16:21-24; Gal. 6:11; Col. 4:18; and II Thess. 3:17 (on which see N.T.C. on I and II Thessalonians, pp. 208, 209). (For details with respect to the life and character of Timothy see N.T.C. on The Pastoral Epistles, pp. 33-36.)

Paul calls himself and Timothy **servants**. James (1:1), Peter (II Peter 1:1), and Jude (verse 1) introduce themselves similarly. The Greek word is *doulos* (δοῦλος) singular, *douloi* (δοῦλοι) plural. Some prefer the translation *slaves*. It is true that *something* can be said in favor of that rendering. In a sense even deeper than that which pertains to ordinary slaves and their earthly masters, Paul and Timothy had been *bought* with a price and were therefore *owned* by their Master (I Cor. 3:23; 7:22) on whom they were *completely dependent* and to whom they owed *undivided allegiance*. If by thus defining the concept *doulos* as used here in Phil. 1:1 its meaning were exhausted, and if our word *slaves* conveyed nothing of a sinister nature, the translation *slaves* might be unobjectionable. But such is definitely not the case. As Paul uses the term, a *doulos*, in the spiritual sense, is one who *ministers* to his Lord with gladness of heart, in newness of spirit, and in the enjoyment of perfect freedom (Rom. 6:18, 22; 7:6), receiving from him a glorious reward (Col. 3:24). Love and good will toward God and man fill the heart of this *doulos* (Gal. 5:13; Eph. 6:7). But with the English word *slave* we immediately associate the ideas of involuntary service, forced subjection, and (frequently) harsh treatment. Hence, in the light of Paul's own use of this noun and of the cognate verb, it is clear that the rendering *slaves* in passages such as Phil. 1:1 is not the best, and that the translation *servants* (as in A.V., and as in the text of A.R.V. and of R.S.V.), though not fully adequate, is the better of the two. It must be borne in mind, however, that these servants serve their Lord all the more heartily

because they know that they have been redeemed by his blood from the
bondage of sin, and accordingly belong to him, who is the Disposer of their
destinies, the Director of their lives.[27]

By adding **of Christ Jesus** Paul accomplishes two things: (1) He directs
the attention to *his Lord* and away from himself and from Timothy. Not
Paul and Timothy are all-important; Christ Jesus is. In the deepest sense
Philippians is *Christ's* letter to the church. Let the Philippians remember
that. (2) He focuses the light upon *his heavenly Master rather than upon
Rome* which considered itself to be the master of the earth. It is not surprising that Paul, being a prisoner who by dint of circumstances was being
constantly reminded of the servile attitude of Roman soldiers, and writing
to people living in a Roman colony many of whose citizens worshipped the
Roman emperor, was comforted by the fact that the Anointed One, the
Savior, and not the emperor, was his real Master. (For a detailed treatment of the names *Jesus* and *Christ* see N.T.C. on I and II Thessalonians,
pp. 41, 42; and for the order in which the words occur here — *Christ Jesus*
instead of *Jesus Christ* — see N.T.C. on The Pastoral Epistles, p. 51, footnote 19.)

Now in the opening salutation of every one of his letters, with the exception of Philippians, I and II Thessalonians, and Philemon, Paul calls himself *apostle*. In fact, even in Rom. 1:1 and Titus 1:1, where as in Phil. 1:1
he refers to himself as *servant,* he still immediately adds *apostle*. Why then
does he omit the designation *apostle* here in Phil. 1:1? The probable reason is that the Philippians were Paul's "beloved and longed for," his "joy
and crown" (Phil. 4:1), with whom he knew himself to be on the most
pleasing and intimate terms of Christian fellowship and among whom his
authority stood unassailed. It is possibly for this same reason that in writing to this church founded by himself Paul does not deem it at all necessary
to indicate any distinction between himself and Timothy. Humbly he
writes, "Paul and Timothy, servants of Christ Jesus." Compare with this
II Cor. 1:1 and Col. 1:1 (apostle . . . brother), and Philemon, verse 1
(prisoner . . . brother). The thoroughly sympathetic and understanding
Philippians did not have to be told that Paul was the apostle and that
Timothy was his delegate. Besides, in Christ, the two, though differing in
age, authority, and experience, were equal in the sense that both were
saved by the same grace and were engaged in the same exalted task.

Paul addresses his letter **to,** and pronounces his salutation upon **all the
saints in Christ Jesus who are in Philippi.** He is not merely interested in

---

[27] In the Old Testament the prophets as a group (Amos 3:7 and other passages) are
called *douloi,* that is, *servants,* and the name *doulos,* translated *servant,* is also applied to individual men of God, such as Joshua (Judg. 2:8), David (Ps. 35:27 =
LXX 34:27), Solomon (I Kings 8:28), and the author of Psalm 116 (Ps. 116:16 =
LXX 115:7). And see the great Servant passages in Isaiah (42:1-9; 49:1-9a; 50:4-11;
and 52:13-53:12).

certain prominent individuals, "the pillars of the church," for instance. Moreover, he hates cliques or unnecessary dissensions (cf. Phil. 4:2 and see also I Cor. 1:12, 13; 3:4; 11:21). He prays for *all* (Phil. 1:4), loves *all* (1:7), yearns for *all* (1:8), hopes to continue with them *all* (1:25), and greets *all* (4:21).

In writing or in preaching, the character of the message will be affected by the writer's or preacher's opinion of the addressed. It will make a difference whether he views them as *sinless ones in their own right* or, on the other hand, as nothing else than *gross sinners*, mere pagans, whether baptized or unbaptized. Paul avoids both extremes. He views the addressed as they exist not in themselves but in Christ. As such they are the saints. A *saint* is someone who by the Lord has been *set apart* to glorify him. It is in that sense that the addressed are called *holy*. Thus also during the old dispensation there were certain places, objects, and people that had been *set apart* or *consecrated* unto the service of God; for example, the holy place of the house of Jehovah (I Kings 8:10), the most holy place (Exod. 26:33), the tithe of the land (Lev. 27:30), the place of the bush (Exod. 3:5), holy water (Num. 5:17), the ark and the Levites (II Chron. 35:3), the priests (Lev. 21:6, 7) and the Israelites, in distinction from other nations (Exod. 19:6; Lev. 20:26; Deut. 7:6; Dan. 7:22; and cf. Num. 23:9; Amos 3:2). It is this latter idea which in the New Testament is applied to Christians generally. They are the Israel of the new dispensation, *set apart* to proclaim God's excellencies (I Peter 2:9). A saint, then, is a person to whom the Lord has shown great favor and upon whom, accordingly, there rests a great responsibility. He who is a *saint* (II Cor. 1:1) must remember that he has been *called to be a saint* (Rom. 1:7; I Cor. 1:2). Ideally, saints are, indeed, *believers* (Eph. 1:1; Col. 1:1).

But even redeemed sinners are never saints *in their own right*. Hence, Paul addresses the members of the church at Philippi as saints **in Christ Jesus,** that is, *by virtue of union with him*. Of this phrase ("in Christ," "in him," etc.) the apostle is very fond. So was also our Lord ("in me") as reported by the disciple whom he loved (see John 15:1-7). Paul uses the phrase repeatedly throughout his epistles. The union indicated is not "an actual physical union," as some have thought. Neither is it true that in Paul's writings there are two contradictory "ways of salvation," the one forensic or legal (Jesus paid for my sins, delivering me from guilt and condemnation), and the other experimental, mystical, or practical (I live in him, having died with him and having risen with him). On the contrary, the forensic and the experiential are two essential elements in the one great work of salvation. Christ's death *for* the believer must never be separated from the faith exercised *by* the believer. There is, moreover, a link between these two, namely, the regenerating and sanctifying work of the Holy Spirit *within* the believer. That Spirit applies to the believer's heart the merits of Christ's death, and, having planted in that heart the principle of faith, qualifies him to embrace his Lord by means of a living faith. Thus *for* and *within* and *by* form one golden chain, and the person who slights any one of these three links is wrong in theory and in practice. Paul, in some of the very passages in which the expression *in Christ (Jesus)* is used, combines the two ideas (what Christ did *for* the believer and what is now done *by* the latter) and also shows that the Bond of union between the two is *the Holy Spirit* working *within* the heart.

Examples:

FORENSIC	PRACTICAL
"There is therefore now *no condemnation* to them that are *in Christ* Jesus	*who walk* not after the flesh but after *the Spirit"* (Rom. 8:1, 4).
"And *he died for* all	that they who live should no longer *live* for themselves . . . wherefore if any man is *in Christ* he is *a new creature"* (II Cor. 5:17).

See also the explanation of another famous *in him* passage, which beautifully combines the related ideas, namely, Phil. 3:9, 10; and cf. I Cor. 6:19, 20; Titus 2:14.

Paul addresses his letter in general and his opening salutation in particular to all the saints in Christ Jesus that are in Philippi **together with** (that is, in association with) **overseers and deacons.** Against the traditional view according to which it was Paul who wrote Philippians the objection has been advanced that during the apostle's life there were as yet no "overseers and deacons." The sources, however, do not sustain the objection. Note the following:

As to *overseers* (Acts 20:28; Titus 1:7) or *elders,* that is, *presbyters* (Acts 20:17; Titus 1:5), these are mentioned again and again from early apostolic times on. The Lucan and Pauline references are as follows:

Acts 11:27-30

About A. D. 44, during a famine, a relief commission, consisting of Barnabas and Saul, is sent to Judea with a gift for the needy believers in that province. This gift is delivered to *the elders.* It is no surprise to find *elders* in this Jewish-Christian community. Surely, the much-debated view that this Christian eldership was a divinely sanctioned outgrowth of the eldership in ancient Israel (Josh. 24:31) and even more directly of the eldership in the contemporary non-Christian Jewish community right here in Jerusalem and surroundings is hard to refute. After all, the people who started the Judean churches were *Jews,* and the church is the true *Israel.*[28]

Acts 14:23

Sometime between A. D. 44 and 50, on his first missionary journey, Paul appointed *elders* in every church.

I Thess. 5:12, 13

About the year 52, on his second missionary journey, the very journey on which the church at Philippi was founded, the apostle writes to the Thessalonians, "Now we request y o u, brothers, to appreciate those who labor among y o u and are over y o u in the Lord and admonish y o u, and to esteem them very highly in love because of their work." See N.T.C. on that passage. That *overseers* or *elders* were included in this reference would seem probable.

Acts 20:17-38

In the year A. D. 57 or 58, Paul, on his third missionary journey, comes to Miletus on the coast of Asia Minor, and sends for the *overseers* (verse 28) or *elders* (verse 17) of the Ephesian region, and bids them farewell in a touching address.

I Tim. 3:1-7; Titus 1:5-9

A little later than Philippians, but not much later than A. D. 63, Paul after his release from the first Roman imprisonment, writing from Macedonia, enumerates the requirements for the office of *overseer* (I Tim. 3:1; Titus 1:7) or *elder* (Titus 1:5), and states that the *elders* who rule well should be counted worthy of double honor (I Tim. 5:17). See N.T.C. on The Pastoral Epistles; pp. 117-129; 179, 180; 344-349.

Though there are those who dispute it, yet a comparison between verses 17 and 28 of Acts 20, and between verses 5 and 7 of Titus 1, would seem to indicate that *elder* and *overseer* indicate the same person. The man who with respect to age and dignity is called *elder* is called *overseer* or *superintendent* with respect to the nature of his task.

As to *deacons,* about the year A. D. 33, when Greek-speaking Christians from among the Jews complained that their widows were being neglected in the daily distributions, seven men were chosen to attend to this matter and, no doubt, to matters of similar nature. The term *deacon* is not used in Acts 6:1-6, but that makes no material difference: the purpose for which these men were chosen is clearly indicated. The requirements for the office of *deacon* (the very term is used now) are found in I Tim. 3:8-12. (Other

---

[28] From the well-nigh endless literature on this subject I wish to select only two articles of very recent date and excellent contents. Both occur in *The Twentieth Century Encyclopedia of Religious Knowledge* (An Extention of *The New Schaff-Herzog Encyclopedia*), Grand Rapids, Mich., 1955. They are F. C. Grant, "Organization of the Early Church," pp. 823, 824; and D. J. Theron, "Presbyter, Presbyterate," p. 905.

supposed New Testament references to the office of deacon are debatable. See N.T.C. on The Pastoral Epistles; pp. 129-134.)

Now into this frame of references the mention of *overseers* and *deacons* here in Philippians (written probably A. D. 62/63) fits very well. It is definitely not an anachronism.

Another question is: Just why did Paul make special mention of these overseers and deacons in *this* (and in no other) opening salutation? Some answer: because these leaders had taken the initiative in gathering the gifts sent to Paul by the Philippians both now and on previous occasions. The apostle wishes to express his appreciation to them. Others are of the opinion that the particular reference to these leaders was in the nature of a hint to them that they must see to it that the instructions contained in the letter are carried out. And still others stress the idea that Paul by making special mention of these men thereby furnishes a needed endorsement of their authority (in view of the *dogs* and the *enemies of the cross of Christ* who were threatening the church, and who might lead some astray, Phil. 3:2, 18). Any or all of these explanations may be correct. And there may also have been an entirely different reason. We do not know.

2. The rest of the salutation — one might also say *the salutation proper* — is as follows: **grace to y o u and peace from God our Father and the Lord Jesus Christ.** Thus, there is pronounced upon all the saints in Christ Jesus that are in Philippi, together with overseers and deacons, *grace,* that is, God's spontaneous, unmerited favor in action, his sovereign, freely bestowed loving-kindness in operation, and its result, *peace,* that is, the conviction of reconciliation through the blood of the cross, true spiritual wholeness and prosperity, these two blessings (grace and peace) coming from God our Father and the Lord Jesus Christ.

This salutation is exactly as in Rom. 1:7; I Cor. 1:3; II Cor. 1:2; Gal. 1:3; Eph. 1:2; Philemon 1-3; and substantially also as in II Thess. 1:1. For further details of explanation and for a discussion of the question whether this salutation is an exclamation, a declaration, or perhaps merely an expression of a pious wish, see N.T.C. on I and II Thessalonians, pp. 40-45, 153, 154.

---

3 I thank my God in all my remembrance of y o u, 4 always in every supplication of mine in behalf of y o u all making my supplication with joy, 5 (thankful) for y o u r fellowship in the gospel from the first day until the present, 6 being confident of this very thing that he who began a good work in y o u will carry it on toward completion until the day of Christ Jesus; 7 just as it is right for me to be thus minded in behalf of y o u all, because I am holding y o u in my heart, y o u all being partakers with me of grace (as evidenced) both in my bonds and in the defense and confirmation of the gospel. 8 For God is my witness how I am yearning

for y o u all with the deeply-felt affection of Christ Jesus. 9 And this is my prayer that y o u r love may abound more and more with full knowledge and keen discernment, 10 so that y o u may approve the things that are excellent and may be pure and blameless with a view to the day of Christ, 11 filled with the fruits of righteousness that come through Jesus Christ to the glory and praise of God.

1:3-11

II. *The Thanksgiving and Prayer*

1:3-8

A. *The Thanksgiving*

3. In the letters that present themselves as coming from Paul (and, we firmly believe, actually did come from him) the salutation is in all except two cases (Galatians and Titus) followed by hearty words of thanksgiving. This praise is addressed not to the gods or to any particular deity (as was customary in Paul's day among pagans) but to that glorious Being whom Paul here (and in Rom. 1:8; Philem. 4) calls *my God*. His words are **I thank my God.**[29] The apostle is jubilant. He reflects on the wonderful way in which he has been led and on the evidences which the church at Philippi has given of its love for the gospel and for himself. Hence, he says, I thank *my God*. Cf. Ps. 42:11; 63:1. He continues **in all my remembrance of y o u.**[30] The many individual reflections on the work of grace in the lives of the Philippians are grouped together in the phrase *all my remembrance* (literally "all *the* remembrance," but in the light of the immediate context the article surely has possessive force).

4. Now thanksgiving, by causing a person to reflect on *blessings,* increases his *joy.* Hence, there now follows the parenthesis, which indicates a circumstance accompanying the thanksgiving: **always in every supplication of mine in behalf of y o u all making my supplication with joy.** (For *prayer* and its synonyms see N.T.C. on The Pastoral Epistles pp. 91, 92). A *supplica-*

---

[29] Not, "I, however, thank God," based on a reading preferred by Ewald, Zahn, Moffatt, and others. No more here than in comparable passages (Col. 1:3; I Thess. 1:2) is Paul trying to draw a contrast between (a) himself and Timothy, or (b) himself and the Philippians. As to the latter, the view that he wishes to say, "I for my part do not feel as meanly as y o u do about this last gift y o u sent me," rests upon a fanciful reconstruction of the historical background.

[30] Not "in all y o u r remembrance of me." Here as well as elsewhere μνεία is followed by the objective genitive (see Rom. 1:9; Philem. 4). Besides, the parallelism is evident: "my remembrance of y o u" underlies "in every petition of mine in behalf of y o u." In both cases it is *Paul's* activity that is indicated: *Paul* remembers, *Paul* makes petition.

tion is a petition for the fulfilment of a definite need that is keenly felt. Even in Philippi there were definite spiritual needs. There were imperfections (Phil. 1:9-11; 2:2, 4, 14, 15; 4:2) and dangers (Phil. 3:2, 18, 19). So Paul again and again (always . . . in every supplication) beseeches the Lord that these needs may be supplied. In these supplications Paul omitted no one (in behalf of y o u all). The main point, however, is this: since there was much room for thanksgiving, Paul is ever making his supplication *with joy,* for prayer with thanksgiving is joyful prayer.

5. The *immediate* reason for the thanksgiving is given in verse 5, the *ultimate* reason in verse 6. These two must not be separated. What Paul is saying is in substance this, "Y o u r *perseverance* in sympathetic participation in the work of the gospel (verse 5) has convinced me that y o u are the objects of divine *preservation* (verse 6). For all this I thank my God (verse 3), making my supplication with joy (verse 4)." We find exactly the same reasoning in I Thess. 1:2-5, where the believers' day-by-day Christian living is regarded as the unquestionable evidence of their election from eternity. And for all that Paul gives thanks to God (see N.T.C. on I and II Thessalonians, pp. 45-51).

Returning then to the immediate reason for thanksgiving we read: **thankful** (supplied from verse 3) **for y o u r fellowship in the gospel.**

The Fellowship of all Believers in Christ [31]

(1) It is a fellowship *of grace.* It is not a natural or Platonic fellowship, nor is it man-made, that is, called into being or organized by men, like a club or society. It is not even *merited* by men. It is sovereignly effected by Jesus Christ (I Cor. 1:9), and is the gift of the Spirit (II Cor. 13:13; Phil. 2:1) sent from the Father. Apart from Christ and his Spirit this fellowship is entirely impossible. Ideally speaking, the fellowship between Christ and his people even precedes *time,* for they were chosen in him *from eternity* (Eph. 1:4).

In time, Jesus Christ is, as it were, the Magnet, for it is he who *draws* to himself those given to him by the Father (John 12:32; 17:2, 9, 11, 24). He draws them through his Word and Spirit. This Spirit applies to them the merits of the Savior's death. Jesus, by means of his crucifixion, resurrection, ascension, and coronation, attracts to himself (that is, to abiding faith in himself) all of God's elect, from every age, clime, and nation. Moreover, in the person of their Surety, Jesus Christ, they themselves were tried, condemned, and crucified. They also were made alive and raised with him. With him they live in heavenly places. Their life is hid with Christ in God. This truth, accordingly, concerns both their state and their condition. Their santification as well as their justification is mediated through Christ

---

[31] Because of its length this footnote has been placed at the end of the chapter, page 93.

alone. *It is all of grace.* And it is a very close fellowship. In fact, so closely connected with him are believers that while they are on earth they even complete what is lacking in his suffering (see on Col. 1:24).

(2) It is, consequently, a fellowship *of faith.* Just as *Christ* draws sinners to himself through his redemptive acts, revealed to them by the Word and applied by *the Spirit, so they* approach and embrace Christ through a living, Spirit-given, *faith.* There is accordingly a faith-participation in Christ's sufferings, body, and blood (Phil. 3:10; I Cor. 10:16; II Cor. 1:7; and cf. Philem. 6), as well as in his resurrection and glory (Phil. 3:10; Col. 3:1). Faith commemorates Christ's death, rejoices in his presence, and awaits his revelation in glory.

(3) It is a fellowship *in prayer and thanksgiving.* Faith comes to expression in these devotions. Believers pray both individually and unitedly. Through their prayers they glorify *God.* Also they remember *one another* in prayer and thanksgiving (Phil. 1:3, 5, 9-11). Hence,

(4) It is a fellowship *of believers with one another; a fellowship in love for one another.* The same Magnet who attracts sinners *to himself,* also, in the very act of doing so, draws them into a close relationship with *each other.* Thus, the believer enshrines his fellow-believers in his heart and yearns for them (Phil. 1:7, 8; 2:2; 4:2; cf. John 13:34).

(5) It is therefore a fellowship *in helping each other; hence also, a fellowship in contributing to each other's needs.* Believers make their fellowship of love felt by remembering the poor among their number, no matter who they are, to what race they belong, or where they are living (Rom. 15:26; II Cor. 8:4). They, moreover, also make it a practice to support the missionaries in their needs. This was true especially with respect to the *Philippian* believers. These had even "entered into a partnership" with Paul in an account of expenditures and receipts (Phil. 4:15, which also belongs under 6).

(6) It is, accordingly, a fellowship *in promoting the work of the gospel.* It is an active co-operation in gospel-activity (Phil. 1:5; cf. I Cor. 9:23). Those who in this joint-participation are brothers give each other the right hand of fellowship with a view to hearty co-operation in kingdom-work (Gal. 2:9).

(7) It is a fellowship in *separation.* This sounds paradoxical but is true. The **koinonia** is a fellowship over against the world. Attachment to Christ always means detachment from the world, that is, from worldly thoughts, purposes, words, ways, etc. For what fellowship could there possibly be between light and darkness? (II Cor. 6:14; cf. James 4:4; I John 2:15).

(8) Finally, it is a fellowship in *warfare.* Believers struggle side by side against a common foe (Phil. 1:27-30; 2:25).

It is with all this in mind that the expression "I thank God for y o u r fellowship in the gospel" must be considered. It will then be clear that it indicates not only that the Philippians had "received the gospel by faith" (John Calvin), but much more. This acceptance by faith is implied, of course. But the emphasis is on *hearty co-operation in the work of the gospel* (cf. I Cor. 9:23), a *sympathetic participation* which had been shown **from the first day until the present** (for "the present" see also Rom. 8:22). As soon as the Lord had opened Lydia's *heart* for the gospel, that wonderful woman had opened her *home* for the gospel-workers (Acts 16:14, 15), and she had *kept* it open; in fact, she had opened it ever wider, so that what had been "headquarters" for the missionaries became "church" (place of assembly) for all the early converts at Philippi (Acts 16:40). How tenderly also the jailer had washed the missionaries' stripes and placed food before them (Acts 16:19-34). Is it not logical to believe that the man continued to reveal this same spirit? Moreover, when on his second missionary tour Paul had reached the very next place after Philippi, namely, Thessalonica, the Philippians had once and again sent gifts to him to further the work of the gospel (Phil. 4:16). When, on that same journey, the apostle had gotten to be in want at Corinth, he had not found it necessary to burden the Corinthians, for his needs had once more been supplied by "the brothers who came from Macedonia" (II Cor. 11:9). And thus, whenever the opportunity had presented itself — sometimes it had not presented itself (Phil. 4:10) — this noble band of Christians had proved the truth of the proverb, "A friend in need is a friend indeed!" The recent heroic mission of Epaphroditus, who had risked his very life in the interest of the good cause, was, as it were, the climax of this glorious manifestation of "fellowship in the gospel from the first day until the present" (Phil. 2:25; 4:13, 18).

There are several facts which cause this active co-operation to stand out all the more remarkably:

(1) It was a fellowship *for the furtherance of* (note εἰς) *the gospel*, not only in the interest of a good friend, Paul. In fact, in the hearts of the Philippians there was room for others besides Paul. Thus, for example, they (and also other believers in Macedonia) had given a magnificent example of Christian charity in supplying the needs of the poor saints at Jerusalem (II Cor. 8:1-5).

(2) It was *exceptional*. No other church had manifested such a high degree of fellowship (Phil. 4:15).

(3) It was *spontaneous*. Whenever there was need and opportunity to supply it, the Macedonians (surely including the Philippians) had given of their own free will and joyfully (II Cor. 8:2, 3).

(4) It included a giving *according to* their means, yes, *and at times even beyond their means* (II Cor. 8:3).

(5) It was *not a matter of fleeting impulse but of lasting principle*. The very phrase (here in Phil. 1:5) "from the first day until the present" stresses *perseverance* in spite of all obstacles. The prayers, the sympathies, the tes-

timonies, the willingness to make a pecuniary contribution, all these had
never ceased. The Philippians had not lost their first love (contrast Rev.
2:4) during this entire decade.

6. Paul thanks God for this, for it was God who had grafted his own
image in the hearts of the Philippians. Hence, to the *immediate* reason for
the thanksgiving the apostle now adds the *ultimate* reason: **being confident
of this very thing that** [32] **he who began a good work in y o u will carry it
on toward completion.** Note how closely the apostle links *human perseverance* ("y o u r fellowship in the gospel from the first day until the present")
with *divine preservation* ("*he who* began a good work in y o u will carry it
on toward completion"). Any doctrine of salvation which does not do full
justice to both of these elements is unscriptural. See Phil. 2:12, 13; II Thess.
2:13. Although it is true that God brings his work to completion, it is
equally true that when God has once begun his work in men, the latter by
no means remain merely passive instruments!

"*He who* began a good work in y o u," is God, as is evident from the context, "I thank *my God* . . . being confident that *he who* began a good work
in y o u, etc." When God's name, attitude, or activity is clearly implied, he
is not always mentioned by name. In fact by *not* mentioning his name but
merely saying *he who* there is often in such instances a greater opportunity
to stress his disposition or his activity: "*He who* does *this* will also certainly
do *that*." Thus William Cullen Bryant says beautifully (in his poem "To
A Waterfowl") :

> "*He who,* from zone to zone,
> Guides through the boundless sky thy certain flight,
> In the long way that I must tread alone,
> Will lead my steps aright." [33]

The good work which God had begun within the hearts and lives of the
Philippians was that of *grace,* whereby they had been transformed. This
work, indeed, was good in origin, quality, purpose, and result. The result
had been their own willing and working for God's good pleasure (Phil.

---

[32] The connective ὅτι is, of course, anticipatory: "confident of this very thing,
namely, that he, etc." The main clause (verse 3) , "I thank my God in all my remembrance of y o u," has as its object, "for y o u r fellowship in the gospel from
the first day until the present" (verse 5) . That is the *immediate* reason for the
thanksgiving. The adverbial modifiers of accompanying circumstance (modifying
"I thank my God") are a. "always making my supplication with joy" (verse 4) and
b. "being confident of this very thing, etc." (verse 6) . However, verse 6 expresses
more than this: also the *ultimate* reason for the thanksgiving.

[33] Other instances where God's name does not occur in the very phrase or clause
but the divine being or one of his attributes is mentioned in the immediate context or is clearly implied are Luke 2:14b (men of good pleasure = of *God's* good
pleasure) ; Rom. 8:11; Gal. 1:6; 2:8; 3:5; 5:8; I Thess. 5:24.

2:12, 13) ; specifically, their own hearty co-operation in whatever pertained to the advancement of the gospel.

Now Paul is confident that God will not permit his good work of transforming and qualifying grace to remain unfinished. The expression "will carry it onward toward completion" implies "and will present it complete."

Accordingly, out of the darkness and the distress of a prison in Rome a message of cheer reaches each Philippian believer, enabling him to say:

"The work thou hast in me begun
Shall by thy grace be *fully* done."

God, accordingly, is not like men. Men conduct *experiments*, but God carries out *a plan*. God never does anything by halves. Men often do.

This teaching of divine *preservation* for a life of service (hence, with implied human *perseverance*) is in harmony with that of the entire Bible, which tells us about:

a faithfulness that will never be removed (Ps. 89:33; 138:8),

a life that will never end (John 3:16),

a spring of water that will never cease to bubble up within the one who
    drinks of it (John 4:14),

a gift that will never be lost (John 6:37, 39),

a hand out of which the Good Shepherd's sheep will never be snatched
    (John 10:28),

a chain that will never be broken (Rom. 8:29, 30),

a love from which we shall never be separated (Rom. 8:39),

a calling that will never be revoked (Rom. 11:29),

a foundation that will never be destroyed (II Tim. 2:19),

and an inheritance that will never fade out (I Peter 1:4, 5).

It should be stressed, however, that according to the present context (and all of Scripture) this preservation is not for a purely selfish purpose but is *for service*. God's work of grace qualifies men *for work*.

Now God will carry his good work on toward completion **until,** and will actually have it all completed on, **the day of Christ Jesus.** This day is also called:

the day of Christ (Phil. 1:10; 2:16),

the day of our Lord Jesus (Christ) (I Cor. 1:8; cf. II Cor. 1:14),

the day of the Lord (I Thess. 5:2; II Thess. 2:2; cf. I Cor. 5:5),

the day (I Thess. 5:4),

that day (II Thess. 1:10),

the parousia (of the Lord, of our Lord Jesus, etc.) (I Thess. 2:19; 3:13; 4:15; 5:23; II Thess. 2:1, 8; cf. I Cor. 15:23; etc.). See also N.T.C. on I and II Thessalonians, pp. 76, 122-124, 141, 146-150, 161, 167, 168.

It is called the day *of Christ Jesus* because on that day *he* will be manifested in glory, will be met by his bride (the church), will judge, and will thus be publicly vindicated.

Not until that day has arrived will *that* work of God be completed which qualified the addressees for hearty co-operation in spreading the gospel and which ends in the completed fellowship. Moreover, it takes *all* God's ransomed children to make *one* ransomed child complete. A brick may have the appearance of a finished product, but it will still look rather forlorn until it is given its proper place in row and tier, and all the rows and tiers are in, and the beautiful temple is finished. So also God's children, like so many living stones, will form a finished temple when Jesus returns, not until then. Believers are like the dawning light that shines brighter and brighter unto the coming of the perfect day, for it is then that he who began a good work in them will have completed it.

7. The confidence (see verse 6) which Paul has with respect to the Philippians is well-founded, as he shows by adding: **just as it is right for me to be thus minded in behalf of y o u all, because I am holding y o u in my heart.**[34] Paul's *attitude* toward the Philippians (not just his *opinion* about them) has been made clear in the beginning of this long sentence: he thanks God for them, makes supplication for them with joy, being thankful for their fellowship in the gospel, etc. For this *disposition* on his part the apostle does not claim any special credit. He says, "It is *right* (morally obligatory) for me to be thus *minded* (or *disposed*)" (cf. Phil. 2:5; 3:15, 19; 4:2; also Rom. 8:5; 11:20; I Cor. 13:11; Gal. 5:10). Ill-will toward the Philippians, a refusal to thank God for them, while in his inmost being he is convinced of their loyalty to God's cause, would have been highly improper. The apostle is holding them in his *heart,* and the heart is the mainspring of dispositions as well as of feelings and thoughts (see Matt. 15:19; 22:37; I Tim. 1:5). Out of it are the issues of life (Prov. 4:23). And the fact, in turn, that the apostle is cherishing the Philippians in his heart finds its ready explanation in the situation upon which the emphasis really falls, namely, **y o u all being partakers with me of grace.** These Philippians have given proof that they belong to *the fellowship* (see on Phil. 1:5). Accordingly, Paul calls them "my fellow-partakers of the grace" (thus literally), that is, of that operation of God's grace which enables one to work in the interest of the gospel, to suffer for it, and to assist those who proclaim and defend it. (On the word *grace* see N.T.C. on I and II Thessalonians, p. 42). Paul continues: **(as evidenced) both in my bonds and in the defense and confirmation of the gospel.**[35]

---

[34] "*I* am minded," and "*I* am yearning"; hence also (in parallelism with "*I* am yearning") "*I* am holding y o u in my heart"; not: "Y o u are holding me in y o u r heart." Note also the word-order in the original.
[35] The word-order is as follows: ". . . because I am holding y o u in my heart both in my bonds and in the defense and confirmation of the gospel my fellow-partakers of the grace y o u all being." This raises the question. Does Paul mean that he is holding the Philippians in his heart both in his bonds and in the defense and con-

The Philippians had given evidence of their participation with Paul in the grace of God. They had proved it in his *bonds,* that is, his *imprisonment* (see on this word N.T.C. on The Pastoral Epistles, p. 251) and they had also proved it in something which, as it stood in the closest possible association with this imprisonment, is mentioned immediately afterward, namely, *the defense and confirmation of the gospel.*[36] It is evident from this clause that when these words were written Paul had already appeared before the Roman authorities. He had given an account *of himself as a herald of the gospel.*[37] He had *defended* the gospel by removing doubts and suspicions, and had *confirmed* it by setting forth its meaning positively. Naturally the two activities (defense and confirmation) overlapped. And the Philippians had shown that they were deeply concerned in all this. They had prayed for Paul. They had sympathized with him in his experiences — Were not their own experiences similar? Were not they engaged in the same conflict? See on Phil. 1:29, 30. — And they had even sent their personal representative to him with a gift and in order to assist him in every possible manner. (Phil. 2:25; 4:10-14, 18). Epaphroditus had delivered the gift and had begun his work in Rome. The fact that subsequently for a certain space of time he had not been able to assist Paul was nobody's fault. The reason for that was that this worthy ambassador, probably while busily engaged as Paul's attendant and assistant, had become a very sick man, on the verge of death! (Phil. 2:27).

8. Paul has just written: I am holding y o u in my heart (verse 7). He now shows that this is no exaggeration: **For God is my witness how I am yearning for y o u all with the deeply-felt affection of Christ Jesus.** Because it is important that the Philippians shall know how ardently he loves them, that they may be confirmed in the truths which he conveys and may take to heart his admonitions, the apostle appeals to the God who cannot lie and who judges the hearts of men (I Sam. 15:29; Jer. 11:20; John 14:6; 15:29; Rom. 2:23; II Tim. 2:13; Titus 1:2; Heb. 6:18).[38] That is the mean-

firmation of the gospel: or does he mean that all these Philippian saints are his fellow-partakers of God's grace, and that this participation is evidenced both in the apostle's bonds and in the defense and confirmation of the gospel? Obviously the latter. See verse 5. *Y o u all being* (πάντας ὑμᾶς ὄντας) is in apposition with *y o u* (ὑμᾶς). Hence, the clause means: I am holding y o u in my heart, y o u all being my fellow-partakers of grace (as evidenced) both in my bonds, etc.
[36] Some commentators seem to dissociate these two (a. bonds and b. defense and confirmation of the gospel), and regard b. as referring to Paul's preaching in general over the course of the years. But the fact that the apostle mentions b. immediately after a. is significant and shows that in the present instance the two should not be thus separated.
[37] See on Phil. 1:27 for a word-study of the concept *gospel.*
[38] As Calvin says aptly: *neque enim parum hoc valet ad fidem doctrinae faciendam cum persuasus est populus a doctore se amari:* "for it tends in no small degree to

ing of the words, "For God is my witness." Cf. Rom. 1:9; II Cor. 1:23; I Thess. 2:5, 10. The fact with reference to which Paul calls upon God to be witness is that the apostle yearns deeply for all these Philippians. He is tenderly attached to them and longs to see them again (cf. Phil. 4:1; Rom. 1:11; I Thess. 3:6; II Tim. 1:4). In fact, he yearns for them all "with the deeply-felt affection (or: "in the tender mercies") of Christ Jesus." Meaning: Paul's love is patterned after (cf. Phil. 2:5) and energized by Christ's indwelling love (Gal. 2:20).[39]

---

secure faith in the doctrine when the people are persuaded that they are loved by the teacher" (*Commentarius In Epistolam Pauli Ad Philippenses,* Corpus Reformatorum, vol. LXXX, Brunsvigae, 1895, on this passage).

[39] The word "deeply-felt affection" or "tender mercies" has given rise to much discussion. The original has σπλάγχνα (ἐν σπλάγχνοις) A.V. renders "bowels"; A.R.V., "tender mercies"; R.S.V. "affection." The primary, literal meaning is *inward parts, intestines, entrails.* See Acts 1:18, "He (Judas) burst open in the middle and all his *entrails* gushed out." It is when Scripture links the affections (love, mercy, pity) with the σπλάγχνα that objections arise. We are told that on this point the Bible is untrustworthy. Paul, being a child of his own day, is simply perpetuating a crude notion of the ancients.

However, over against this attack on Scripture and on Paul stand the following facts:

(1) Experience has proved again and again that emotions (sorrow, joy, pity, love, hatred, anger, etc.) do, indeed, affect the internal organs. A person, let us say, attends a joyous banquet. The feasting is suddenly interrupted by a message of sadness. Moved by grief and sympathy the banqueters — particularly those most directly concerned — lose their appetite.

(2) Science confirms this fact, and has shed some light on the function which the autonomic nervous system performs with respect to it.

(3) We are dealing here with figurative language. Paul has just as much right to use the term σπλάγχνα *figuratively* as we have to make a similar use of the term *heart.* The word σπλάγχνα which literally means *entrails* — and often especially the nobler entrails: heart, liver, lungs — , by way of metonymy, begins to indicate the spiritual center of the emotions, what we today call *the heart,* and even the emotion of *tender love* itself.

In our translation of the term σλπάγχνα we must remember that metaphorical terminology differs in various languages. With this in mind, I suggest the following rendering of the word in the New Testament passages in which it occurs:

(1) The literal rendering *entrails* (Acts 1:18, already quoted).
(2) Figurative usage:
     a. The heart:
         Luke 1:78: "merciful heart."
         II Cor. 6:12: "in y o u r own hearts."
         II Cor. 7:15: "his heart goes out to y o u."
         Col. 3:12: "compassionate heart."
         Philem. 7: "the hearts of the saints have been refreshed by you."
         Philem. 12: "my very heart."
         Philem. 20: "refresh my heart."
         I John 3:17: ". . . and closes his heart against him."
     b. Deeply-felt affection, tender mercies:
         Phil. 1:8: "the deeply-felt affection (or: the tender mercies) of Christ Jesus."
         Phil. 2:1: "deeply-felt affection (or: tender mercies) and compassion."
         Cf. L.N.T. (A. and G.) entry σπλάγχνον

1:9-11

B. *The Prayer*

9. Having thus reaffirmed his great love for the Philippians, Paul is able to proceed as he does; for, though the words which immediately follow imply that perfection had not yet been attained among those to whom this epistle would be read, the very tactful introduction (verses 3-8) has removed every legitimate reason for taking offense.

Verses 9-11 contain the substance of the prayer to which reference was made in verses 3 and 4. This should be compared with Paul's recorded prayers found in the other epistles of this first Roman imprisonment: Eph. 1:17-23; 3:14-21; Col. 1:9-14. Combining them we noticed that the apostle prays that those addressed may abound in wisdom, knowledge, power, endurance, longsuffering, joy, gratitude, and love. Also, we observe that Jesus Christ is regarded as the One through whom these graces are bestowed upon the believer; and that the glory of God is recognized as the ultimate purpose. Truly, one cannot afford to ignore Paul's lessons in prayer-life.

Accordingly, in the present section we have:

(1) *Its Burden:* **And this is my prayer that y o u r love may abound more and more.** The word *love* (ἀγάπη) crowds the pages of Paul's epistles. For its use in Philippians see, besides our present passage, 1:16; 2:1; 2:2. He views this love as being entirely dependent upon and caused by God's love which it strives to imitate (Eph. 4:32-5:2; 5:25-33). Though it is true that when the apostle speaks about the love which believers should exercise, he generally does so in a context which makes *men* the object of that love (Rom. 13:10; 14:15; I Cor. 4:21; II Cor. 2:4, 8; Gal. 5:13; Eph. 1:15; 4:2; etc.), yet no one who has made an earnest study of the closeness of *the fellowship,* which involves both God and men (see on 1:5), can long cling to the idea that for Paul *God* would be removed from the range of this object. (See Rom. 8:28; I Cor. 2:9; 8:3; Eph. 6:24; II Tim. 4:8.) And particularly when, as in the present passage and its context, there is nothing which in any way restricts this object, such rigid limitation seems unjustifiable. The love of which Paul speaks is, accordingly, intelligent and purposeful delight in the triune God, the spontaneous and grateful outgoing of the entire personality to him who has revealed himself in Jesus Christ, and consequently, the deep and steadfast yearning for the progress of his kingdom and for the true prosperity of all his redeemed. This yearning becomes manifest in one's attitude (humility, tenderness, the forgiving spirit even toward "enemies"), in words (of encouragement, truthfulness, and mildness) and in deeds (of self-denial, loyalty, and kindness). The best description of love is found in I Cor. 13.

Now Paul does not pray that the Philippians may *begin* to exercise this love, but that the ocean of their love may rise to its full height, overflowing its entire *perimeter;* in fact, that it may thus abound *more and more.* It is characteristic of Paul that he is never satisfied with anything short of perfection (see Phil. 2:11, 12; 3:13; 4:17; then also I Cor. 15:58; II Cor. 4:15; I Thess. 3:12; 4:1, 9, 10; II Thess. 1:3; Eph. 3:14-19; 4:12, 13; Col. 1:9, 10; 3:12-17; and cf. N.T.C. on The Pastoral Epistles, p. 75).

However, *fully developed* love never travels alone. It is accompanied by all the other virtues. It functions in beautiful co-operation **with full knowledge and keen discernment.** Though knowledge apart from love leaves its possessor a spiritual zero (I Cor. 13:2), and though "knowledge puffs up but love builds up" (I Cor. 8:1), love also needs knowledge, particularly *real, full, advanced spiritual knowledge* (ἐπίγνωσις) in the sense in which the word is used in Rom. 10:2; and cf. also the related verb used similarly in I Cor. 13:12). With the blessing of God such penetrating insight into God's wonderful, redemptive revelation will produce gratitude in an ever-increasing measure, which, in turn, will increase the supply and enhance the quality of love to God and to the brotherhood.

The apostle prays that as a further ingredient of their love the Philippians may have *keen discernment,* the taste and feeling for that which in any concrete situation is spiritually beautiful, *the aesthetic sense* in the sphere of Christian duty and doctrine (αἴσθησις is the Greek word, occurring only here in the New Testament). Love, in other words, should be *judicious.* This keen discernment or perception, born of experience, is the ability of mind and heart to separate not only the good from the bad, but also the important from the unimportant, in each case choosing the former and rejecting the latter. This is, indeed, necessary. A person who possesses love but lacks *discernment* may reveal a great deal of eagerness and enthusiasm. He may donate to all kinds of causes. His motives may be worthy and his intentions honorable, yet he may be doing more harm than good. Also, such an individual may at times be misled doctrinally. There must have been a good reason why Paul here stressed the necessity of abounding in love "with full knowledge and keen discernment" (see Phil. 3:1-3; 3:17-19).

(2) **10.** *Its Purpose:* **so that y o u may approve the things that are excellent.** That naturally follows from what has just been said. Certain commentators here prefer the rendering "so that y o u may distinguish the things that differ." In the abstract this translation is possible. Besides, the difference between the two is not great, for the ability to distinguish between the good and the bad would be for the purpose of electing the former and rejecting the latter. Nevertheless, the rendering found (with slight variations) in A.V., A.R.V. (text), and R.S.V. is to be preferred. It best suits the context: the man who not only has the ability to distinguish but also actually chooses

the things that really matter, in preference to those that are either bad or of little importance, does this with a view to being "pure and blameless," etc. Besides, Paul is his own best interpreter. Phil. 1:10 finds its best commentary in Phil. 4:8, 9 (see on that passage).[40] The prayer, accordingly continues, **and may be pure and blameless.** Underlying the first adjective is probably the image of precious metal from which the dross has been removed; hence, *unmixed, without alloy;* and so, in the moral sense, *pure.*[41] Underlying the second is that of arriving at one's destination *not stumbled against,* i.e., *uninjured* by any obstacles in the road; hence, morally uninjured, and so, *not worthy of blame, blameless* (the word is used in that passive sense also in Acts 24:16; for the active sense see I Cor. 10:32). The prayer, then, is that the Philippians, their faculties having been trained to prefer the good to the evil, and the essential to the trivial (cf. Heb. 5:14), may be pure and blameless **with a view to the day of Christ.** For the expression "the day of Christ" see on verse 6. Their whole life must be a preparation for that great day, for it is then that the true character of every man's life will be revealed (I Cor. 3:10-15), and everyone will be judged according to his work (Dan. 7:10; Mal. 3:16; Matt. 25:31-46; Luke 12:3; I Cor. 4:5; Rev. 20:12).

11. It is not enough, however, to pray that with a view to the day of Christ's return no flaw and no blame may be found in the Philippians. The implication of this negative petition must now also be stated positively. Hence, the prayer continues: so that y o u may be . . . **filled with the fruits of righteousness.**[42] Paul prays that in the hearts and lives of the Philip-

---

[40] As to the verb δοκιμάζω here –ειν, this does not settle the issue either way. It may mean *to put to the test, examine* (I Cor. 11:28; II Cor. 13:5) ; *to prove by means of testing* (cf. I Cor. 3:13 and I Peter 1:7); or *to approve* (I Cor. 16:3). As to the *diaphora,* these are opposed to the *adiaphora* (the things that do not matter). Hence, the *diaphora* would seem to be the things that really matter, the important or excellent things. Although basically the verb διαφέρω, used intransitively, means *to differ,* yet the sense *to be of (more) value, to be superior or excellent* finds abundant illustration not only in the New Testament (Rom. 2:18; see the context there; Matt. 6:26; 10:31; 12:12; Luke 12:7, 24) but also elsewhere (see the entry διαφέρω in L.N.T., A. and G.). The context and the parallel passage (Phil. 4:8, 9) must decide the issue. And these favor the rendering "approve the things that are excellent."

[41] The actual *usage* of the word favors this explanation. The etymology is not of much help, because of its uncertainty.

[42] Literally *fruit,* where (after "filled with") we could also say *fruits.* Moreover, according to the best reading, the word *fruit* is here in the accusative, καρπόν, the accusative of the remote object (cf. also Col. 1:9; II Thess. 1:11) ; elsewhere the apostle uses πληρόω with the dative (Rom. 1:29; II Cor. 7:4) or with the genitive (Rom. 15:13, 14). This simply shows that there is no fixed rule with respect to the case which follows this verb. The tendency, moreover, was toward the accusative.

pians there may be a rich spiritual harvest, consisting of a multitude of the fairest fruits of heaven; such as, love, joy, peace, longsuffering, kindness, goodness, faithfulness, gentleness, self-control (Gal. 5:22, 23), and the works which result from these dispositions. One of these works, a very important one, is soul-winning (Prov. 11:30). As is shown by the passage just mentioned (and see also Amos 6:12, cf. James 3:18), the expression "fruits of righteousness" is taken from the Old Testament. These are fruits that are produced by the right relation between God and believers. No mere man is ever able to produce them by his own unaided efforts. They are fruits **that come through Jesus Christ,** for apart from him the disciple can do nothing (John 15:5). It is Christ who by means of his sacrifice secured for the believer a new state and consequently also a new condition, so that by virtue of that new relationship the believer by the power of the Holy Spirit is now able to produce fruit, more fruit, much fruit (John 15:2, 5; cf. Matt. 7:17, 18). In fact, believers are "his workmanship, created in Christ Jesus for good works, which God prepared beforehand that we should walk in them" (Eph. 2:10).

Paul concludes his prayer by beseeching God that the ultimate purpose of all that is mentioned in the entire sentence, beginning with verse 9, may be **to the glory** [43] **and praise of God.** The circle must be completed. Fruits

---

[43] Paul uses the word δόξα, *glory,* more than seventy-five times in his epistles. Since it is a word with many different, though related, meanings, a closer study is profitable. The noun is related to the verb δοκέω; hence, has the primary meaning *opinion* (IV Macc. 5:18). It is but a small step to the meaning *good opinion* concerning someone; hence, *praise, honor, homage.*

The Hebrew *kābhôdh,* which is the most common word for *glory* in the Old Testament, has the primary meaning *weight, heaviness, burden* (Is. 22:24); hence, *substance, wealth, dignity.* It is used to describe Jacob's *substance,* his flocks and herds (Gen. 31:1). At times the element of brightness, radiance, splendor is added to that of substance. Thus, the word is used to indicate *the brilliant physical manifestation of Jehovah's presence* (Exod. 16:7; Is. 6:1-5).

In a study of the meaning of δόξα in Paul's epistles both the Greek derivation and use and the Hebrew background must be borne in mind. Accordingly, the different senses in which the word is used by Paul may be summarized as follows:

(1) *praise, honor bestowed upon creatures, or belonging to them* (their *reputation*). Here the antonym is *dishonor* (II Cor. 6:8) or *shame* (Phil. 3:19). The synonym of δόξα, so used, is τιμή (Rom. 2:7; 2:10).

(2) *adoration or homage rendered to God.* Thus the word is used here in Phil. 1:11, as is shown by its synonym *praise.* See also Rom. 3:7; 3:23; 4:20; 11:36; I Cor. 10:31, etc.

(3) *the thing which reflects honor or credit on someone, or the person whose virtues redound to the glory of another* (I Cor. 11:7; 11:15; II Cor. 8:23; I Thess. 2:20).

(4) *external splendor, brightness, brilliance, or radiance* (of the heavenly bodies, I Cor. 15:40, 41).

(5) *the bright cloud by which God made himself manifest, the Shekinah* (Rom. 9:4).

(6) *the manifested excellence, absolute perfection, royal majesty or sublimity of*

descending from heaven must waft their fragrance back to heaven again. The chief end of man is "to glorify God and enjoy him forever" (cf. Matt. 5:16; John 15:8; 17:4). Call this Calvinism if you wish; every man who loves the Word, be he a Baptist, Methodist, Lutheran, Calvinist, or whatever he may be, subscribes to it from the bottom of his heart. It was a thought embedded very securely and deeply in the heart and thoughtlife of Paul (I Cor. 10:31; Eph. 1:6, 12, 14). God must be magnified. His virtues must be extolled. The majesty of the redeeming love and power of him who when his people rejoice rejoices over them with singing (Zeph. 3:17) must be acknowledged gratefully, in spontaneous anthems of praise and adoration.

Synthesis of 1:1-11

This section consists of three parts: salutation, thanksgiving, and prayer. Thanksgiving and prayer are, however, so closely connected that they may be considered together.

In the salutation Paul associates Timothy with himself, so that the letter must be regarded as coming from both, though Paul alone is the author. Paul calls himself and Timothy servants of Christ Jesus, for they recognize Christ Jesus as their sovereign Lord, whom they serve willingly and with gladness of heart. The salutation — of grace and peace — is officially pronounced upon all the spiritually consecrated people in Philippi, viewed as gathered for worship. For a reason unknown to us Paul adds, "together with overseers and deacons." Happy the church with overseers and deacons whom a man like Paul can trust.

Paul thanks God because whenever he thinks of and prays for the Philippians, joy wells up in his heart. Truly, he is writing as Christ's *joyful servant*, yes joyful even though he writes from a Roman prison. The Philippians have always shown that the work of God's grace, proof of their eternal security and preservation, is functioning in their hearts and lives. They have shown and are showing, by their very deeds, that they understand the implications of the blessed *fellowship* of all those who are in Christ. Hence, though from a distance, they co-operate with Paul in his defense. In response to this splendid sharing, he yearns for them all with the deeply-felt affection of Christ Jesus.

God (Rom. 1:23; II Cor. 4:6), or of Christ (II Cor. 3:18; 4:4), *particularly also at his second coming* (Titus 2:13; II Thess. 1:9).

(7) *God's majestic power* (Rom. 6:4).

(8) *the light that surrounds those who are, or have just been, in contact with God* (II Cor. 3:7).

(9) *the state and/or place of blessedness into which believers will enter* (Rom. 8:18) *and Christ has already entered* (I Tim. 3:16).

(10) in general, *the pre-eminently excellent or illustrious condition of something or of someone, manifested excellence, either now or in the future* (I Cor. 15:43; II Cor. 3:10; Eph. 1:6; 1:14; 1:18; Phil. 3:21; 4:19).

He prays that their love may increase not only, but may also become fully rounded so as to include the graces of deep insight into the way of salvation and keen discretion in every concrete situation of life, that sense of true values which always chooses whatever is best. Thus may they all be filled with the fruits of righteousness to the glory and praise of God.

Summary of Chapter 1

Paul, the Optimistic Prisoner

rejoicing in his imprisonment for the advantage of the gospel, and in the fact that Christ will be magnified in his (Paul's) person whether by life or by death; and exhorting the Philippians to remain steadfast, united, and unafraid.

1:12-18a   The Imprisonment for the advantage of the gospel.

1:18b-26   Christ magnified in Paul's person whether by life or by death.

1:27-30   Exhortation to steadfastness, unity, and fearlessness.

12 Now I want y o u to know, brothers, that the things that have happened to me have in reality turned out to the advantage of the gospel; 13 so that it has become clear throughout the whole praetorian guard and to all the rest that my bonds are for Christ, 14 and most of the brothers have been heartened in the Lord through my bonds and are showing far more courage in telling the message of God without being afraid.

15 Some, to be sure, are heralding Christ from envy and rivalry, but others from good will. 16 The latter do it out of love, knowing that I am appointed for the defense of the gospel; 17 the former proclaim Christ out of selfish ambition, not sincerely, thinking to raise up affliction (for me) in my bonds. 18 What then? Only that in every way, whether in pretense or in truth, Christ is being proclaimed, and in this I rejoice.

1:12-18a

I. The Imprisonment for the Advantage of the Gospel

12. Being the Joyful Servant of Christ Jesus, Paul is also the Optimistic Prisoner. The Christ whom he so willingly serves will take care of him; in fact, is doing so already, and not of *him* alone, but what is far more important, of *the gospel* also. For the concept *gospel* see on 1:27.

In all probability this optimism was not wholly shared by those whom Paul addresses. The church at Philippi was on tenterhooks. "What is going to happen to Paul; will he be condemned or will he be acquitted?" That was the question which everyone was anxiously asking. "Too bad for him . . . and for the cause of the gospel, this imprisonment!" That was what many people were thinking.

Now on both of these points Paul was of a different mind. With him the primary question was not, "What is going to happen to me?" It was, "How is the gospel-cause affected by whatever happens to me?" And his answer was not, "It is being retarded." It was, "It is actually being advanced by my imprisonment." Accordingly, Paul writes first about "the gospel," "the message of God," "the Christ" (verses 12-18), and then about his own hope of release (verses 19-26). And even in that second paragraph he writes not so much about himself as about "Christ magnified" in his (Paul's) person and work.

The opening clause, **Now I want y o u to know, brothers,** is substantially the same in meaning as the slightly differently worded one in I Cor. 11:3 and Col. 2:1. Similar is also the expression, "I (or *we*) do not wish y o u to be in ignorance" (Rom. 1:13; I Cor. 10:1; 12:1; II Cor. 10:1; 12:1; II Cor.

1:18; I Thess. 4:13) ; and cf. "I (or *we*) make known to y o u" (I Cor. 15:1; II Cor. 8:1; Gal. 1:11). Introductions of this character serve to call attention to the fact that something of considerable interest or importance is going to follow. The word *brothers* (also in 1:14; 3:1, 13, 17; 4:1, 8, 21) is one of endearment, and indicates that the apostle regards these Philippians as being, along with himself, children of the same heavenly Father, by virtue of the merits of Christ and the work of the Spirit, and accordingly as being included in the glorious fellowship (see on verse 5 above).

Paul continues, **that the things that have happened to me have in reality turned out to the advantage of the gospel.** The apostle's recent experiences (literally, "the things concerning me" or "my affairs"; cf. Eph. 6:21; Col. 4:7) have had the same effect on the gospel-message as the work of sturdy engineers has on the progress of an army. These men are sent ahead in order to remove obstructions and clear the roads for the rest of the army. Now in the path of the gospel, too, there had been formidable obstructions. On the part of those who had heard vague rumors but were unacquainted with the real essence of the gospel, there had been mistrust and hostility. And on the part of many a church-member there had been fear and cowardice. Paul's experiences and reactions — his bonds, trial, constant witness for Christ, conduct in the midst of affliction — had served the purpose of tending to remove these obstacles. Thus, road-blocks set up by Satan to hinder and stop the progress of the gospel (see N.T.C. on I Thess. 2:18; cf. I Cor. 9:12) had become stepping-stones to better understanding and deeper appreciation of God's redemptive truth and to rising courage in defending it. Paul had been bound, but the word of God could not be bound (see II Tim. 2:9; cf. Isa. 40:8; 55:11). When the apostle went to Rome as a prisoner, it was in reality *the gospel* that went to Rome.

Thus it has ever been. Joseph, cast into a pit and sold into slavery, by and by magnifies God and praises his providence (Gen. 37:23, 24; 50:20). Israel, pursued by Pharaoh's army, a moment later is heard singing a song of triumph (Exod. 14 and 15). Job, deprived of his children, earthly goods, and health, arrives at a deeper insight into the mysteries of God's wisdom than ever before (Job 1 and 2; then 19:25-27 and 42:5, 6). Jehoshaphat, threatened by the Ammonites and Moabites, offers a soul-stirring prayer in the midst of his distress. There follow praise, victory, and thanksgiving (II Chron. 20). Jeremiah, cast into a muddy cistern and suffering other afflictions, coins the famous phrase immortalized in Scripture and song, "Great is thy faithfulness" (Jer. 38:6; Lam. 3:23; cf. verses 2 and 7). Our Lord Jesus Christ, crucified, by means of his very cross gains the victory over sin, death, Satan, causing every true believer to exclaim, "Far be it from me to glory save in the cross of our Lord Jesus Christ" (Matt. 27:5; Acts 4:27, 28; Gal. 6:14; cf. Heb. 12:2). Peter and John, imprisoned, become bolder than ever in proclaiming Christ to be the only Savior (Acts 4). The early church, scattered abroad, improves that very opportunity to go about preaching the word (Acts 8).

The manner in which this wonderful progress has been achieved is now described. First, Paul's experiences have affected the outside-world, notably, the praetorian guard (verse 13). Secondly, they have exerted their wholesome influence upon insiders, the "brothers" (verse 14).

13. Beginning with the first group, Paul states, **so that it has become clear throughout the whole praetorian guard and to all the rest that my bonds are for Christ.** On the expression *the praetorian guard* see *Introduction,* II, V. Paul was under constant guard (cf. Acts 28:16, 20). The guards relieved each other. In this way ever so many of them came into contact with this apostle to the Gentiles. They took note of his patience, gentleness, courage, and unswerving loyalty to inner conviction. They were deeply impressed. Yes, even these hardened soldiers, these rude legionaries, who presumably would be the very last to be affected in any way by the gospel, were deeply moved by what they saw and heard and felt in the presence of Paul. They listened to him as he talked to friends who came to visit him, or to his secretary to whom he dictated his letters, or to his judges, or to God in prayer, or even to themselves. It is not difficult to imagine that at first they listened with a measure of disdain or hardly listened at all. But after a while they became interested, and then . . . enthusiastic. And what they learned they began to spread. "We are guarding a very remarkable prisoner," they would say, "and we are firmly convinced that his imprisonment is not for any crime he has committed but solely *for his connection with the Christ* whom he proclaims." And so the news spread, from guard to guard, to the families of the guards, to Caesar's household (see on Phil. 4:22), and thus to "all the rest," the inhabitants of Rome, in general. Paul's *case* and, even better, Christ's *cause,* became "the talk of the town." That meant *progress* for the gospel, for *the real issue* was being clarified.

14. And now the effect upon "the brothers": **and most of the brothers have been heartened in the Lord** [44] **through my bonds and are showing far more courage in telling the message of God without being afraid.**

---

[44] What does "in the Lord" modify? Must we read, "brethren in the Lord" (A.V.)? This is possible, but it would be the only instance in the New Testament in which the noun *brothers* is so modified. However, we do have "brothers in Christ" in Col. 1:2. Hence, "brothers in the Lord" cannot be entirely dismissed. Or is it "bonds in the Lord"? But the order of the words in the original pleads against this meaning. Besides, the interpretation, "trusting in my bonds in the Lord" makes little sense. Probably the best is "heartened in the Lord through my bonds." That is entirely in harmony with the context here: Paul's bonds have become manifest as being for the sake of Christ, and so by means of these bonds and the testimony of the man in bonds most of the brothers have been heartened in the Lord. And see also Phil. 2:24 and 3:3, 4 (in the original).

Who were these *brothers?* Clearly, the believers in Rome. Here, years ago, a congregation had been established to which the apostle had addressed his famous Epistle to the Romans. That congregation consisted largely of converts from the Gentile world. However, when Paul, as prisoner, arrived in Rome, he immediately proclaimed the gospel to the *Jews,* with the result that "some believed . . . some disbelieved" (Acts 28:24). The Jews who believed founded *their own* churches in Rome. Nevertheless, we may be sure that between the members of the first group, the believers from the Gentiles, and the second, those from the Jews, there existed a bond of Christian fellowship, so that when Paul here speaks of the *brothers* he has reference to members of both groups, that is, to those among them who had not left Rome.[45] Similarly we read in Acts 28:30 that during his two years of imprisonment in Rome Paul welcomed *all* who came to him, proclaiming the kingdom of God and teaching about the Lord Jesus Christ openly and without hindrance (Acts 28:30, 31).

Now what had been the brothers' attitude to Paul and his message? And what had been the attitude of their leaders? As soon as they knew that Paul was on trial had they offered help? Had they remained steadfast in spreading the tidings of salvation, the good news? Here in verse 14 it seems to be implied that at first they had not shown a very commendable degree of courage. *Some* courage here and there, yes, but not very much. Instead, they seem to have been "frightened by the adversaries" (verse 28), definitely in need of the warning that each man should look out not only for his own interests but also for the interests of others (2:4). All had been looking after their own affairs (cf. 2:21). At his defense no one had been at Paul's side but all had deserted him.

But things were changing now. Let it be borne in mind that when this letter was written, the author speaks as a man who is awaiting not *a trial* but *a verdict.* The trial had reached its crisis; the case was about to be terminated (Phil. 2:19, 23, 24). Everyone had had a chance to observe Paul's steadfastness and courage while "under fire." The Lord had sustained him most wonderfully (Phil. 4:13), and this not only during his trial but even earlier, on his way to Rome as a prisoner (Acts 23:11; 27:23). So now at last, as a result of having seen what the grace of God is able to accomplish in the heart of his "bound" apostle, *most* of the brothers (not just "many," A.V.) have taken courage, the courage which is "in the Lord," imparted and kept alive by him. Not only was there official proclamation of "the message of God," that is, the gospel, but this message had even become the theme for discussion without restraint, the topic for ordinary conversation or *talk,* and this now *far more* than ever before. Yet this was the case not among *all* but only among *most* of the brothers. The fact that even

---

[45] See also my *Bible Survey,* pp. 206, 207; 210-212; 353-357; 427.

now conditions were not exactly ideal even among the preachers at Rome is clear from that which follows, which, however, also shows Paul's magnificent optimism:

15. Some, to be sure, are heralding Christ from envy and rivalry, but others from good will.

It stands to reason (and should never have been denied) that when Paul now begins to speak about those who "are heralding Christ from envy and rivalry . . . out of selfish ambition, not sincerely, *thinking to raise up afflic-tion (for me) in my bonds*" he is no longer referring to those people for whom he has nothing but praise because they have been *"heartened in the Lord through my bonds* and are showing far more courage in telling the message of God without being afraid."* The apostle approaches the subject from a different angle now. He has already indicated two favorable results of his imprisonment experiences: a. *the issue has been clarified for the out-siders* (praetorian guard, etc.), so that these now realize that Paul's bonds are *for Christ;* b. *most of the believers in the great metropolis have shaken off their former fears,* and are now at last telling the message of God cou-rageously. He now accentuates a third reason for his optimism (a reason in reality already implied in a. and b.), namely, c. *Christ is being proclaimed!* Now with this thought uppermost in his mind he is saying that this herald-ing of the Christ is, sad to say, not always actuated by the proper motives.

The men of whom Paul is thinking are *all heralding* Christ (see verses 15, 17, 18).[46] They are exercising their ambassadorship, and are publicly and authoritatively proclaiming him as the one only name under heaven that is given among men by which we must be saved. (On this verb *to herald* or *to preach* and its synonyms see N.T.C. on The Pastoral Epistles, pp. 309, 310.) As far as one is able to gather from the text, none of the heralds is a preacher of false doctrine. None of them, for example, is giving undue prominence to the observance of the law as a means of salvation. None of those referred to here in Phil. 1:15-18 is "preaching a different gospel" (Gal. 1:6; cf. 5:1-6) or "another Jesus" (II Cor. 11:4). None of them is "a dog" or "an evil worker" (Phil. 3:2). But while all are proclaiming the true gospel, not all are actuated by pure motives. *That* is the point! It is with respect to this point that Paul is here dividing the preachers at Rome into two groups.

The first group consists of those who are heralding Christ from *envy* and *rivalry.* (For this combination see also I Tim. 6:4. For a word-study of *envy* see N.T.C. on The Pastoral Epistles, p. 388). It should be borne in

---

[46] The contention of S. Greydanus, that the verb κηρύσσουσιν belongs only with "others from good will," because those who are filled with envy and rivalry cannot really be said to herald Christ, must be considered an error. Words have a history and cannot be so strictly circumscribed or delimited. Besides, if τινὲς . . . διὰ φθόνον καὶ ἔριν does not have κηρύσσουσιν as its predicate, what is its predicate? It would be a subject without a predicate.

mind that there was a church in Rome long before Paul arrived there. It can scarcely be doubted, therefore, that certain preachers in Rome had attained a degree of prominence among the brothers. With the arrival of Paul and especially with the spreading of his fame throughout the city (see verses 13 and 14) is it easy to understand that these leaders were beginning to lose some of their former prestige. *Their* names were no longer mentioned so often. Hence, they became envious of Paul. Their motives in preaching Christ were not pure or unmixed.

16. *The second group* consisted of those who were motivated by *good will* (used here of *human* good will; in Phil. 2:13; Luke 2:14; 10:21; Eph. 1:5, 9 of *divine* good pleasure). That the essence of this *good will* was love for Paul and for the gospel which he proclaimed is evident from the words which immediately follow: **The latter do it out of love, knowing that I am appointed for the defense of the gospel.**[47] These men do not begrudge Paul the authority which he exercised by divine appointment, nor the great gifts he had received from God and the honor which was bestowed upon him by many people. They heralded Christ out of *love* (see on verse 9), a love for Christ, hence also for his gospel and for the man whom they knew to have been *set, destined, or appointed* (see for this verb I Thess. 3:3; cf. Luke 2:34) for *the defense* (see on verse 7) of *the gospel.*

17. The former proclaim Christ out of selfish ambition. Like many a hired servant discards idealism and has his mind set chiefly on the wages which he will receive, so also these envious preachers are actuated by selfish motives (cf. Phil. 2:21). They crave honor and prestige, at least they have permitted this motive to crowd the nobler incentives into a corner. Hence, Paul continues: these men proclaim Christ **not sincerely,** that is, not from unmixed motives, not purely, **thinking to raise up**[48] affliction (for me) in

---

[47] The A.V., on the basis of the Textus Receptus, reverses the order found in the A.R.V. and R.S.V. (so that A.V. verse 16 is A.R.V. and R.S.V. verse 17; and A.V. verse 17 is A.R.V. and R.S.V. verse 16). This change was probably made in order that the sequence in verses 16 and 17 might be the same as that in verse 15. But the *chiastic* arrangements, so that the third clause parallels the second, and the fourth parallels the first, is based on the best texts (see textual apparatus in N.N.).

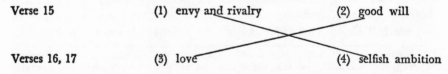

Verse 15   (1) envy and rivalry   (2) good will

Verses 16, 17   (3) love   (4) selfish ambition

For another illustration of chiastic parallelism in Paul see N.T.C. on The Pastoral Epistles, pp. 138, 139; cf. Prov. 13:24; 23:15, 16.
[48] This verb, rather than "to add to" is supported by the best texts.

my bonds. They would just as soon aggravate Paul's affliction, as long as their own selfish interests are served.

18a. What then? or "What really matters?" **Only that[49] in every way, whether in pretense or in truth, Christ is being proclaimed, and in this I rejoice.** Paul's self-forgetfulness excites affectionate admiration. We love him all the more for having written this beautiful passage. Sensitive soul though he was, he does not begin to pity himself because certain jealous preachers were trying to win applause at his expense. What really matters to him is not what they are doing to *him* but what they are doing for *the gospel.* But is it possible, then, that such selfish individuals can render service to the gospel in any way? Yes, for it must be borne in mind that those who hear them do not know what Paul knows. The listeners hear only the *good* preaching. They do not see the *bad* motive. What matters then is that *in every way,* that is, whether *in pretense* — as by those who know how to cover up their selfish ambition — or *in truth* — as by those whose sole aim is actually the glorification of their Lord and Savior — Christ is proclaimed. In *this,* says Paul, *I rejoice* (see also 1:25; 2:2, 17, 18, 28, 29; 3:1; 4:1, 4, 10). It would seem that the apostle's joy is so great that it crowds out every other consideration.

18b Yes, and I shall continue to rejoice. 19 For I know that through y o u r supplication and the help supplied by the Spirit of Jesus Christ this will turn out for my salvation, 20 in accordance with my eager expectation and hope that in not a single respect I shall ever be put to shame, but that now as always by my unfailing courage Christ will be magnified in my person, whether by life or by death. 21 For to me to live (is) Christ, and to die (is) gain. 22 Now if (what awaits me is) to live in the flesh, this for me means fruit resulting from work; yet which I shall choose I cannot tell. 23 So I am hard pressed between the two, having the desire to depart and be with Christ, for that is very far better; 24 but to remain in the flesh is more necessary for y o u r sake. 25 And being convinced of this, I know that I shall remain, yes remain with y o u all, for y o u r progress and joy in the faith, 26 in order that in connection with me, because of my being with y o u again, y o u r exultation in Christ may abound.

1:18b-26

II. *Christ Magnified in Paul's Person whether by Life or by Death*

18b, 19. Paul is the Optimistic Prisoner not only because he realizes that his imprisonment is for the advantage of the gospel (1:12-18), but also be-

---

[49] B has ὅτι; D,E,K, and L have πλήν without ὅτι. But πλὴν ὅτι, Aleph, A,F,G,P, though rather unusual not only fits the context very well but is also used by Paul as reported by Luke in Acts 20:23.

cause he is deeply convinced that in his person Christ will be magnified, and that this happy result will be attained whether he, the apostle, is set free (as he rather expects) or is put to death (1:19-26).

At first glance it might seem as if from the lofty height of glorying in the fact that Christ is being proclaimed — verse 18 — Paul now descends to the somewhat lower plane of rejoicing in his own salvation — verse 19. However, by reading not only verse 19 but also verse 20 it will be seen that for Paul *salvation* consisted in this — to quote his own words — "that . . . Christ be magnified in my body, whether by life or by death." Christ's glory and Paul's salvation cannot be separated.

Yet there is progress in thought. The apostle advances from the consideration of his joy in the present (verse 18) to the consideration of his joy in the future. He writes: **Yes, and I shall continue to rejoice.** He states as the reason for his continued rejoicing: **For I know that through y o u r supplication and the help supplied by [50] the Spirit of Jesus Christ this will turn out for my salvation.** This present imprisonment with all its attending woe will result in Paul's truest welfare, his highest good, namely, Christ magnified more than ever in Paul's person. Note that this glorious result will be brought about by means of *two factors* which because of their great difference in magnitude — the one human, the other divine — we would probably hesitate to place next to one another: *y o u r supplication . . .* and *. . . the help supplied by the Spirit of Jesus Christ!* Yet, they certainly belong together: the very same Spirit which sustained Jesus Christ, the Mediator, in *his* trials, will cause all things to work together for good in the case of Paul also, and this in answer to the prayer of fellow-believers. The apostle sets much store by the intercession (here *supplication,* that is, fervent petition or request for the fulfillment of a definite need; cf. Phil. 1:4; 4:6; see N.T.C. on I Tim. 2:1) of his friends (cf. Rom. 15:30, 32; II Cor. 1:11; Col. 4:2; I Thess. 5:25; II Thess. 3:1). Note that *Paul* makes supplication for the Philippians (1:4), and that he knows that *they* are doing the same thing for him (1:19). The *fellowship* is operating (see on verse 5).

20. The "knowledge" of which Paul speaks is in complete harmony with an underlying conviction born of experience. Hence, the apostle continues:

---

[50] The verb χορηγέω means basically *to lead a chorus* i.e., to furnish a chorus at one's own expense, *supplying* whatever is necessary to fit out the chorus. Hence, it comes to mean simply *to supply or furnish,* with the added idea *abundantly* (II Cor. 9:10; I Peter 4:11). Similarly, the compound verb ἐπιχορηγέω means *to furnish or provide* (II Peter 1:5); *to give or grant* to someone (II Cor. 9:10; Gal. 3:5; passive II Peter 1:11). Without acc. the verb becomes *to support* (Col. 2:19). Hence, also the noun as used here in Phil. 1:19 means *support* or *help.* In Eph. 4:16 the reference is to a ligament that serves as support. The idea that this support is *generous* may well be implied in Phil. 1:19. See L.N.T. (A. and G.) pp. 892, 305; also M.M., pp. 251.

in accordance with my eager expectation and hope that in not a single respect I shall ever be put to shame, but that now as always by my unfailing
courage Christ will be magnified in my person. The apostle is not bragging.
Quite the opposite is true. He ascribes nothing to self but everything to the
power of the Spirit of Jesus working within him. It is his *eager expectation*
(see Rom. 8:19; yearning, looking forward to something with head erect)
and well-founded hope that this Spirit will never put him to shame. He will
never permit Paul to seek an easy way out of his imprisonment; for example,
by denying his Lord. On the contrary, he will equip the apostle with *unfailing courage;* literally, *complete outspokenness,* a courage which reveals
itself in a frank and unhesitant proclamation of the good tidings of salvation to all who are willing to listen, and which has as its source confidence
in God and in his promises, the confidence of one who knows that at all
times he can approach his God without fear (cf. Eph. 3:12).[51]

Thus Christ will be magnified in Paul's *person;* literally *body,* but here
body indicates *the entire personality* (cf. also Rom. 12:1; Eph. 5:28),[52] as
is evident from the addition of the words whether by life or by death. If
Paul is acquitted and released, he will continue his apostolic labors. If he
is condemned to death, he will go to his Lord with unwavering faith and
with a song in his heart. Either way it will become evident what the Lord
through his grace can accomplish in the heart of his child. Thus Christ will
be magnified.

21. There is no sharp division between verses 20 and 21. They should
stand together. Paul says that he knows that in his person Christ will be
magnified, **For to me to live (is) Christ, and to die (is) gain.** Were this not
true, Christ would not be magnified in him.[53]

What Paul means by saying, "For to me to live is Christ," may be learned
from the familiar lines of the well-known hymn by Will L. Thompson:

> "Jesus is all the world to me,
> My life, my joy, my all;
> He is my strength from day to day,
> Without him I would fall.

---

[51] See D. Smolders, "L'audace de L'apôtre selon saint Paul. Le thème de la parrêsia (suite et fin)," *Coll Mech* 43 (Feb., 1958), 117-133.

[52] L.N.T. (A. and G.), p. 807.

[53] It is clear that both here and also in verse 22 we are dealing with abbreviated
language: "is" has to be inserted (cf. N.T.C. on John, Vol. I, p. 206). There should
also be no doubt about the fact that the expression "to live" and "to die" belong
to the same physical sphere: "to live" means "to live in the flesh," and "to die"
means "to depart" from this earthly scene (see verses 22 and 23).

> When I am sad to him I go,
> No other one can cheer me so;
> When I am sad he makes me glad,
> He's my friend."

And the stanzas which follow.

When the apostle says so emphatically "to me" placing this word at the very beginning of the sentence, he is giving a personal testimony and is at the same time drawing a contrast between himself and those to whom he has just been referring and who, no doubt, are still very much in his mind; namely, preachers "who proclaim Christ out of selfish ambition." *Paul*, then, in contrast with them, is not *self*-centered but *Christ*-centered. He is concerned with the honor and glory of his wonderful Redeemer.

To determine even more exactly just what the apostle has in mind when he says, "to live (is) Christ," parallel Pauline passages must be consulted. It means: to derive one's strength from Christ (Phil. 4:13), to have the mind, the humble disposition of Christ (Phil. 2:5-11), to know Christ with the knowledge of Christian experience (Phil. 3:8), to be covered by Christ's righteousness (Phil. 3:9), to rejoice in Christ (Phil. 3:1; 4:4), to live for Christ, that is, for his glory (II Cor. 5:15), to rest one's faith on Christ and to love him in return for his love (Gal. 2:20).

"And to die (is) gain." Dying physically means gain *for Paul*. It will mean that he will actually be *with* Christ (see verse 23), "at home with the Lord" (II Cor. 5:8). But gain for Paul can never be dissociated from gain for the cause of Christ, for the one objective in which Paul rejoices most is that in *his* person Christ may be magnified. Death will be a distinct gain because it will be the gateway to clearer knowledge, more wholehearted service, more exuberant joy, more rapturous adoration, all of these brought to a focus in Christ. Surely, if even now Christ is magnified in Paul's person, he will be thus magnified even more on the other side of death. Cf. I Cor. 13:12. Death is gain because it brings more of Christ to Paul, and more of Paul to Christ.

22. From the words "whether by life or by death" and "For to me to live (is) Christ, and to die (is) gain," it follows that the apostle was weighing the two possibilities, and was asking himself, "Now if the choice between these two were mine, which would I choose?" This thought, which in verses 20 and 21 is in the background, comes to the fore now, as Paul continues **Now if (what awaits me is) to live in the flesh, this for me (means) fruit resulting from work.** The words placed in parentheses show that here again we are dealing with abbreviated expression, but the sense is clear enough.[54]

---

[54] Both A.V. and R.S.V. are better here than the text of A.R.V., which reads as follows, "But if to live in the flesh, — if this shall bring fruit from my work, then what

If Paul is acquitted, so that his life *here on earth* is prolonged,[55] this will mean *fruit:* souls won for eternity through his further ministry, the edification of believers, the establishment of churches, etc. The prospect is wonderful. Paul knows that, should he be acquitted and released, he will again avail himself of every opportunity to proclaim the gospel far and wide. What is more, *he knows that this work will not be in vain.* In the realm of the Spirit there is *always* fruit of labor. When one abounds in the work of the Lord, his labor is never futile (I Cor. 15:58). To be sure, not every seed germinates, nor does every plant bear fruit (Matt. 13:1-9). Many people there are who experience "so many things" *in vain* (Gal. 3:4). But it is equally true that by no means all the seeds that are scattered are wasted. He who goes forth weeping, bearing the seed for sowing, will come home with shouts of joy, bringing his sheaves with him (Psalm 126:6). The word that proceeds from the mouth of Jehovah never returns to him empty (Is. 55:11). Hence, blessed are those who sow beside all waters (Isa. 32:20, cf. also 32:17). And let no one think that if the seed does not *at once* appear above·the ground and if the plant does not rush to maturity like Jonah's gourd, the work of sowing has been in vain. Rather, *at God's own time* the seeds scattered broadcast will ripen into a blessed harvest (Eccles. 11:1; cf. Mark 4:26-29). And in this fruit-bearing Christ will be glorified, *the Christ who was Paul's very life.*

And since for Paul to live was Christ, hence for him to die was gain (vs. 21). In fact it was better by far, by *very* far (vs. 23). Hence, it is not surprising that the apostle continues **Yet which I shall choose I cannot tell.**[56]

I shall choose I know not." In addition to several other objections to this reconstruction there is the basic one that it would imply that the apostle doubted whether a prolonged ministry on earth would mean fruitful labor. However, as is clear from verse 24, he entertained no doubts with reference to this.

[55] The expression "to live in the flesh" means to go on living *in this world.* In Paul's epistles the word σάρξ (flesh) has the following meanings:

a. the chief substance of the body, whether of men or of animals (I Cor. 15:39);
b. the body itself, in distinction from the spirit, mind, heart (Col. 2:5);
c. earthly existence (Gal. 2:20; Phil. 1:22, 24);
d. a human being, viewed as a weak, earthly, perishable creature (I Cor. 1:29; Gal. 2:16). This usage depends heavily on the Hebrew. Cf. Isa. 40:6, "All flesh is grass," etc.
e. physical descent or relationship (Rom. 9:8);
f. the human nature, without any disparagement (Rom. 9:5);
g. human worth and attainment, with emphasis on hereditary, ceremonial, legal, and moral advantages; the self apart from regenerating grace; anything apart from Christ on which one bases his hope for salvation (Phil. 3:3).
h. the human nature regarded as the seat and vehicle of sinful desire (Rom. 7:25; 8:4-9, 12, 13; Gal. 5:16, 17, 19; 6:8).

[56] A.V. has "What I shall choose I wot not." Similarly A.R.V. "What I shall choose I know not." This rendering is possible. That γνωρίζω can have the meaning *to know* is clear. See N.T.L. (A. and G.), p. 162. However, in all other New Testament occurrences this verb probably has the meaning *to cause to know, to make*

23, 24. The apostle loves Christ, and loves to be with him to glorify him forever, free from sin and from suffering. But he also loves the Philippians and knows that they have definite spiritual needs, and that a further ministry among them will be very fruitful and to the glory of the Redeemer. The choice is a difficult one, which is expressed even more clearly in the words: **So I am hard pressed between the two, having the desire to depart and be with Christ, for that is very far better; but to remain in the flesh is more necessary for yo u r sake.** Torn between conflicting considerations Paul is being pressed from both sides:

On the one side there is the desire,[57] the strong yearning, *to strike* (literally, to loosen) *the tent* of his earthly, temporary existence; the desire "to break camp," or "to loosen the cables of a ship," hence, *to depart.* See II Tim. 4:6. Note the words: to depart *and be with Christ.* The apostle knows that when his soul departs from this earthly life, it is immediately *with Christ.* It does not "go out of existence" until the day of the resurrection, nor does it "go to sleep" (cf. Ps. 16:11; 17:15; Matt. 8:11; Luke 16:25; John 17:24; I Cor. 13:12, 13; II Cor. 5:8; Heb. 12:23; Rev. 6:10; 20:4). It at once enjoys blessed fellowship with the Savior. That is "very far better" [58] than to remain in the flesh. Just why is this far more appealing, subjectively considered? Consult such passages as Rom. 8:18; II Cor. 5:8; II Tim. 4:7, 8; and Phil 3:14 for the answer. Note the contrast between

Remaining here	and	*Departing to be with Christ*
****		****
Here:		There:
a. A temporary residence, a mere tent-dwelling		A permanent abode
b. Suffering mixed with joy		Joy unmixed with suffering
c. Suffering for a little while		Joy forever
d. Being absent from the Lord		Being at home with the Lord
e. The fight		The feast
f. The realm of sin		The realm of complete deliverance from sin, positive holiness.

On the other side there is the need of the Philippians. The apostle places this objective need over against his own subjective desire. He is convinced

---

known (hence, *to tell*). This is definitely true of all other occurrences in the Prison Epistles (Eph. 1:9; 3:3, 5, 10; 6:19, 21; Phil. 4:6; Col. 1:27; 4:7, 9). The causative rendering makes excellent sense also in the present passage, though the possibility of the other meaning must be admitted.

[57] legitimate desire; see N.T.C. on The Pastoral Epistles, pp. 271-274, especially footnote 147.

[58] This rendering of the A.R.V. is more exact than that of either the A.V. or the R.S.V., for it preserves the flavor of the *triple* comparative used in the original: "much more the better."

that his continued life on earth, enabling him to bestow further pastoral care upon the believers at Philippi, must be given serious consideration. The church had existed for not much longer than a decade. Only yesterday some of its members had emerged from the idolatry and immorality of heathendom. Though it was a wonderful church in many ways, it had its weaknesses and it was confronted with real dangers (see Phil. 3:1-3; 3:19; 4:2). Accordingly, big-hearted Paul is ready for the present, if that be God's plan, to forego the entrancing glories of heaven in order that his span of life on earth may be lengthened in the interest, among others, of the Philippians. The *need* of the church weighs heavier with him than the *desire* of his own soul.

25, 26. He therefore continues, **And being convinced of this, I know that I shall remain, yes remain with y o u all.** Because the apostle is convinced of *this*, namely, of that which he has just written: that the lengthening of his life's span would mean fruit resulting from work, and that such work was needed by the church at Philippi, he regards it as altogether probable that he will remain on earth a while longer. "It is my definite opinion," says he, as it were, that "I shall even remain by the side of *y o u all.*" This *y o u all* probably includes more than the church at Philippi.

The purpose of this expected release and prolonged ministry is expressed in *the phrase* **for y o u r progress and joy in the faith,** and in *the clause* that stands in apposition with it (see verse 27).

Again and again in Philippians and also in Paul's other epistles the idea of spiritual *progress* is stressed. Such progress means growth in love (Phil. 1:9), in knowledge (1:9), in fruitfulness (1:11), and in obedience (2:12). Why is it important that believers progress? Because *not to progress* means *to regress*. Standing still spiritually is impossible. And *regression produces depression* (dejection). But *progress means happiness,* the joy unspeakable and full of glory. Hence, Paul very neatly unites these two concepts and writes that he expects to remain with his friends on earth for their *progress and joy* in the faith. There follows the elucidation: **in order that in connection with me, because of my being with y o u again, y o u r exultation in Christ may abound.** The apostle's release — should it please God to grant this, as Paul rather expects — would result in more than merely sentimental rejoicing. Not only would the Philippians exclaim, "Paul, we are very happy to have you with us once more." They would also thank their Anointed Savior. In connection with God's mercies bestowed upon Paul they would make their boast in the Lord, praising *him,* and this particularly for bringing their dear friend to them *again.* Note that word *again.* It implies that the apostle had been in Philippi before (on the second missionary journey, Acts 16:11-40; the third, outward bound, II Cor. 8:1-5; and the third, homeward bound, Acts 20:5).

All the historical evidence points to the fact that Paul's expectation was fulfilled, and that, having been released, he actually visited the Philippians once more. For proof see N.T.C. on The Pastoral Epistles, pp. 23-27, 39, 40.

---

27 Only continue to exercise y o u r citizenship in a manner worthy of the gospel of Christ, that whether I come and see y o u or am absent, I may hear of y o u that y o u are standing firm in one spirit, with one soul striving side by side for the faith of the gospel, 28 and not frightened in anything by the adversaries, which is for them a clear sign of destruction, but of y o u r salvation, and this from God. 29 For to y o u it has been granted in behalf of Christ not only to believe in him but also to suffer in his behalf, 30 being engaged in the same conflict which y o u saw me having and now hear me having.

1:27-30

III. *Exhortation to Steadfastness, Unity, and Fearlessness*

27, 28. It is in keeping with his character as Optimistic Prisoner that Paul now exhorts the Philippians to remain steadfast, united, and unafraid, and to regard it a privilege to be counted worthy to suffer for Christ. He writes, **Only continue to exercise y o u r citizenship in a manner worthy of the gospel of Christ.** Paul says, "Only," that is, "whatever happens to *me* personally, whether I come and see y o u or am absent," *in any event* be sure to conduct yourselves as believers. With respect to the words, "Continue to exercise y o u r citizenship," commentators differ rather sharply. According to some the meaning is, Continue to discharge y o u r obligations as citizens and residents of Philippi faithfully. According to others the idea that there is even so much as an allusion here to Roman citizenship is far-fetched.[59] But why should it be necessary to accept either of these rather extreme positions? In opposition to the first opinion the question may be asked, Does not Phil. 3:20 ("For *our* homeland is in heaven") clearly indicates that the apostle is referring to *heavenly* citizenship? And in answer to the second view, the question is pertinent, Does not that very passage and also the position of the Philippians as Roman citizens make it altogether probable that this Roman citizenship is *the underlying idea?* Paul is drawing a parallel, making a comparison. It is as if the apostle were saying, "Y o u are Roman citizens and proud of it (and so am I, Acts 16:21, 37). But constantly bear in mind that what matters *most* is the fact that y o u are citizens of *the kingdom of heaven.* Continue, therefore, to exercise *that* citizenship in a manner worthy of the gospel of Christ." The verb has reference, accordingly, to Christian conduct, a manner of life that befits a citizen-soldier who be-

---

[59] For the first idea see Raymond R. Brewer, "The Meaning Of POLITEUESTHE In Philippians 1:27," *JBL* 73 (June, 1954), 76-83. For the second, R.C.H. Lenski, *op. cit.,* p. 756.

longs to the kingdom and army of Jesus Christ.[60] Naturally, good citizens
of the realm of Christ will also be good citizens of the Roman realm.

To exercise their citizenship "in a manner worthy of the gospel of Christ"
means to conduct it in harmony with the responsibilities which that gospel
imposes and with the blessings which it brings. The word *gospel* occurs
twice in this verse, and not less than six times in this one chapter. This is
therefore the proper place to answer the question:

What Is the Gospel?

It is the God-spell, the *spell* or *story* that tells us what God has done to
save sinners. Hence, it is *evangel* or *message of good tidings*. It is *the glad
news of salvation which God addresses to a world lost in sin*.[61] Not what *we*
must do but what *God* (in Christ) has done for us is the most prominent
part of that news. This is clear from the manner in which the noun *evangel*
and the related verb *to proclaim an evangel, to bring good news* are used in
the Old Testament. See LXX on Psalm 40:9; 96:2; Isa. 40:9; 52:7 in relation to Chapter 53; 61:1; and Nahum 1:15.

Isa. 61:1

"The Spirit of the Lord Jehovah is upon me,
because Jehovah has anointed me,
to bring good tidings to the afflicted.
He has sent me to bind up the broken-hearted,
to proclaim liberty to the captives,
and the opening (of the prison) to those who are bound;
to proclaim the year of Jehovah's favor;
and the day of vengeance of our God;
to comfort all who mourn;
to grant to those who mourn in Zion —
to give them a garland instead of ashes,
the oil of gladness instead of mourning,
the garment of praise instead of the spirit of heaviness;
that they may be called oaks of righteousness,
the planting of Jehovah, that he may be glorified."

---

[60] Thus interpreted, the meaning of the verb πολιτεύομαι approaches, but is not entirely identical with, that of περιπατέω (Phil. 3:17, 18 and frequent in Paul) . This
emphasis on conduct is also found in the only remaining New Testament instance
of the verb πολιτεύομαι (Acts 23:1) . For its use both in and outside of the New
Testament see also L.N.T. (A. and G.) , p. 693.

[61] In Paul the emphasis falls at times on *the contents* of God's message, namely,
salvation; at other times on *the proclamation* of this message. These two meanings
may occur side by side: Rom. 1:1, 2; I Cor. 9:14. In the sense of Gospel (with a
capital "G") "a *book* containing the story of Christ's life and teaching" the word
is not used in Scripture. See G. Friedrich's article on this concept in Th.W.N.T.,
Vol. II, pp. 705-735.

In his sermon at Nazareth Jesus referred these words to himself, quoting the first part of the passage (Luke 4:18; cf. Isa. 61:1, 2b) .

Isaiah 52:7 in relation to Chapter 53; cf. Nahum 1:15:
"How beautiful upon the mountains (are) the feet of him *who brings good tidings,* who publishes peace, *who brings good tidings of good,* who publishes salvation" (thus Isaiah, and cf. Nahum) .
In Romans 10:15 Paul refers to these words. According to the contexts in Nahum and Isaiah freedom from the foreign yoke or return to the native soil was good tidings for Israel of old. But even during the old dispensation the good news had reference to blessings far beyond the national and physical horizon. One has no right to exclude from the glad tidings of Isaiah 52 the precious contents of Chapter 53; e.g.,

> "Surely, he has borne our griefs
>   and carried our sorrows;
> yet we esteemed him stricken,
>   smitten by God, and afflicted.
> But he was wounded for our transgressions,
>   he was bruised for our iniquities;
> the chastisement of our peace was upon him;
>   and by his stripes we are healed."

Between the evangel of the old dispensation and that of the new there is a very close connection. Thus, for example, apart from Isaiah 53 the New Testament cannot be understood:
When John the Baptist proclaimed his gospel, pointing to Jesus as the Lamb of God who takes away the sin of the world, was he not thinking of Isaiah 53? (I John 1:29; cf. Isa. 53:7, 10) .
When Matthew referred to Christ's humble origin and the lowly conditions of his birth, was there not a clear reference to Isaiah 53? (Matt. 2:23; cf. Isa. 11:1; 53:2) .
When this same Matthew-passage and also many other New Testament references showed that Christ was despised, was not this in fulfilment of Isaiah 53? (Matt. 2:23; Luke 18:31-33; 23:35, 36; John 1:46; I Peter 2:4; cf. Isa. 53:3) .
When John, the apostle and evangelist, summarized Israel's reaction to Christ's earthly ministry, did he not do it in words taken from Isaiah 53? (John 12:36-38; cf. Isa. 53:1).
When Jesus healed the sick, gave himself a ransom "for many," and "was reckoned with the transgressors," did he not fulfill Isaiah 53? (Matt. 8:16, 17; cf. Isa. 53:4; Matt. 20:28; Mark 10:45; cf. Isa. 53:11, 12; Luke 22:37; cf. Isa. 53:12) .

When Matthew stated, "And there came a rich man and asked for the body of Jesus," was he not thinking of Isaiah 53? (Matt. 27:57; cf. Isa. 53:9).

When Jesus stressed that he regarded not only his suffering and death but also his entrance into glory (resurrection, etc.) as fulfilment of prophecy, was he not thinking of a series of Old Testament passages which included Isaiah 53? (Luke 24:25, 26; cf. Isa. 53:10-12).

When Philip *the evangelist* told the Ethiopian eunuch the evangel or good news of Jesus, was not his text taken from Isaiah 53? (Acts 8:32, 33; cf. Isa. 53:7, 8).

When Peter described Christ's sinlessness and vicarious suffering for his wandering sheep, did he not do so in the very terms of Isaiah 53? (I Peter 2:22-25; cf. Isa. 53:4, 5, 6, 9, 12).

When the author of Hebrews dwelt on Christ's self-sacrifice for many, was not his source Isaiah 53? (Heb. 9:28; cf. Isa. 53:12).

When to John on Patmos the Lamb revealed himself in visions, was it not *the slaughtered Lamb* of Isaiah 53? (Rev. 5:6, 12; 13:8; 14:5; cf. Isa. 53:7).

And so also when Paul proclaimed what he delighted to call "my gospel," did he not base it on God's glorious redemptive revelation found in principle even in the Old Testament, and did he not include Isaiah 53 among his sources? (Rom. 4:25; I Cor. 15:3; cf. Isa. 53:5; Rom. 10:16; cf. Isa. 52:7; 53:1). *Note that not a single verse of Isa. 53 is ignored in the New Testament!*

The *evangel of the new dispensation is that of the old dispensation, gloriously amplified.* The gospel of the Coming Redeemer is transformed into the gospel of the Redeemer who came, who is coming again, and who imparts salvation, full and free, *to every believer on a basis of perfect equality.*[62]

The following elements are included in the concept *gospel* as set forth by Paul:

(1) *Its Power*

Romans 1:16 states: "For I am not ashamed of *the gospel:* for it is *the power* (δύναμις, cf. our *dynamite*) *of God unto salvation* to every one who believes, to the Jew first and also to the Greek."

The person who accepts the gospel by a true and living faith is saved, delivered, reconciled, redeemed, justified, etc. See Rom 3:23, 24; 7:24, 25; 8:1; I Cor. 15:1, 2; II Cor. 5:18-21; I Tim. 1:15. Dynamite, by being *destructive,* can be very *constructive.* So is the gospel when it takes hold of a person.

---

[62] In Paul the noun *gospel* (εὐαγγέλιον) occurs about 60 times; the verb (εὐαγγελίζω) in the original, nontheological sense, *to bring or announce good news,* once (I Thess. 3:6), and in the theological sense, *to proclaim the divine message of salvation,* twenty times. In addition there is the noun *evangelist* (εὐαγγελιστής). which Paul uses twice (Eph. 4:11; II Tim. 4:5); and the verb *to proclaim good news in advance* (προευαγγελίζομαι) which he uses once (Gal. 3:8).

(2) *Its Author*

The Author, both of salvation itself and of the gospel which promises salvation, is *God in Christ:*

"the gospel of God" (I Thess. 2:9).

"the gospel of Christ" (I Thess. 3:2).

Paul stresses the fact that his gospel is not man-made. The apostle has received it by revelation from God (Gal. 1:11, 12; 2:16). Man by nature is totally unable to devise a gospel or to save himself. He is dead through trespasses and sins, a child of wrath. His works have no merit unto salvation (Eph. 2:1, 5, 9). God, and he alone, can save him. From start to finish it is *God* who saves, never man.

(3) *Its Emphasis*

Accordingly, the gospel places all the emphasis on sovereign, unmerited *grace.* Paul calls it:

"the gospel of the grace of God" (Acts 20:24). Other Pauline passages in which this doctrine of the gospel of grace is set forth most beautifully are such as Rom. 3:23, 24; Eph. 2:6-10; and Titus 3:4-7.

(4) *Its Message*

What, then, is *the message* or *the news* which this gospel brings? What has *grace* done to effectuate salvation? This message centers in *Christ:*

"Now I make known to y o u, brothers, *the gospel* . . . that Christ died for our sins according to the scriptures; and that he was buried; and that he was raised on the third day according to the scriptures," etc. (I Cor. 15:1-11). See also Gal. 2:20: "Christ lives in me . . . loves me, and gave himself up for me." Hence also, "I have been crucified with Christ, have been raised with him, sit in heavenly places with him."

(5) *Its Implication*

The implication is clearly this, that the sinner should accept this gospel, that he should appropriate this salvation, *repenting* (II Cor. 7:10; II Tim. 2:25), and embracing Christ by living *faith:*

"For I am not ashamed of *the gospel:* for it is the power of God unto salvation to *every one who believes;* to the Jew first and also to the Greek. For in it the righteousness of God is revealed *from faith to faith;* as it is written, the just shall live *by faith*" (Rom. 1:16, 17). See also Gal. 3:11; Eph. 2:8; Phil. 2:12, 13. It is, therefore, definitely the "whosoever-*believes*" gospel.

(6) *Its Ambassadors*

Some have been set apart in a special way by God to proclaim this gospel. Thus, for example, Paul had been

"separated unto the gospel of God" (Rom. 1:1). The apostle was so deeply convinced of this and so thoroughly enthused about his solemn obligation that he cried out, "Woe to me if I preach not the gospel!" (I Cor. 9:16). In a broader sense all believers are ambassadors of the gospel of God's marvelous grace.

(7) *Its Appeal*

Since, then, apart from the gospel there is no salvation and no life that is truly to the glory of God, an earnest, emphatic, ringing appeal is addressed to men, urging them to be reconciled with God:

"We are ambassadors therefore for Christ, God as it were making his appeal through us. We beseech y o u for Christ's sake, be reconciled to God" (II Cor. 5:20).[63] This clearly is more than a mere *implication* (see 5 above). What is *implied* is also *urged*.

Are the Philippians living in harmony with this gospel? And are they doing this regardless of whether they are being watched by Paul? Hence, the apostle says, Only continue to exercise y o u r citizenship in a manner worthy of the gospel of Christ, **that whether I come and see y o u or am absent, I may hear of y o u that,** etc. It is certainly in harmony with Paul's compressed emotional style that we interpret these words as meaning, ". . . that whether I come and see y o u, or am absent and hear about y o u, I may learn that," etc.[64]

What the apostle hopes to learn with respect to the Philippians he expresses as follows: that **y o u are standing firm in one spirit, with one soul striving side by side for the faith of the gospel, and not frightened in anything by the adversaries.** We see here not only

What Paul Expects Of The Philippians

but also

What God Expects Of His Children

(1) *Their attitude toward God and his gospel must be one of Tenacity*

They must *stand fast* in the Lord, rooted in him, trusting him, loving him, hoping in him, clinging to the traditions, the authoritative teachings which they have received, the *faith* (body of redemptive truth)[65] that pertains to and is revealed in *the gospel*. For this idea of *standing firm* see also Rom. 14:4; Gal. 5:1; I Thess. 3:8; II Thess. 2:15; and especially the beautiful passage, I Cor. 16:13, 14. There must be no compromise with error. That Paul has in mind loyalty *to the Lord* is clear from the context (and see 4:1), and that this firmness must be exercised *over against the opponents or adversaries* and *in the midst of persecution* appears clearly from verses 28-30. Divine *preservation* does not cancel but implies human *perseverance*.

(2) *Their attitude toward each other must be one of Harmony*

---

[63] For the *contents* of the gospel-message see also N.T.C. on the Gospel according to John, Vol. I, pp. 139-142; for the concept *salvation* see N.T.C. on The Pastoral Epistles, pp. 76-82; and on *heralding* or *preaching* this gospel see N.T.C. on The Pastoral Epistles, pp. 309, 310.
[64] On the general subject of Abbreviated Style in the New Testament see N.T.C. on John, Volume I, p. 206.
[65] Used in this sense also elsewhere in Paul's epistles (Gal. 1:23; 6:10, and frequently in the Pastoral Epistles). See the discussion in N.T.C. on The Pastoral Epistles, pp. 11 and 12.

Note: "in one *spirit,* with one *soul* striving side by side." [66]

Paul's central thought here reminds one of a song popular in The Netherlands (I refer to *Één in Geest en Streven*), which may be rendered as follows:

> One in our endeavor,
> One in song forever,
> One in word and deed,
> One in adoration,
> One in thank-oblation,
> One in praise: our creed.
> One glorious aim,
> Our goal the same
> One in strength and one in striving,
> Help from God deriving.
>
> Lift now hearts and voices
> While our soul rejoices
> In our God above.
> Render adoration,
> Grateful exultation
> for his changeless love.
> Bless, bless the Lord,
> To him accord
> Praise in song, in all our striving
> Help from God deriving.

This matter of Christian unity, active harmony, was much on Paul's mind as he wrote Philippians (see also Phil. 2:2, 3; 4:1). Conditions in the Philippian church were not entirely ideal in this respect. Are they *ever* ideal *anywhere?* For other passages in which the apostle stresses the desirability of believers acknowledging their oneness in Christ, living together in peace, and working together in harmony, see Rom. 12:5; 12:12; I Cor. 1:10; 10:17; II Cor. 13:11; Gal. 3:28; Eph. 2:11-22; 4:3, 4; 4:13. Note also what was said above on the subject of Christian "fellowship" (Phil. 1:5). The danger of mutual discord is pointed out in I Cor. 11:17-22; Gal. 5:15. Paul and Peter were in full agreement also on this point (see I Peter 3:8-12).

The unity here envisioned is one of *striving or struggling side by side, like*

---

[66] Although it is true that when the word *spirit* ($\pi\nu\epsilon\tilde{\nu}\mu\alpha$) is used, the reference is often to man's power of grasping divine things, the thinking and reasoning mind, and that when the word *soul* ($\psi\nu\chi\acute{\eta}$) occurs, this same invisible substance is viewed as the seat of sensations, affections, desires, feeling and will, it is probably best to view the sequence "in one spirit, with one soul" as meaning "united in heart and soul," "with common purpose and ardor." (See also N.T.C. on I Thess. 5:23, pp. 146-150.)

gladiators, against a common foe. In Phil. 4:3 the apostle also speaks about those who struggled side by side with him. This struggle, moreover, is not only *against* a foe, but *for* the gospel-truth. Some people are always struggling *against*, never *for*. Paul is interested not only in fending off attacks, but also and mainly in spreading God's glorious redemptive truth which centers in Jesus Christ and salvation in him.

(3) *Their attitude toward the foe must be one of Intrepidity*

They must not be frightened, like a timid horse shying in view of an unexpected object.[67] Over against the adversaries the Philippians must show undaunted courage, never even for a moment becoming frightened as did Peter when he denied his Lord.

But who are these *adversaries?* Several commentaries simply skip this question. Some (for example, R. Johnstone, *Lectures on the Epistle of Paul to the Philippians,* p. 125; R. C. H. Lenski, *op. cit.,* p. 759) are positive that the opponents cannot have been Jews, but must have been pagans. The arguments for this view are as follows: Is it not true that the Jews in the Roman colony of Philippi were so few in number that Paul did not even find a synagogue there? Besides, does not the apostle state in verse 30 that the Philippians are engaged in *the same conflict* which they had seen Paul having and now hear him having? Surely, Paul suffered *Roman* imprisonment both at Philippi and now again at Rome!

In spite of these arguments others continue to adhere to the view that it is not at all necessary to exclude either Jew or Gentile, either legalist or sensualist, from the category of the adversaries which Paul has in mind. I believe that this is the right solution. We should permit Paul to explain his own terms. In other words, when in Chapter 3 he warns against *dogs, evil workers, the concision;* also against *the enemies of the cross of Christ, whose end is destruction, whose god is their belly, and whose glory is in their shame, who set their mind on earthly things,* then, unless the immediate context forbids, we must be willing to accept such descriptive terms as giving meaning and content to the term *the adversaries* here in 1:28. This all the more because in Chapter 3 the apostle states that *he is there repeating his previous warnings* (3:1). This is the proper procedure, unless we have solid evidence that Chapter 3 belongs to another letter. Such evidence is lacking.

It is a well-known fact that among *the Gentiles,* not only in Rome but also certainly in its *colonies,* etc., the early Christians were suspected of being atheists (because they worshipped no *visible gods*), haters of mankind, etc. In the pursuit of their daily vocations and in their social intercourse the followers of Jesus, who condemned all idol-worship and emperor-worship, were

---

[67] This does not necessarily mean, however, that Paul was thinking of a chariot-race. The word is applied not only to animals but also to people. Thus Polycrates says in Eusebius, *Ecclesiastical History* V. xxiv. 7 "I am not *frightened* at what is threatened us." For other sources see the entry πτύρω in L.N.T. (A. and G.).

subjected to all manner of hardships, and this was happening long before Christianity had been declared an illegal religion. Besides, the Gentile world of that day was steeped in immorality. The Church was still young. Many of its members had been drawn from these Gentile circles. There were tares among the wheat. It is therefore altogether probable that some would-be converts who had come out of an immoral environment distorted their new faith by making Christian liberty an excuse for license (cf. Rom. 3:8; 6:1; Jude 1). Whether some of these voluptuaries had actually become *members* of the Philippian church is an open question. At any rate, they constituted a real threat. They were *adversaries*.

But what about *the Jews?* Is it really true that when Paul wrote about *the adversaries* he was altogether leaving them out of consideration? Is it not natural to assume that he included at least those Jews who had nominally accepted Jesus, but refused to see in him the *complete Savior?* In Chapter 3 he warns the church against Jewish, that is *Judaistic,* errorists ("the concision"). He does this in language that is clear and cutting (3:2). Is it psychologically probable that in this short epistle the opponents who are condemned in such scathing terms in Chapter 3 would be totally absent from the mind of the writer when in Chapter 1 he makes mention of the *adversaries?* Besides, the readily explainable fewness of the Jews in Philippi in the year when this church was founded (about 51/52) does not prove that a full decade later (62/63), when this letter to the Philippians was written, the Jews (Judaizers) could not have been *present or passing through in sufficient numbers* to have become a menace. Cf. Acts 15:1. If Thessalonica was troubled by Jews A. D. 51/52, why could not nearby Philippi be troubled by Judaizers A. D. 62/63? [68]

---

[68] The fortunes of the Jews under various political rulers were constantly changing. Under Augustus 27 B. C. – A. D. 14) and Tiberius (14-37) the Jews enjoyed a measure of tolerance. At the beginning of the reign of Caligula (37-41) they were even somewhat optimistic. Did they not have a good friend at court? But when that emperor, driven by insane ambition, demanded divine honor, a real clash was in the making, and would have occurred had not his death intervened. Under Claudius (41-54) their fortunes varied. Their tumultuous action in Rome led to *the order* for their expulsion from that city (Acts 18:2, probably about the year 49/50). Shortly after this, Paul came to *the Roman colony* of Philippi and not surprisingly found few Jews there. But does this prove that also afterward the Jewish population in Rome and its colonies remained at a minimum? According to the testimony of Cassius Dio it is by no means true that all the Jews were even actually driven out of Rome. At any rate, when Paul arrives in Rome for his first Roman imprisonment the Jews are living there in goodly numbers (Acts 28:17-28). Would it have been so strange if some Jews, including *nominal* Christians, had entered or re-entered Philippi, with the purpose of stopping a few days to make propaganda for their views, or of establishing a temporary or even a more or less permanent residence there? This at any rate would seem to be a more obvious explanation of Phil. 3.2 than that of those who, having based too much on Acts 16:13, regard Phil. 3:2 as nothing but *prophecy!* When Paul wrote Philippians (A. D. 62/63) the reigning emperor was Nero (54-68). He was at first rather reason-

Moreover, whether the struggle is against Jew or Gentile, legalist or sen-sualist, it is "the same conflict" in any case. See on verse 30. Let not the Philippian church be frightened by these enemies of the gospel.

Now of this calm endurance and undaunted courage in the face of formi-dable adversaries the apostle says **which with respect to them is a clear sign of destruction, but of y o u r salvation.**[69] Paul is ever cognizant of the higher hand that rules the affairs of men (see N.T.C. on I Thess. 1:3, 4). The failure of the adversaries to intimidate believers, and the latter's fear-lessness, is *proof* that God is carrying out his program. The word which I have rendered *clear sign* occurs also in Rom. 3:25, 26; II Cor. 8:24 (its only other New Testament occurrences), and in each case has the meaning of *proof,* here in Phil. 1:28 with the added touch of *prophecy.* The point is not that the adversaries themselves see this, though perhaps they may have a dim awareness of it, but that for God's children this intrepidity on their own part is solid evidence of the doom which threatens their enemies unless they repent, and of their own salvation, now in principle and by and by in perfection. For the concept *salvation* see N.T.C. on I Tim. 1:15. *Destruc-tion* or *perdition* is in every way the opposite of *salvation.* The reason why this undaunted courage is proof of salvation and of invincibility is that it is not man-made. Hence, Paul adds **and this**[70] **from God.** If intrepidity

---

able and tolerant. And *even after* the celebrated quinquennium or first five years (54-58), Poppaea Sabina, who proved to be Nero's evil star, a very ambitious and scheming woman who was regarded by the Jews as a proselyte to their religion, ex-erted enough influence upon the emperor to protect the Jews. The Jewish faith was regarded as a *religio licita* (religion to be tolerated). The blame for the dev-astating conflagration of Rome during the night of the 18th to the 19th of July 64 was by Nero placed not on the Jews but on the Christians. *Christianity* became a *religio illicita* (a religion not to be tolerated). Poppaea died (as a result of a cruel kick inflicted by Nero in a fit of rage?) in the year 65. But even before her death, Nero's character had shown evidences of deterioration. Led by evil counsellors he had become very extravagant. The great fire added to the expenses of the empire. As a result, the taxation of conquered peoples, including the Jews, became more and more unbearable. Related to this was the maladministration of Gessius Florus in Judea, and the consequent Jewish insurrection which resulted in the fall of Jeru-salem (66-70).

If this brief summary of historical detail is borne in mind, it will be understood why the scarcity of Jews in Philippi shortly after the edict of Claudius cannot be used to prove the theory that when Paul wrote Philippians a full decade later and spoke about *the adversaries* he could not have been thinking about Jews (who had nominally accepted Christ; hence, Judaizers) as well as Gentiles. Besides, Phil. 3:2 remains an insuperable barrier to this view.

[69] The reading upon which the A.V. is based — "to them of perdition . . . *to you* of salvation" instead of "of y o u r salvation" is clearly a change for the sake of balancing the clauses, smoothness of style.

[70] To what exactly does τοῦτο refer? There has been much controversy on this point. According to many the antecedent is ἔνδειξις. The sense, as some of these interpreters see it, is something like this: in order to know what will happen to them, believers do not need to wait, like stricken gladiators, for a sign — say, the flick of a thumb or the wave of a handkerchief — from the fickle crowd. They get

were merely a homemade article, a state of mind into which a person enters without divine assistance, it would prove nothing as to *salvation*. But if, without in any way cancelling human responsibility, such fearlessness can and must be considered a gift of God, the product of his Spirit working in the heart, then certainly the conclusion follows that he who began a good work will carry it on toward completion (see the context, Phil. 1:6). This is entirely in the spirit of Ps. 27:1-3; 56:11; Rom. 8:31-39.

29, 30. What follows in these verses is elaboration of what has already been said. The proposition "Fearlessness is a gift of God, hence proof of salvation," is true "For," or "Seeing that," etc. Says Paul, **For to y o u it has been granted in behalf of Christ not only to believe in him but also to suffer in his behalf.** It has been *granted* to y o u, says Paul; that is, as *a privilege,* a gift of God's *grace.* The double blessing is this: in behalf of Christ not only to believe in him but also to suffer in his behalf.

First, *to believe in him,* that is, to rest on Christ, surrendering oneself to his loving heart, depending on his accomplished mediatorial work. The form of the expression as used in the original shows that here genuine, personal trust in the Anointed One is meant. (See also N.T.C. on John, Vol. I, pp. 76, 77, 141, footnote 83; Vol. II, p. 51.) Whether or not one regards Eph. 2:8 as proof for the proposition that such faith is God's gift, the conclusion is at any rate inescapable that here in Phil. 1:29 faith — not only its inception but also its continued activity — is so regarded. It is at one and the same time God's gift and man's responsibility.

Secondly, *to suffer in his behalf.* The emphasis falls on this in the present connection. There are *adversaries* who cause believers to suffer. Now suffering is not a privilege *in itself.* One should not court suffering. But suffering *in behalf of Christ,* in the interest of him and his gospel is different. Such suffering is indeed a blessing, a gracious privilege (Acts 5:41), because:

a. It brings Christ nearer to the soul of the Christian. In his suffering for Christ's sake the believer begins to understand the One who suffered redemp-

---

their *sign* directly from God. Others, however, hesitate to accept the view which regards ἔνδειξις as antecedant. With some this hesitancy seems to be connected with the idea that the neuter demonstrative pronoun τοῦτο cannot very well refer to a feminine noun. That theory, however, is grammatically debatable. Better, it would seem to me, is the argument that Paul does not elsewhere use the word ἔνδειξις in any sense other than *proof, positive evidence,* a sense which, with the added touch of *prophecy,* also fits very well in the present context. The strongest argument for the position that τοῦτο refers here not so much to a single word as to the entire idea of the believers' standing firm is supplied by the context, both preceding and following. Note: "standing firm in one spirit . . . not frightened in anything by the adversaries . . . and this from God. *For* to y o u it has been granted (or 'graciously, freely granted') in behalf of Christ not only to believe in him but also to suffer in his behalf." This firmness, this willingness to suffer for Christ and his cause, is God's gracious gift to the church.

tively for him and receives the sweetness of his enduring fellowship. It is "without the gate" that God's child, reproached by the enemy, meets his Lord (Heb. 13:13). See also such other wonderful passages as Job 42:5, 6; Psalm 119:67; II Cor. 4:10; Gal. 6:17; Heb. 12:6.

b. Accordingly, it brings assurance of salvation, the conviction that the Spirit of glory and the Spirit of God rests upon the sufferer (I Peter 4:14; cf. John 15:19-21).

c. It will be rewarded in the hereafter (Rom. 8:18; II Cor. 4:17; II Tim. 2:12; 4:7, 8; I Peter 4:13).

d. It is often a means of winning unbelievers for Christ and of encouraging fellow-believers (that thought is stressed in the very context; see Phil. 1:12-14).

e. By means of all these avenues it leads to the frustration of Satan (book of Job) and the glorification of God (Acts 9:16).

In a most amiable manner Paul now comforts the Philippians by telling them that they are standing on common ground with him. This is a tactful little touch which we often find in Paul's letters. It is beautiful because it is genuine. See I Thess. 1:6; 3:3; II Tim. 1:8; 3:10-15; 4:5-8; Titus 1:4, to mention only a few instances. Cf. N.T.C. on I and II Thessalonians, pp. 28, 29. Says Paul, with reference to the believing and suffering Philippians: **being engaged in the same conflict which y o u saw me having and now hear me having** (literally, "the same conflict having which y o u saw in me and now hear in me").

In Philippi Paul had been "advertised" by a demon-possessed girl, had been slandered, mobbed, stripped, flogged, thrown into a dungeon, his feet locked in gruesome stocks. The devil was behind all this. Influenced by Satan the masters of the slave-girl, the infuriated rabble, and many others had joined in inflicting upon him this "shameful treatment" (Acts 16:16-24; I Thess. 2:2; see also Introduction III). The Philippians had *seen* this conflict between the kingdom of light and that of darkness. And now, through this very letter (see, for example, Phil. 1:12-17; 4:14), and through Epaphroditus (Phil. 2:25-30), they *are hearing* about Paul's bonds and about those people who, encouraged by Satan, were raising up affliction for him in his bonds. For Paul it was like being engaged in a gladiatorial *contest* or *conflict*, a life or death *fight* or *struggle*.[71] It implied prodigious exertion of energy against that very powerful foe, namely, Satan. And the Philippians, vexed in a variety of ways by idol-and-emperor-worshippers, legalistic Judaists, paganistic sensualists, quarrelling church-members, all of these the result of Satanic influence, were engaged in *the same conflict*. The conflict is *the same* because at bottom the arch-enemy is the same! Even more definitely, as Paul himself in this very context stresses by saying it *twice*, the conflict

---

71 Paul's epistles contain numerous references to athletic and gladiatorial contests. See N.T.C. on The Pastoral Epistles, pp. 150, 151, 203, 314, 315.

is the same because it is "in behalf of Christ," in the interest of his cause and kingdom. If then the suffering which this conflict brings upon them is God's gracious gift, the victory is sure, both for Paul and for them. Thus, by divine inspiration, speaks The Optimistic Prisoner.

Synthesis of 1:12-30

In the first subdivision of this section Paul points out that, far from what others may be saying, he himself regards his imprisonment as having turned out for the advantage of the gospel. He speaks, therefore, as *optimistic prisoner*. Road-blocks set up by Satan have become stepping-stones for the progress of the message of salvation. Paul's bonds have had a good effect, *first* on the members of *the praetorian guard,* who have begun to see that this noted prisoner is not a criminal at all but is suffering as a proponent of a very worthy cause, namely, that of Christ and his gospel. From the mouths of the guards Rome's population in general has heard about this and has begun to take an interest in the gospel. *Secondly, believers in Rome,* too, though fearful at first, have of late received courage, so that they are telling the message of God without being afraid.

This does not mean, however, that all is wonderful. *Rome's heralds of salvation,* preachers of the gospel, can be divided into two classes. Some are filled with envy and would just as soon add to Paul's suffering, if only they can harvest popular acclaim. Others, however, proclaim the gospel from good will, being motivated by love both for God and for Paul. The thing that really matters, though, is this, that in every way Christ is being proclaimed. In this Paul rejoices.

In the second subdivision the optimistic prisoner expresses his deep conviction that whatever happens to him, whether it be life or death, acquittal or condemnation, Christ will be magnified in his (Paul's) person. Though he desires to be with Christ, regarding this as being very far better, yet he is willing to place the need of the Philippians above his own immediate enjoyment of eternal bliss.

In the final subdivision Paul urges upon the addressees the spirit of:

a. *tenacity.* Paul's absence or presence should make no difference. They should *stand firm,* and continue to exercise their heavenly citizenship in a manner worthy of the gospel of Christ.

b. *unity:* "with *one* soul striving side by side for the faith of the gospel."

c. *intrepidity.* Whether the enemies be emperor-worshipers, Judaizers, sensualists, or whoever they may be, let the God-given fearlessness of the Philippians be a double sign, namely, of the destruction of their enemies and of their own salvation. Let them meditate on the fact that suffering in behalf of Christ is a privilege, and that Paul himself shares with them in this suffering, as they know very well.

[31] The following sources have been consulted:

Campbell, J. Y., "*Koinonia* and its Cognates in the New Testament," *JBL* 51 (1932) 352-380.

Cranfield, C. E. B., art. "Fellowship, Communion," in *A Theological Word Book of the Bible* (A. Richardson, editor), New York, 1952.

Endenburg, P. J. T., *Koinonia bij de Grieken in den klassieken tijd*, 1937.

Ford, H. W., art. "The New Testament Conception of Fellowship," Shane Quarterly 6 (1945), 188-215.

Groenewald, E. P., *Koinonia (gemeenskap) bij Paulus*, doctoral dissertation, Amsterdam, 1932.

Hauck, D. F., entry κοινός and cognates, Th.W.N.T., Vol. III, pp. 789–810.

Jourdan, G. V., "*Koinonia* in I Cor. 10:16," *JBL* 67 (1938), 111-124.

L.N.T. (Th.) entries κοινός and cognates.

L.N.T. (A. and G.) entries κοινός and cognates.

Liddell and Scott, *Greek-English Lexicon*, Oxford, 1940, entries κοινός and cognates.

M. M., entries κοινός and cognates.

National Herald English-Greek, Greek-English Dictionary, entries κοινός and cognates.

Tenney, M. C., *Philippians, the Gospel at Work*, Grand Rapids, 956, pp. 35-50.

The concept *koinonia* — *fellowship* or *communion* — merits more than passing notice. Examples of usage:

Plato uses the phrase: "the dissolution of a *koinonia*" (*business-partnership, Republic*, 343 D).

He also writes, "Where there is no *koinonia* (*communion*), there can be no friendship" (*Gorgias*, 507 E).

The word *koinonia* lives on in modern Greek in various meanings; such as *society, communication*, and (holy) *communion*.

Throughout it has also been used to indicate *the marriage-bond*.

Does the term also indicate fellowship between God (or the gods) and men?

In ancient Greece, since in so many respects the gods resembled men, a certain amount of contact between the two was considered possible. In fact, the Age of Fable records many instances of such contact.

Even when in the more enlightened circles mythology was shorn of its cruder elements, the idea of fellowship between the gods and men persisted. For example, Plato wrote "Wise men tell us, Callicles, that *heaven and earth and gods and men* are held together by *koinonia* (fellowship) and friendship . . . and that is the reason, my friend, why they call the whole of this world *order* (kosmos) . . ." (*Gorgias*, 508 A).

Plato evidently had no eye for the fact that sin has brought about *separation* between God and man. Apart from special revelation and from saving faith that philosopher was not able to appreciate the truth with respect to the sovereign majesty and holiness of God, on the one hand, and the enormity of sin, on the other. Fellowship between the divine and the human seemed altogether normal and natural to the Greek, for the simple reason that his mind, darkened by sin, was unable to discover the truth.

Accordingly, between the teachings of Plato and those of the Old Testament there is a sharp contrast. The Old Testament stresses *the distance* between God and man. Jehovah is the Holy One. He is separate from all that is sinful, and exalted above all that is weak. He is seated above all people and even above all the gods, which are but vanities. He is unsearchable in his judgments and "terrible" in his mighty acts (Ps. 47:2; 65:5; 66:3, 5; 68:35; 99:3; Is. 61:1-5; 45:15; 55:8, 9; etc.). In fact, the transcendence of God is stressed to such an extent that although the Hebrews did have words indicative of fellowship (from the root ḥ b r; e.g., Prov. 28:24; Is. 1:23), these words were never used to indicate the relation between God and man (Ps. 94:20 is a very doubtful exception). Moreover, the LXX never employs the word *koinonia* to describe any communion between the two.

Nevertheless, the *existence* as such, of the fellowship, even during the old dispensation, must be granted. Though after the entrance of sin with its devastating effect upon the human race, such communion was no longer *natural*, it was present *as a special gift of God to his children*. Thus, Enoch walks with God (Gen. 5:22). Jehovah knows Moses face to face (Deut. 34:10). Jehovah is his people's Shepherd (Ps. 23). He dwells in the hearts of those who are of a contrite and humble spirit (Is. 57:15). He loves, pities, and redeems his own, and even hides them in his own pavillion (Ps. 103:13, 14; Is. 63:9; Ps. 27:5). But *the word koinonia* is not used to indicate this divinely bestowed favor.

As we turn to the New Testament we observe that it was *the incarnation of the Son,* so that God came to dwell *with* men, and *the outpouring of the Holy Spirit,* so that God came to dwell *in* men, that gave the word *koinonia* its full scope. It was Jesus who spoke of himself as the Vine and of his followers as the Branches, adding, "Abide in me, and I (will abide) in y o u." See N.T.C. on John, Vol. II, pp. 293-304 (on John 15:1-11). The disciple whom Jesus loved (John) was glad to record this marvelous truth. It was also he who used the word *koinonia* no less than four times in the first chapter of his first epistle (twice in verse 3, once each in verses 6 and 7).

Nevertheless, it was not John but Paul who, under the guidance of the Spirit, brought this concept to its fullest development. He uses the word *koinonia* no less than thirteen times (Rom. 15:26; I Cor. 1:9; 10:16, twice, II Cor. 6:14; 8:4; 9:13; 13:14; Gal. 2:9; Phil. 1:5; 2:1; 3:10; and Philem. 6). The only remaining passages of the New Testament (i.e., outside of John and Paul) in which the word appears are Acts 2:42 and Heb. 13:16.

In reality the stress which *Paul* places on this concept is even more striking than has been indicated in the comparative statistics already given. In summary,

(a) He uses *koinonia* more than twice as often as all the other New Testament authors combined.

(b) He employs *koinonos*, in the sense of *participant, sharer* (I Cor. 10:18; II Cor. 1:7) or *partner* (I Cor. 10:20; II Cor. 8:23; Philem. 17). This word occurs in Paul's letters alone as often as in all the rest of the New Testament together (Matt. 23:30; Luke 5:10; Heb. 10:23; I Peter 5:1; II Peter 1:4).

(c) Paul also has *sun-koinonos,* co-sharer, using this word three out of the four times that it occurs in the New Testament (Rom. 11:17; I Cor. 9:23; Phil. 1:7; only other instance of its use: Rev. 1:9).

(d) The main verb is *koinoneo,* occurring in Paul's epistles five out of a total of eight times: have a share in (Rom. 15:27; I Tim. 5:22); give a share to (Rom. 12:13; Gal. 6:6); enter into partnership with (Phil. 4:15). The only other occurrences are in Heb. 2:14; I Peter 4:13; and II John 11.

(e) The related compound is *sun-koinoneo,* used by Paul two out of three times: to share with someone in something (Phil. 4:14); to share in something (Eph. 5:11) non-Pauline occurrence: Rev. 18:4.

(f) Finally, there is *koinonikos,* ready to share. Paul is the only New Testament writer who used this word (I Tim. 6:18).

Even this falls short of being a full summary of the meaning which Paul poured into the idea of the fellowship, as a study of the derivation of the word *koinonia* will now show. It comes from *koinos,* which (not only means but) is by etymologists related to our English word *common. Koinonia, then, is basically a community-relationship. It is a sharing together; a having a share, giving a share, fellowship:* 1. *Anteilhaben,* 2. *Anteilgeben,* 3. *Gemeinschaft* (thus, D. F. Hauck, Th.W.N.T., Vol. III, p. 798). Experts in word-derivation connect *koinos* with *xyn* or *syn* (ξύν, σύν), related to the Latin *cum,* English *syn-, con-,* meaning *with, together with, joined* (*joint-, fellow-*). Thus in English we have:

sympathy (a feeling *with* another, *fellow*-feeling), *symphony, synagogue, synchronism,* etc.

concurrence (an occurring *together*), *con*nect, *com*mon, *com*munity, etc.

Accordingly, in order to obtain a comprehensive view of Paul's use of the word *koinonia* one should take note of the numerous *syn*-compounds (words which in the original begin with the prefix *syn*-), which occur in his letters.

First we have the basic idea: *Believers have fellowship "with" Christ.* They suffer *with* Christ, have been crucified *with* him, died *with* him, were buried *with* him (Rom. 8:17; 6:6; 6:8; cf. II Tim. 2:11; Rom. 6:4; Col. 2:12). But they also are made alive *with* Christ, are raised *with* him, are joint-heirs *with* him, glorified *with* him, enthroned *with* him, and reign *with* him (Col. 2:13; Col. 3:1; Rom. 8:17; II Tim. 2:12. and cf. Rev. 20:4).

Then, there is the implied idea: *Believers have fellowship "with" each other.* They are *joint*-partakers (Phil. 1:7, *joint*-imitators (3:17): *joint*-souled (2:2); *jointly* striving (1:27; 4:11) *jointly* rejoicing (2:17, 18); *joint*- (or *fellow*-) workers (2:25; 34:3). See also the following: *jointly* comforted (Rom. 1:12); *jointly* refreshed (15:32); *joint*- (*fellow*-) prisoners (16:7); *fellow*-citizens (Eph. 2:19); *jointly* framed (2:21); *jointly* built (2:21); *fellow*-heirs, *fellow*-members, and *fellow*-sharers (3:6). Paul can hardly conceive of *Christians* holding themselves aloof from other *Christians!*

Finally, all of this beautifully harmonizes with:

a. the Pauline use of the phrase "in Christ" (or "in him," etc.). *Unitedly* believers are *in* Christ, and he is *in* them.

b. the Pauline metaphor of the body, its head, and its members (Rom. 12:3-8; I Cor. 12:12-31; Eph. 4:16).

c. the Pauline metaphor of the temple with its chief cornerstone and its many stones (Eph. 2:19-22; cf. I Peter 2:4-7).

d. the Pauline teaching (received from the Lord) concerning the Lord's Supper, in which the fellowship of believers with Christ, and with one another, is beautifully set forth (see especially I Cor. 10:17).

Summary of Chapter 2

Verses 1-18

Paul, the Humble Cross-bearer

by an appeal to a fourfold incentive exhorting the Philippians to live the life of *oneness, lowliness,* and *helpfulness,*

after the example of Christ Jesus,

and to shine as lights in the midst of a wicked world, thereby filling the hearts of Paul and of themselves with joy.

2:1-4   The Stirring Appeal with fourfold incentive and threefold directive.

2:5-11   The Example of Christ.

2:12-18 Shining lights producing mutual joy.

CHAPTER II

2   1 If therefore (there is) any encouragement in Christ, if any persuasive appeal springing from love, if any fellowship of the Spirit, if any tender mercy and compassion, 2 make full (the measure of) my joy by being of the same mind, having the same love, with souls united setting y o u r minds on unity; 3 (doing) nothing from selfish ambition or from empty conceit, but in humble-mindedness each counting the other better than himself, 4 each looking not (only) to his own interests but also to the interests of others.

2:1-4

A new section begins here, in which Paul reveals himself as ready to be poured out as a libation upon the sacrificial offering of the faith of the Philippians (see verse 17). Accordingly, he appears here as *the Humble Cross-bearer,* and his very humility is shown in this, that he focusses attention not *on* himself but *away from* himself, *on Christ,* the unique Cross-bearer (verses 5-11).

But though this is indeed a new section, it is closely connected with that which precedes. In the closing paragraph of Chapter 1 the apostle had expressed the ardent wish that he might learn that the Philippians "are standing firm in one spirit, with one soul striving side by side for the faith of the gospel" (verse 27). In the present section (2:1-11) he re-emphasizes the necessity of *oneness* among the brothers, a quality that is possible only then when there is true *lowliness* of mind and *helpfulness* of disposition.

Verses 1-4 are in the nature of a stirring appeal. The intensity of this appeal or plea would seem to indicate that there was among the Philippians, at least among some of them, a measure of personal strife, perhaps for ecclesiastical honor or preferment.

I. *The Humble Cross-bearer's Stirring Appeal*

A. *Its Fourfold Incentive*

1. **If then (there is) any encouragement in Christ, if any persuasive appeal springing from love, if any fellowship of the Spirit, if any tender mercy and compassion. . . .**

To be sure, the church of Philippi was characterized by many excellent qualities. Paul calls its members, "my brothers, beloved and longed for, my joy and crown" (Phil. 4:1). Warmly he praises them for their fellowship in the gospel and for their generosity (Phil. 1:5; 4:10, 14-18). But, as is often the case, the "domestic affairs" of the church were not entirely as ideal as were the "foreign affairs." There was some trouble on the Home Front. Did some of the members see too much of each other? Were they getting on each other's nerves? Were some beginning to exaggerate the weaknesses and to minimize the virtues of other church-members? At any rate, not only Abraham (Gen. 13:7, 8) and James (James 3:16) were acquainted with the disastrous results of disunion, but so was also Paul (Rom. 13:13; I Cor. 3:3; Gal. 5:20; I Tim. 6:4). Brothers *attacking* or even just *belittling* each other make a sorry spectacle before the world. Their inner spiritual growth is retarded and their witness to the world is weakened.

This evil often results from inconsistency. On the one hand men will give glowing accounts of the blessings which they have received since they became Christians and of their spiritual experiences. On the other hand, among *some* of them the fruits of gratitude for all these favors are not particularly impressive *in one area; namely, at home.* Accordingly, the main thrust of what the apostle is saying is this: If then y o u receive any *help* or *encouragement* or *comfort* [72] from y o u r vital union with Christ, and if *the love* of Christ toward y o u does at all provide y o u with an incentive for action; if, moreover, y o u are at all rejoicing in *the marvelous Spirit-fellowship*,[73] and if y o u have any [74] experience of *the tender mercy and compassion* [75] of Christ, then prove y o u r gratitude for all this by loving

---

[72] The word is παράκλησις. For this meaning see also II Cor. 1:4-7; 7:4, 13; Philem. 7; II Thess. 2:16. Cf. N.T.C. on I and II Thessalonians, p. 62, and 189; and on John, Vol. II, p. 276

[73] This genitive transcends both objective and subjective; one might call it adjectival. That it is a fellowship *with* the Holy Spirit, an actual participation in that Spirit and in all his benefits cannot be doubted (cf. I Cor. 10:16; I John 1:3). But Paul also here regards it as the *gift* of the Spirit, just as he here considers the *persuasive appeal* as springing from love, and just as in II Cor. 13:13 he views *grace* as being the gift of the Lord Jesus Christ, *love* the gift of the Father, and *fellowship* the gift of the Holy Spirit. For a discussion of the fellowship see above under Phil. 1:5.

[74] The majority of the oldest manuscripts has τις. Is this an error of an early transcriber (for τινα or else for τι, the τι changed to τις by accidental repetition of the first letter of the following word)? See J. B. Lightfoot, *op. cit.*, p. 108; A. T. Robertson, *Word Pictures*, Vol. IV, p. 443. No better explanation has as yet been advanced. Lenski's defense of the reading τις, by interpreting the passage as if the meaning were, "If any such fellowship, let it be tender mercies and compassions," and so also in the preceding line, "if any fellowship, let it be of spirit," does not satisfy. Paul does not thus separate *fellowship* and *spirit*. The expression κοινωνία πνεύματος is a unit as is κοινωνία τοῦ ἁγίου πνεύματος in II Cor. 13:13.

[75] Literally "tender mercies (deeply felt affections) and compassions. For the literal meaning of σπλάγχνα and the argument resulting from it see on Phil. 1:8.

y o u r brothers and sisters *at home!* (that is what the threefold directive
amounts to, as will become clear). All true Christian activity begins at
home, as the Gadarene demoniac discovered (Mark 5:18-20).

Note: Paul says "If," not as if he doubts whether the condition is really
true, but simply to emphasize that when the condition is present, the conclusion should also be present. One might translate, "If then (there is) any
encouragement in Christ, as there surely is, if any persuasive appeal springing
from love, as there surely is, . . . make full (the measure of) my joy."

B. *Its Threefold Directive*

2-4. The conclusion is a very natural one: "If then to any extent y o u
have all these experiences and share in these benefits, then . . ." and here
follows the threefold directive. Not really three directives, but a *threefold*
directive: essentially the command is *one*, yet *three* graces, very closely related, can be distinguished. The three are:

Verse 2: *oneness*

Verse 3: *lowliness* (of mind or disposition)

Verse 4: *helpfulness*

Paul says, **make full (the measure of) my joy.** The manner in which he
thus prefaces the threefold directive is touching. There was joy in the
heart of the apostle (Phil. 1:4; 4:10). The Philippians, because of their
many virtues, had been a source of this joy. But its measure was not yet
full. A higher degree of oneness, lowliness, and helpfulness on the Home
Front can supply what is still lacking in Paul's cup of joy. While none of
the Philippians would have been able to claim perfection in these virtues,
in the case of some the lack was rather noticeable (see on 4:2). This is
Paul's deep concern. Not speedy release from prison but the spiritual
progress of the Philippians — of *all* of them — is his chief desire. This shows
how big-hearted he is.

(1) Oneness

Paul continues . . . **by being of the same mind, having the same love,
with souls united setting y o u r minds on unity.**[76] Read what has been
said with respect to the general theme of oneness or harmony (see on Phil.
1:27, 28). *The mind or inner disposition* is basic. This fundamental attitude will reveal itself by having *the same love* (for God in Christ, hence for
fellow-members, with emphasis on the latter in the present connection), and
by setting their minds on *the one,* that is, on *oneness* or *unity.*

Note that according to the context the oneness for which Paul pleads is
of a distinctly spiritual nature. It is a oneness in disposition, love, and aim

---

[76] The harmonious connection between the elements of this lengthy apodosis
would seem to demand that no comma be inserted after σύμψυχοι. The construction then is as follows: modifying *be of the same mind* are the four participles *having, minding* ("setting y o u r mind on"), *counting,* and *looking.*

(see also N.T.C. on John 17:21). It is the oneness set forth so strikingly in Ps. 133.

(2) *Lowliness*

Oneness cannot be achieved without lowliness, that is humility. Hence, Paul continues: **(doing)** [77] **nothing from selfish ambition or from empty conceit.** If everyone is constantly thinking of himself alone, how can unity ever be brought about? The Philippians must not be actuated by unholy rivalry, by selfish motives, craving honor and prestige for themselves, like certain preachers in Rome (see on Phil. 1:17, where the identical word — selfish ambition — is used). Selfish ambition and empty conceit (cf. Gal. 5:26) go together, for "the emptier the head the louder the boast." As often so here also Paul balances a negative with a positive formulation of the same idea. Thus, the thought advances to: **but in humble-mindedness each counting the other better than himself.** The word used in the original and here rendered *humble-mindedness* or *lowliness* (of disposition) was by non-Christians used in an evil sense (cowardliness, meanness; see Josephus, *Jewish War* IV.494; *Epictetus* III.24.56). When grace changes the heart, submission out of fear changes to submission out of love, and true *humility* is born. By Paul this virtue is associated with those of tenderheartedness, kindness, forbearance, longsuffering, meekness (Acts 20:19; Eph. 4:2; Col. 3:12). It is the happy condition which arises when in a church each member counts the other to be better than himself. Thus the members, filled with tender affection, will be outdoing one another in showing honor (Rom. 12:10).

But is not this rule impracticable? How can a man who knows that he is industrious regard the rather lazy fellow-member as being better than himself? The answer will probably be somewhat along this line:

a. The rule does not mean that one must consider *every* fellow-member to be *in every respect* wiser, abler, and nobler than he is himself.

b. As a general principle the rule certainly should control our lives, for while to a certain extent (never *completely,* see Psalm 139:23, 24; Jer. 17:9) a Christian is able to scrutinize *his own* motives (I Cor. 11:28, 31), and knows that they are not always good or unmixed, which knowledge leads him at times to utter the prayer, "O Lord, forgive my *good deeds!*" he has no right to regard *as evil* the motives of his brothers and sisters in the Lord. Unless a consistently wicked pattern is clearly evident in the life of one who has with his mouth confessed the Lord, that individual's outwardly good deeds must be ascribed to *good* and never to *evil* motives. On this basis it clearly follows that a truly humble child of God, who has learned to know *himself* sufficiently so that at times he utters the cry of the publican (Luke

---

[77] Or *minding,* that is, *contemplating,* if φρονοῦντες instead of ποιοῦντες is to be supplied here, from the immediately preceding clause.

18:13), or of Paul (Rom. 7:24), will regard *others* to be indeed better than himself. And not only *better* but *in certain respects abler,* for the Lord has distributed his gifts (I Cor. 12). There is generally something, of value to the kingdom, which the brother or sister can do better than y o u or I.

It is easy to see that when this spirit of *genuine* mutual regard and appreciation is fostered, unity will result. True Christianity is still the best answer to the question, "How can I win friends and influence people?" And the ecumenicity which it proclaims is the only kind that is really worthwhile.

It is probably not too bold an assertion to say that Paul himself had grown in this grace of humble-mindedness. He who during his third missionary journey called himself "the least of the apostles" (I Cor. 15:9), styled himself "the very least of all saints" during his first Roman imprisonment (Eph. 3:8), and a little later, during the period that intervened between his first and second Roman imprisonments, climaxed these humble self-descriptions by designating himself "chief of sinners" (I Tim. 1:15).

It took a humble cross-bearer to urge humble-mindedness. Is not Paul's humility also one of the reasons why even in the midst of his imprisonment, facing a verdict, he was filled with joy? The man who has learned to view himself as a great sinner before God appreciates God's saving grace, and thanks God even in the midst of his tears.

(3) Helpfulness

The apostle concludes this paragraph by adding **Each looking not (only) to his own interests but also to the interests of others.**

This follows from the immediately preceding. If one regards the brother very highly, he will wish to look to his interests in order to help him in every possible way. The apostle surely implies that a believer should look to his own interests. But he should obey the command, "You must love your neighbor as yourself" (Matt. 19:19), a commandment which receives added stress when the neighbor is a brother in Christ (John 13:34; Gal. 6:10). The more one realizes how fervently Christ loved the brother, and went all out to save him, the more he will wish to advance that brother's interests. Thus, too, true unity will be promoted, and before the world the glorious fellowship will begin to stand out in all its beauty, as a mighty testimony.[78]

---

5 In y o u r inner being continue to set y o u r mind on *this,* which (is) also in Christ Jesus, 6 who, though existing in the form of God, did not count his existence-in-a-manner-equal-to-God something to cling to, 7 but emptied himself, as he took on the form of a servant, and became like human beings. 8 So, recognized in fashion as a human being, he humbled himself and became obedient even to the extent of death; yes, death by a cross.

---

[78] See the poem "Living For Others," by Charles E. Orr, in *Treasures of Poetry,* published by the Gospel Trumpet Co., Anderson, Indiana, 1913, p. 221.

9 Therefore God raised him to the loftiest heights and bestowed on him the name that is above every name, 10 that in the name of Jesus every knee should bend, of those in heaven, and of those on earth, and of those under the earth, 11 and that every tongue should confess to the glory of God the Father that Jesus Christ is Lord.

2:5-11

By means of *a fourfold incentive* Paul has urged the Philippians to be obedient to *the threefold directive,* namely, that they should manifest to one another the spirit of oneness, lowliness, and helpfulness (Phil. 2:1-4). In order to underscore this exhortation and to indicate the source of the strength needed to live up to it, he now points to *the example of Christ, who with a view to saving others renounced himself, and thus attained to glory.*

John Calvin has given an excellent summary of the present paragraph and has indicated its proper divisions into two parts or "members," (a. verses 5-8; b. verses 9-11) and the reason for both and for each. Says he: "The humility to which he had exhorted them in words, he now commends to them by the example of Christ. There are, however, two members, in the first of which he invites us to imitate Christ because this is the rule of life; in the second he allures us to it because this is the road by which we attain true glory." [79]

II. *The Example of Christ*
Who with a View to Saving Others Renounced Himself

2:5-8

A. *Invitation to Imitate Christ because this is the rule of life*

5. Says Paul, **In y o u r inner being continue to set y o u r mind on** *this,* **which (is) also in Christ Jesus.**[80] The apostle desires that the Philippians keep on cherishing the disposition described in verses 1-4, a disposition that also characterizes Christ Jesus. This admonition is in line with many similar

---

[79] *Humilitatem, ad quam hortatus verbis fuerat, nunc commendat Christi exemplo. Sunt autem duo membra: quorum in priore invitat nos ad Christi imitationem, quia sit vitae regula: secundo allicit, quia sit haec via, qua ad veram gloriam pervenitur* (Commentarius in Epistolam Pauli Ad Philippenses, Corpus Reformatorum, vol. LXXX, Brinsvigae, 1895, p. 23).

[80] K. S. Wuest adopts a similar rendering: "This be constantly setting your mind upon in your inner being, that which is also in Christ Jesus," "When Jesus Emptied Himself," an article in *Bib Sac,* Vol. 115, No. 458 (April, 1958) pp. 153-158. The reading without γὰρ and with φρονεῖτε instead of φρονείσθω has the best support. The rendering, "Have the same thoughts among yourselves as you have in your communion with Christ Jesus," injects into the text an idea that is foreign to it, is not in harmony with the context, and misconstrues ἐν ὑμῖν.

rules that urge us to follow the example of him who is the Anointed Savior.
To be sure, there is an area in which Christ cannot be our example. We
cannot copy his redemptive acts. We cannot suffer and die *vicariously*. It
was he, he alone, who was able to satisfy the divine justice and bring his
people to glory. But with the help of God we can and should copy *the
spirit* that was basic to these acts. The attitude of self-renunciation with a
view to helping others should be present and should grow in the life of
each disciple. And *that* obviously is the point here (see verses 1-4). *Oneness, lowliness,* and *helpfulness* were manifested by our Savior (John 10:30;
Matt. 11:29; 20:28). These should characterize his disciples also. In *that*
sense there is truth in those simple lines:

> "Oh, dearly, dearly has he loved,
> And we must love him too;
> And trust in his redeeming blood,
> *And try his works to do.*"

Other passages which bring out the idea that Jesus is our Example are such
as the following: Matt. 11:29; John 13:12-17; 13:34; 21:19; I Cor. 11:1;
I Thess. 1:6, I Peter 2:21-23; I John 2:6. It is exactly because Jesus is our
Lord that he can be our Example. If he is not our Example, faith is
barren, orthodoxy dead.

6, 7a. Accordingly, the apostle continues: **who, though** [81] **existing** [82] **in the
form of God. . . .** But what is meant by existing in God's *form?* In the
paragraph under study two words — *morphe* (μορφή), that is, *form,* and
schema (σχῆμα), that is, *fashion* — occur in close connection: "existing in
the *form* of God . . . recognized in *fashion* as a human being.[83] Now

---

[81] The preceding context has prepared us for the idea of *sacrifice;* hence, the rendering "though existing" (taking the participle as *concessive*) is correct here as in
II Cor. 8:9 ("*though* being rich").

[82] The present participle ὑπάρχων stands in sharp contrast with all the aorists which
follow it, and therefore points in the direction of continuance of being: Christ
Jesus was and is eternally existing "in the form of God."

[83] In the New Testament the first word *morphe* is found only here in Phil. 2:6, 7
and in Mark 16:12. The second one *schema* is found only here in Phil. 2:8 and
in I Cor. 7:31. Both of these words are, however, also component elements in other
words. Consult the original: (1) for *morphe* as a word-element: a. Rom. 2:20;
II Tim. 3:5; b. Matt. 17:2; Mark 9:2; Rom. 12:2; II Cor. 3:18; c. Phil. 3:10; d. Rom.
8.29; Phil. 3:21; (2) for *schema* as a word-element: a. I Cor. 12:23; b. I Cor. 7:36
13:5; c. Rom. 1:27; Rev. 16:15; d. Mark 15:43; Acts 13:50; 17:12; I Cor. 7:35;
12:24; e. I Cor. 12:23; f. Rom. 3:13; I Cor. 14:40; I Thess. 4:12; g. I Cor. 4:6;
II Cor. 11:13, 14, 15; Phil. 3:21; and h. Rom. 12:2; I Peter 1:14.

Do these two words — *morphe* and *schema* — have the same meaning? At times,
throughout Greek literature, as any good lexicon will indicate, both can have the
meaning *outward appearance, form, shape.* In certain contexts they can be just
about interchangeable. But at other times there is a clear difference in meaning.
The context in each separate instance must decide.

this very transition from *form* to *fashion* would seem to point to a difference in meaning.[84] Besides, from several New Testament passages in which one or the other or both of these words occur, generally as component elements in verbs, it is evident that *in these given contexts morphe or form refers to the inner, essential, and abiding nature of a person or thing, while schema or fashion points to his or its external, accidental, and fleeting bearing or appearance.*[85]

---

[84] Cf. the change from ἀγαπάω to φιλέω in John 21:15-17 see N.T.C. on John Vol. II, pp. 494-500.

[85]

MORPHE, FORM	SCHEMA, FASHION
Rom. 8:29	I Cor. 7:31
"whom he foreknew he foreordained to be *conformed* to *the image* of his Son." An *inner change* takes place. A person's *nature* is renewed.	"the *fashion* of this world passes away." Though the universe is not destroyed as to its inner essence, the *scheme* or *outward aspect* of things is rapidly changing. "Change and decay in all around I see, O thou that changest not abide with me."
II Cor. 3:18	II Cor. 11:14
"we are . . . *transformed* into the same *image* from glory to glory." Again, an abiding change takes place, a change that affects *the inner nature.*	"Satan *fashions* himself into an angel of light." He cannot change his inner self, but can and does assume *the garb* of a good angel. He *masquerades!*
Gal. 4:19	I Peter 1:14
"My little children, for whom I am again suffering birth-pangs, until Christ be *formed* in y o u." Paul is not satisfied with mere beginnings. He wants to see the completed *image* of Christ in *the inner life and character* of the Galatians. — Similar is the following example:	"Be sober . . . not *fashioning* yourselves according to y o u r former lusts." Those addressed must show that their *scheme of life* — words, habits, actions, manner of dress, etc. — is not suggestive of the passions that were formerly in control of them. *Outward bearing and conduct* must be in harmony with the new life.
Phil. 3:10	
"that I may gain Christ. . . . becoming *conformed* unto his death."	

Rom. 12:2
"Stop being *fashioned* after the pattern of this (evil) age, but be constantly *transformed* by the renewal of y o u r mind." Here we have both words (each occurring in a compound verb): *fashion* and *form*. Stop adopting the external customs of the world round about y o u. There must be a *gradually progressing and abiding inner change, a metamorphosis.*

What Paul is saying then, here in Phil. 2:6, is that *Christ Jesus had always been (and always continues to be) God by nature, the express image of the Deity.* The *specific character of the Godhead as this is expressed in all the divine attributes was and is his eternally.* Cf. Col. 1:15, 17 (also John 1:1; 8:58; 17:24).

This thought is in harmony with what the apostle teaches elsewhere: II Cor. 4:4; Col. 1:15; 2:9 (and cf. Heb. 1:3).

A closely related question, namely, "Is Paul speaking here in Phil. 2:5-8 about the pre-incarnate or about the incarnate Christ?" is not difficult to answer. The two must not be separated. The One who in his pre-incarnate state exists in a manner equal to God is the same divine Person who in his incarnate state becomes obedient even to the extent of death, yes, death by a cross. Naturally, in order to show the greatness of our Lord's sacrifice, the apostle's *starting-point* is the Christ in his pre-incarnate state. Then follows of necessity Christ in his incarnate state. This strongly reminds one of II Cor. 8:9, "Though he was rich, yet for y o u r sake he became poor." One might compare this transition to what is found in the Gospel of John, Chapter 1:

"In the beginning was the Word, and the Word was face to face with God, and the Word was God. He himself was in the beginning face to face with God . . . And the Word became flesh, and dwelt among us as in a tent, and we beheld his glory."

Thus, though existing in the form of God, he **did not count his existence-in-a-manner-equal-to-God** [86] **something to cling to** [87] but emptied himself.

He did not regard it as *something that must not slip from his grasp.* On

---

Similarly, we immediately recognize the fact that *basically and in certain contexts* there is a difference between:

forma	and	*habitus* (Latin)
Gestalt	and	*Gebärdung* (German)
gestalte	and	*gedaante* (Dutch)
And so also between		
form	and	*fashion* or *figure* (English)

The fact that *in certain contexts* the word *form* is the more basic one is clear also from the following two examples:

A de*form*ed individual is generally in a worse condition than a dis*figured* person.

The *form* or *inner nature* of an apple tree remains the same throughout the year: short and stocky trunk, scaly bark, gnarled branches, rounded head. But the *fashion* of the tree changes with the seasons. As the year progresses we see the tree budding, blossoming, bearing fruit, picked clean, and finally entirely bereft of both leaf and fruit.

[86] The word ἴσα is adverbial, meaning "in a manner of equality."

[87] Because of its length this footnote has been placed at the end of the chapter, page 129.

the contrary, *he* . . . and here follow the two words that have given rise to much discussion and dispute: *emptied himself.*[88]

The question is: of what did Christ Jesus empty himself? Surely *not* of his existence "in the form of God." He never ceased to be the Possessor of the divine nature. "He could not do without his deity in his state of

---

[88] Tyndale's rendering "he made him silfe of no reputacion" was taken over by Cranmer, the Geneva Version, and the A.V. Cf. also The New English Bible "he made himself nothing." Similarly, the Dutch (*Statenvertaling*) has, "*hij heeft zichzelven vernietigd.*" In favor of that translation it is usually argued that in all the other instances in which the apostle employs the verb κενόω a metaphorical sense must be given to it (see Rom. 4:14; I Cor. 1:17; 9:15; and II Cor. 9:3). Dr. B. B. Warfield even goes so far as to call the alternative rendering ("emptied himself") a mistranslation (*Christology and Criticism*, p. 375).

But is this argument against the translation "emptied himself" really valid? Is it not possible to retain the translation "emptied himself" and still give a metaphorical — at least a non-strictly-literal — meaning to the verb? R.S.V. renders I Cor. 1:17 as follows, ". . . let the cross of Christ *be emptied* of its power." And cf. the use of this verb in I Cor. 9:15. At any rate the meaning that must be given to the verb in these other instances of its New Testament use hardly proves the position that here in Phil. 2 it cannot mean *he emptied*.

It is significant that the rendering *he emptied himself* has always had defenders; for example,

Latin: *sed ipse sese inanivit*
French: *il s'est aneanti lui-même*
English (Rheims translation of 1582) : he exinanited himself.

This rendering "is nearer the Greek and in every way more satisfactory than that of the A.V." (J. H. Michael). It is accepted by: *The Amplified New Testament,* W. G. Ballentine (*The Riverside New Testament*), R. C. H. Lenski, J. Moffatt, A. T. Robertson, G. Verkuyl (*The Berkeley Version*), K. S. Wuest, R. Young (*Literal Translation of the Holy Bible*), as well as by A.S.V. and R.S.V. Similarly, the new Dutch translation has, "*maar Zichzelf ontledigd heeft*"; the South African, "*maar het Homself ontledig*"; and the Swedish, "*utan utblottade sig själv.*"

A strong argument in favor of this rendering is the fact that it expresses precisely the idea that one expects after "he did not count his existence-in-a-manner-equal-to-God something to cling to." If a person refuses to cling to something, he empties or divests himself of it. Note: *of it.* Most commentators agree that when one empties himself, he empties himself *of something.*

Some excellent exegetes, whose doctrinal position and emphasis I share, reject the secondary object, "of it." In line with their preference for a translation other than "he *emptied* himself," they stress the fact that "of it" is not actually in the text. However, the difference between the two groups of interpreters becomes very minor when both accept the following propositions:

(1) Christ Jesus gave *himself,* nothing less.
(2) He did not in any sense whatever divest himself *of his deity.*
(3) The meaning of the clause "he emptied himself" or "he made himself of no reputation" (whichever is preferred) is set forth in greater detail in the words which follow it, namely, "as he took on the form of a servant . . . humbled himself and became obedient even to the extent of death; yes, death by a cross."

Many translators, though not actually using the verb *emptied,* express the same idea by their translation: "stripped himself of his glory" (R. F. Weymouth), "stripped himself of all privilege" (J. B. Phillips), or "laid it aside" (E. J. Goodspeed, M. R. Vincent, C. B. Williams).

humiliation. . . . Even in the midst of his death he had to be the mighty
God, in order by his death to conquer death" (R. C. H. Lenski).[89]

The text reads as follows:

"Christ Jesus . . . though existing in the form of God, did not count
his existence-in-a-manner-equal-to-God something to cling to, but emptied
himself."

The natural inference is that *Christ emptied himself of his existence-in-a-manner-equal-to-God.*[90]

On the basis of Scripture we can particularize as follows:

(1) *He gave up his favorable relation to the divine law.*

While he was still in heaven no burden of guilt rested upon him. But at
his incarnation he took this burden upon himself and began to carry it
away (John 1:29). And so he, the spotlessly righteous One, who never committed
any sin at all, "was made to be sin in our behalf, that we might
become the righteousness of God in him" (II Cor. 5:21). This is basic to
all the rest.

---

[89] The Kenotists who teach otherwise are clearly wrong. These defenders of the
Kenosis-theory in any of its many forms teach that in one way or another Christ at
the incarnation divested himself *of his deity,* whether absolutely or relatively.
Christ's human nature is just "shrunken deity." Of the vast literature of this subject
I select only the following titles:

Karl Barth on Phil. 2:5-8 in his *Erklärung des Philipperbriefes;* also the pertinent
pages in his *Kirchliche Dogmatik* IV (for example, IV:1, pp. 138 f, 146, 147;
Engl. transl. pp. 126 f, 133, 134; IV:2, pp. 37, 38; Engl. transl. pp. 35, 36); and
C. Van Til, "Karl Barth on Chalcedon," W. Th. J. XXII (May 1960), pp.
147-166.

C. A. Beckwith, article "Kenosis" in *The New Schaff-Herzog Encyclopedia of Religious Knowledge,* Vol. VI, pp. 315-319

L. Berkhof, *The History of Christian Doctrine,* pp. 124-126

A. B. Bruce, *The Humiliation of Christ,* pp. 134-192

E. D. La Touche, *The Person of Christ in Modern Thought,* pp. 351-366

H. R. Mackintosh, *The Doctrine of the Person of Jesus Christ,* pp. 223-284

J. J. Müller, *Die kenosisleer in die christologie sedert die Reformatie,* doctoral disseration, Amsterdam, 1931

W. Sanday, *Christologies Ancient and Modern* (advocates the rather strange theory
that the divinity of Christ was located in the subliminal consciousness)

B. B. Warfield, *Christology and Criticism,* pp. 371-389

[90] This is the position of L. Berkhof: ". . . the verb *ekenosen* [he emptied] does not
refer to *morphe theou* [form of God] but to *einai isa theo*, that is, his being on an
equality with God" (*Systematic Theology,* p. 328).

That is also the view of A. T. Robertson (*Word Pictures in the New Testament,*
Vol. IV, p. 444): "Of what did Christ empty himself? Not of his divine nature.
That was impossible. He continued to be the Son of God. . . . Undoubtedly
Christ gave up his environment of glory."

Of Greijdanus (*De Brief van den Apostel Paulus aan de Philippenzen,* in Korte
Verklaring, p. 50): "He laid aside his majesty and glory (John 17:5) but remained
God."

And of H. Ridderbos (*Commentaar op het Nieuwe Testament, Romeinen,*
p. 25): "He divested himself of his divine power and majesty by becoming like
human beings."

(2) He gave up his riches

". . . because for y o u r sake he became poor, though being rich, in order that y o u through his poverty might become rich" (II Cor. 8:9).

He gave up everything, even *himself,* his very *life* (Matt. 20:28; Mark 10:45; John 10:11). So poor was he that he was constantly *borrowing:* a place for his birth (and what a place!), a house to sleep in, a boat to preach from, an animal to ride on, a room in which to institute the Lord's Supper, and finally a tomb to be buried in. Moreover, he took upon himself a debt, a *very heavy* debt. His debt, voluntarily assumed, was the heaviest that was ever incurred by anyone (Isa. 53:6). One so deeply in debt is surely *poor!*

(3) He gave up his heavenly glory

Very keenly did he feel this. That is why, in the night before his crucifixion, out of the very depths of his great heart he uttered the prayer: "And now Father, glorify thou me in thine own presence with the glory which I had with thee before the world existed" (John 17:4).

From the infinite sweep of eternal delight in the very presence of his Father he willingly descended into this realm of misery, in order to pitch his tent for a while among sinful men. He, before whom the seraphim covered their faces (Isa. 6:1-3; John 12:41), the Object of most solemn adoration, voluntarily descended to the realm where he was "despised and rejected of men, a man of sorrows and acquainted with grief" (Isa. 53:3).

(4) He gave up his independent exercise of authority

In fact, he became a servant, *the* servant, and "even though he was a Son, learned obedience by what he suffered" (Heb. 5:8). He said: "I do not seek my own will, but the will of him who sent me" (John 5:30; cf. 5:19; 14:24).

Impatiently we voice an objection, namely, "But if Christ Jesus actually *gave up* his favorable relation to the divine law, riches, glory, and independent exercise of authority, *how could he still be God?"*

The answer must be that he, who was and is and ever remains the Son of God, laid aside all these things *not* with reference to his *divine* nature but with reference to his *human* nature, which he voluntarily took upon himself and in which he suffered all these indignities.

In his Commentary on this passage Calvin reasons as follows: It was *the Son of God himself* who emptied himself, though he did it *only with reference to his human nature.* This great Reformer uses the illustration: "Man is mortal." Here the word "Man" refers to *man himself,* man in his entirety, yet man's mortality is ascribed *to the body only,* not to the soul.

Further than this we cannot go. We stand before an adorable mystery, a mystery of power, wisdom, *and love!*

7b. It has become clear by this time that the clause, "He emptied himself" derives its meaning not only from the words which immediately precede it (namely, "he did not count his existence-in-a-manner-equal-to-God something to cling to") but also from those that follow, namely, **as he took on the form of a servant.** In fact, this clause, "he emptied himself," "includes all the details of humiliation which follow, and is defined by these" (Vincent). In the likeness of a human being taking on the form of a servant, so that he was recognized in looks and manners as a human being, humbling himself and thus becoming obedient to the extent of death; yes, death by a cross — *all this* is included in "he emptied himself." When he laid aside his existence-in-a-manner-equal-to-God, he in that very act took upon himself its very opposite (that is, *as to his human nature*).

The type of reasoning which we have here in verses 6-8 is not at all similar to that which goes on in the mind of a child who is building with blocks, each block being a unit in itself, separate from all the rest. On the contrary, it is *telescopic* reasoning: the various sections of the telescope, present from the start, are gradually drawn out or extended so that we see them.

Hence, he emptied himself *by taking* the form of a servant. "He emptied himself by taking something to himself" (Müller). Moreover, when he became a servant, he was not play-acting. On the contrary, *in his inner nature* (the *human* nature, of course) he became a servant, for we read, "He took on *the form* of a servant." (Read what was said previously with respect to the meaning of the word *form* in distinction from *fashion*.) This is great news. It is, in fact, astounding. He, the sovereign Master of all, becomes servant of all. And yet, he remains Master. The text cannot mean that "he *exchanged* the form of God for the form of a servant," as is so often asserted.[91] He took the form of servant while he retained the form of God! It is exactly that which makes our salvation possible and achieves it.

It was, moreover, the form of *a servant* — and *not* that of a *slave* — which he took upon himself. From the very beginning of his incarnation he was the thoroughly consecrated, wise and willing servant pictured by Isaiah (42:1-9; 49:1-9a; 50:4-11; and 52:13-53:12), the spontaneously acting servant who resolutely fulfills his mission, so that with reference to him Jehovah said: "Behold, my servant, whom I uphold; my chosen, in whom my soul delights."

The passage under study has as its starting-point the very beginning of this servant-career, the point where Christ *took* the form of a servant. But it implies, of course, that he remained servant to the very end of that career. Of his earthly mission it has been truly said, "The only person in the world who had the right to assert his rights waived them" (Wuest). It was Christ Jesus who said, "I am in the midst of y o u as one that serves" (Luke 22:27). In the very act of being servant to men (Matt. 20:28; Mark 10:45), he was accomplishing his mission as servant of Jehovah. We see

---

91 Even H. Bavinck commits that error (*Gereformeerde Dogmatiek*, Vol. III, third edition, p. 456).

him, Jesus, the Lord of glory . . . with a towel around his waist, pouring water into a basin, washing the feet of his disciples, and then saying to them: "Do y o u know what I have done to y o u? Y o u call me Teacher and Lord, and y o u say (this) correctly, for (that is what) I am. If therefore, I, y o u r Lord and Teacher, have washed y o u r feet, y o u also ought to wash each other's feet, for I have given y o u an example, in order that just as I did to y o u, so also y o u should do" (John 13:12-15).

And that is exactly Paul's point. He is saying to the Philippians and to us, "Follow the example of y o u r Lord" (see verse 5).

Never did any servant serve with more unswerving loyalty, unwavering devotion, and unquestioning obedience than did this one.[92]

Paul continues, **and became like human beings** (or more literally, "in the likeness of human beings having become"). When Christ took the form of a servant, he, who from all eternity had the divine nature and who continues to have it unto all eternity, took upon himself the human nature. Accordingly, the divine Person of the Christ now has two natures, the divine and the human (John 1:1, 14; Gal. 4:4; I Tim. 3:16). But he assumed that human nature not in the condition in which Adam had it before the fall, nor in the condition in which Christ himself now has it in heaven, nor in the condition in which he will reveal it on the day of his glorious return, but in its *fallen* and therefore *weakened* condition, burdened with *the results* of sin (Isa. 53:2).

Surely, that human nature was *real,* and in so far just like that of other human beings (Heb. 2:17). But though it was real, it differed in two respects from that of other men:

(1) His, and only his, human nature from its very conception was joined in personal union with the divine nature (John 1:1, 14); and

(2) Though it was burdened with *the results* of sin (hence, subject to death), it was not sinful in itself. Therefore this passage "*in the likeness* of human beings having become," and the similar one, "God sending his own Son *in the likeness* of sinful flesh" (Rom. 8:3) must be read in the light of Heb. 4:15, "One who was in all points tempted as we are, *yet without sin.*" There was likeness, similarity. There was no absolute, unqualified identity.

8. Paul continues, **So, recognized in fashion as a human being.**

When Jesus had come into the flesh, how did men regard him? What did they find him to be? The answer is: in their estimation he was a human being, just like themselves in ever so many respects:

---

[92] See further what has been said with reference to the meaning of δοῦλος in Phil. 1:1. Dr. John A. Mackay wrote an excellent article on this subject in The Princeton Seminary Bulletin (Jan., 1958). The title is "The Form of a Servant." He states, "The servant image is the most significant symbol in the Bible and in the Christian religion. . . . It denotes a complete absence of external compulsion. It means voluntariness, spontaneity, a certain inner joy and even exultancy."

Had they come into this world through the natural process of birth? So had he (Luke 2:7). (The mystery of the *virgin*-birth they did not fathom.)

Had they been wrapped in swaddling clothes (cf. Ezek. 16:4)? So had he (Luke 2:7).

Had they grown up? So had he (Luke 1:80).

Did they have brothers and sisters? So did he (Matt. 13:56).

Had they learned a trade? So had he (Mark 6:3).

Were they at times hungry, thirsty, weary, asleep? So was he (Matt. 4:2; John 4:6, 7; Mark 4:38).

Were they ever grieved or angry? So was he (Mark 3:5).

Did they weep at times? So did he (John 11:35).

Did they rejoice, for example, at weddings? He too attended a wedding (John 2:1, 2).

Were they destined to die? So was he, though in *his* case that death was physical, eternal, voluntary, and vicarious (John 10:11), and *this* they did not understand.

In his entire *fashion,* therefore, he was recognized as a human being. He had the looks and outward bearing of men. His way of dress, customs and manners resembled those of his contemporaries.

To a considerable extent *they were right* in so regarding him. Accordingly, it is open to doubt whether the following very familiar lines really tell the truth:

"The cattle are lowing, the Baby awakes,
  But little Lord Jesus, *no crying he makes.*"

Should it not be assumed that a normal baby cries at times, but that in the case of Jesus this crying, too, like everything else, was "without sin"?

Better are the words composed by Susanne C. Umlauf, of which I shall quote only two stanzas:

"Hast thou been hungry, child of mine?
  I, too, have needed bread;
For forty days I tasted naught
  Till by thy angels fed.
Hast thou been thirsty? On the cross
  I suffered thirst for thee;
I've promised to supply thy need,
  My child, come unto me.

"When thou art sad and tears fall fast
  My heart goes out to thee,
For I wept o'er Jerusalem —
  The place so dear to me:

111

> And when I came to Lazarus' tomb
> I wept — my heart was sore;
> I'll comfort thee when thou dost weep,
> Till sorrows all are o'er."

But though they were right in recognizing his humanity, *they were wrong* in two respects: they rejected a. his *sinless* humanity and b. his *deity*. And so, though his entire life, particularly also his mighty words and acts, implied the command, "Veiled in flesh the godhead see!" yet, by and large, they disavowed his claims and hated him all the more because of them (John 1:11, 5:18, 12:37). They heaped scorn upon him, so that "he was despised and rejected of men" (Isa. 53:3).

The amazing fact is, however, that "when he was reviled, he reviled not again" (I Peter 2:23), but **he humbled himself.** (For the meaning of the concept *humblemindedness* see on verse 3.) From the very beginning of his incarnation he bowed himself under the yoke. Implied in this act of humbling himself is: **and became obedient,** namely, to God the Father, as verse 9 clearly indicates (note, "Therefore *God,*" etc.). Moreover, his obedience knew no bounds: **even to the extent of death.** In that death he, functioning both as Priest and Guilt-offering, gave himself as an expiatory sacrifice for sin (Isa. 53:10). Hence, this death was not just an ordinary death. Says Paul, **yes death by a cross.**

Such a death was very *painful*.

It has been well said that the person who was crucified "died a thousand deaths."

It was also very *shameful*.

Compelling the condemned person to carry his own cross, expelling him from the city to a place "outside the gate," and there executing him by means of a death which, as we learn from Cicero, was considered the death of a slave (*Actio in Verrem.* i. 5, 66; *Oratio pro P. Quinto* viii. 4), was surely shameful. See John 19:31; I Cor. 1:23. "Let the very name of the cross be far removed not only from the body of a Roman citizen, but even from his thoughts, his eyes, his ears" (Cicero, *Pro Rabirio* 5). Hence, being a Roman, Paul, even should he after all be sentenced to die, would in all probability not have to die such a shameful death! Did he think of that when, with reference to his Master's death, he wrote, "yes, death by a cross"?

It was *accursed*.

"He that is hanged is accursed of God" (Deut. 21:23). And if this was true even with respect to a dead body, how much more with reference to a living person! Christ Jesus humbled himself, becoming obedient to a death whereby he vicariously bore the curse of God (Gal. 3:13). See also N.T.C. on John, Vol. II, pp. 425-427.

Thus, while he was hanging on that cross, from *below* Satan and all his hosts assailed him; from *round about* men heaped scorn upon him; from *above* God dropped upon him the pallor of darkness, symbol of the curse; and from *within* there arose the bitter cry, "My God, my God, why hast thou forsaken me?" Into this hell, the hell of Calvary, Christ descended.

The underlying thought of verses 5-8 is this: Surely, if *Christ Jesus* humbled himself so very deeply, y o u Philippians should be constantly willing to humble yourselves in y o u r own small way. Surely, if *he* became obedient to the extent of death, yes death by a cross, y o u should become increasingly obedient to the divine directions, and should accordingly strive more and more to achieve in y o u r lives the spirit of y o u r Master, that is, the spirit of oneness, lowliness, and helpfulness, which is pleasing to God.

Note the chiastic (that is, the crisscross) parallelism:

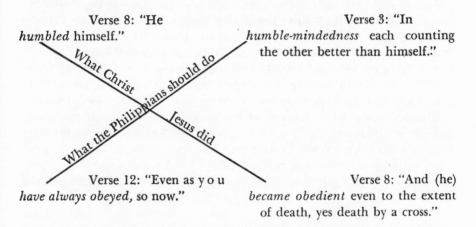

Verse 8: "He *humbled* himself."

Verse 3: "In *humble-mindedness* each counting the other better than himself."

What Christ Jesus did

What the Philippians should do

Verse 12: "Even as y o u *have always obeyed,* so now."

Verse 8: "And (he) *became obedient* even to the extent of death, yes death by a cross."

B. *Invitation to Imitate Christ*
because this is the road by which we attain to glory

9. The glorious reward which Christ Jesus received is described as follows: **Therefore God raised him to the loftiest heights.** He who humbled himself was exalted. The same rule which he had himself laid down for others was now applied in his own case. For this rule see Matt. 23:12; Luke 14:11; 18:14; and cf. Luke 1:52; James 4:10; and I Peter 5:6. It was "because of the suffering of death" that his reward was given to him (Heb. 2:9; cf. Heb. 1:3; 12:2). Yet, there is a difference between *his* exaltation and *ours.* To be sure, he, too, was *exalted.* The very same verb which applies to his followers (II Cor. 11:7) is used at times with respect to him (John 3:14b; 8:28; 12:32, 34; Acts 2:33; 5:31). But in the present passage a verb is used which in the New Testament occurs only in this *one* instance and is here applied only to *him,* namely, the verb *"super-*exalted." God the Father elevated the Son *in a transcendently glorious manner.* He raised him *to the loftiest* *heights.*[93] Do believers go to heaven? See Psalm 73:24, 25; John 17:24; II Cor. 5:8; Heb. 12:18-24. The Mediator "passed through the heavens" (Heb. 4:14), "was lifted high above the heavens" (Heb. 7:26), and even "ascended far above all the heavens" (Eph. 4:10). His super-exaltation means that he received the place of honor and majesty and is accordingly "seated at the right hand of God's throne" (Mark 16:19; Acts 2:33; 5:31, Rom. 8:34; Heb. 1:3, 12:2), "far above all rule and authority and power and dominion and every name that is named not only in this age but also in that which is to come" (Eph. 1:20-22). *Resurrection, ascension, coronation* ("session" at God's right hand), all these are implied and included in the statement, "God raised him to the loftiest heights" (verse 9). Moreover, before the sentence is finished the final step in Christ's exaltation is also described (verses 10 and 11), the *consummation* of his glory when on the day of his coming every knee shall bend before him and every tongue shall proclaim his lordship.

All this happened (and with respect to the last step *will happen*) in fulfilment of prophecy: Gen. 3:15; II Sam. 7:13; Psalm 2:7-9; 8; 47:5; 68:17-19; 72; 110:1; 118:22, 23; Isa. 9:6, 7; 53:10-12; Micah 5:2; Zech. 9:9, 10; cf. Luke 24:26; Rev. 1:7.

The exaltation is the reversal of the humiliation. He who stood condemned in relation to the divine law (because of the sin of the world which rested on him) has exchanged this penal for the righteous relation to the law. He who was poor has become rich. He who was rejected has been accepted (Rev. 12:5, 10). He who learned obedience has entered upon the actual administration of the power and authority committed to him.

As *king,* having by his death, resurrection, and ascension achieved and displayed his triumph over his enemies, he now holds in his hands the reins of the universe, and rules all things in the interest of his church (Eph. 1:22, 23). As *prophet* he through his Spirit leads his own in all the truth. And as *priest* (High-priest according to the order of Melchizedek) he, on the basis of his accomplished atonement, *not only intercedes but actually lives forever to make intercession* for those who draw near to God through him (Heb. 7:25).

Though it was *the person* of the Mediator upon whom these honors were conferred, it was of course *the human nature* in which the exaltation itself took place, since the divine nature is not capable of either humiliation or exaltation. But these two natures, though ever distinct, are never separate. The human nature is so very closely linked with the divine that though it never becomes divine, it shares in the glory of the divine. Therefore Christ's *assumption* of glory is in a sense also *resumption* of glory. There is no real conflict between Phil. 2:9 and John 17:5.

---

[93] Super-combinations are typically Pauline. See N.T.C. on The Pastoral Epistles, p. 75.

Paul continues: **and bestowed on him the name that is above every name.** God the Father *bestowed* on him (literally, he *graciously*, that is *whole-heartedly*, granted to him) *the* name (thus according to the best reading, not merely *a* name). The apostle does not as yet fully tell us what that name is. He does say, however, that it is the name which excels that of every creature in the entire universe.

10. The purpose of the exaltation is: **in order that in the name of Jesus,** that is, *not* in the name *"Jesus"* but in the full name with which Jesus is now rewarded and which he now bears — a name which trembles on Paul's lips but which even now he does not yet fully mention but reserves as a climax — **every knee should bend, of those** [94] **in heaven, and of those on earth, and of those under the earth.** *At his return in glory* Jesus will be worshiped by "the whole body of created intelligent beings in all the departments of the universe" (M. R. Vincent). Angels and redeemed human beings will do this joyfully; the damned will do it ruefully, remorsefully (*not* penitently), see Rev. 6:12-17. But so great will be his glory that all will feel impelled to *render homage* to him (cf. Isa. 45: 23; Rom. 14:11; I Cor. 15:24; Eph. 1:20-22; Heb. 2:8; Rev. 5:13).

Note the three classes of created intelligent beings:

(1) those in heaven: the cherubim and seraphim, yes *all the* ten thousand times ten thousand *good angels,* including archangels; also, of course, *all redeemed human beings who have departed from this earthly life* (Eph. 1:21; 3:10; I Peter 3:22; Rev. 4:8-11; 5:8-12).

(2) those on earth: *all human beings on earth* (I Cor. 15:40).

(3) those under the earth: *all the damned in hell,* both *human beings* and the *evil angels* or *demons* (for if the adjective *heavenly* refers, among others, to the *good* angels, then its antonym, which literally means *under-earthly,* a word occurring only here in the New Testament, in all probability includes the *evil* angels) .[95]

---

[94] In the abstract the three adjectives here used, in their genitive form, can be translated either as neuter or as masculine. A.V. and A.R.V., and also several commentators, prefer the neuter. And it is entirely true that the work of Christ is of value for the entire creation, both animate and inanimate (Isa. 11:6-9; Rom. 8:18-22; II Peter 3:7, 11-13; Rev. 21:1-5). However, we generally associate such actions as *knees bending* and *tongues confessing* with *persons,* not with things. So, unless it can be proved that the context here in Philippians 2:9-11 is very highly poetical (cf. Job 38:7; Ps. 65:13; 98:8; 148:3, 4, 7-10; Isa. 55:12, etc.), the view which refers these designations to *persons* deserves the preference.

[95] *Use of the term* καταχθόνιος-οι *in Greek mythology.*

Zeus (by the Romans identified with Jupiter) becomes the supreme deity and rules the heavens; Poseidon (Rom. Neptune), the ocean; Hades or Pluto (Rom. Dis), the realm of the dead; and the goddess Demeter (Rom. Ceres) the fruitful earth, agriculture.

Daughter of Demeter is Persephone (Rom. Proserpine). Hades abducts Persephone and makes her his wife. Demeter implores Zeus to restore her daughter to her. It is agreed that each year Persephone shall spend part of the time with her

11. Finally Paul arrives at the climax for which he has been preparing. Now at last he actually completes the mention of the name which is above every name: **and that every tongue should confess** [96] **to the glory of God the Father that** *Jesus Christ* **is Lord.** [97] Cf. Isa. 45:23; Rom. 14:11. Not only will all *make obeisance* but in doing so they will also *openly acknowledge and proclaim* the sovereign lordship of Jesus. They will *confess* that JESUS CHRIST (is) LORD, ΚΥΡΙΟΣ ΙΗΣΟΥΣ ΧΡΙΣΤΟΣ.

The solemnity with which the apostle utters this full name, deserves special attention. To him and to others in the early church *this* fact was one of tremendous significance, namely, that the humble "servant" Jesus had even now been crowned with glory and honor and as the great Conqueror is even now celebrating his triumph and actively ruling all things in the interest of his people. *This was the paramount confession of the very early church,* which longed for the day when the marvelous fact would be acknowledged by all. It must have imparted sweet comfort to Paul, the prisoner awaiting a verdict! It must have strengthened the Philippians in all their struggles and afflictions. *Not the earthly emperor but Jesus Christ is the real Ruler!* In order to appreciate somewhat the intense feeling and enthusiasm of the apostles when they thought of *Jesus Christ* as LORD (ΚΥΡΙΟΣ) one should note such passages as the following:

---

husband Hades, and the rest with her mother Demeter. (Here clearly is a symbol of Nature dying and reviving.) Hades and Persephone are therefore, respectively, the god and goddess of the underworld, and in Greek religion are to be counted among *the subterraneans* or καταχθόνιοι.

Use of this term in the New Testament.

In Paul's solitary use of the term the subterraneans are the damned, for according to the context the region "under the earth" is the symbol of that which is opposed to heaven. There are commentators who (with M. R. Vincent) argue that the term in question does not include the infernal spirits or demons, since according to Eph. 2:2; 6:12 demons are not regarded by Paul as being in Hades.

Over against this, note the following:

(1) The context shows that the apostle has in mind the whole body of created intelligences. From this category the demons cannot be excluded.

(2) The reference is to the judgment day. Surely *then* the demons will be assigned to hell, to dwell there forever.

(3) Even now these demons are *hellish ones.* They belong to hell, are hellish in character, and are elsewhere represented as streaming forth upon their sinister missions out of the gates of Hades (Matt. 16:18). The place of "everlasting fire," "is prepared for the devil and his angels" (Matt. 25:41). What Paul says in Eph. 2:2; 6:12 is not in conflict with all this.

[96] Though it is true that the future indicative ἐξομολογήσεται, supported by A,C,-D,F,G, etc., may have been changed to the aorist subjunctive ἐξομολογήσηται, supported by p[46], Aleph and B, in order to conform it to κάμψῃ, yet this is merely a possibility. One expects the aorist subjunctive. Besides, since in subordinate clauses these two forms (future indicative and aorist subjunctive) frequently interchange, there is no essential difference in meaning. See also Gram. N.T., pp. 188, 872.

[97] For alternate translation see footnote 99.

Peter:

"Let all the house of Israel therefore know assuredly that God has made him both Lord and Christ, this Jesus whom y o u crucified" (Acts 2:36).

Paul:

"If you confess with your lips that Jesus is Lord and believe in your heart that God raised him from the dead, you will be saved" (Rom. 10:9).

"No one can say, 'Jesus is Lord' except in the Holy Spirit" (I Cor. 12:3).
"Maranatha" (meaning, "Our Lord, come!") (I Cor. 16:22).

John:

"These will war against the Lamb, and the Lamb will conquer them, for he is Lord of lords and King of kings" (Rev. 17:14).

"And on his robe and on his thigh he has a name inscribed, KING OF KINGS AND LORD OF LORDS" (Rev. 19:16).

This *name* meant very, very much to Paul and to sincere believers everywhere, because a name, as then understood, was not as with us merely a convenient means of distinguishing one individual from another. On the contrary, in biblical usage the name is intimately associated with the person who bears it and is frequently that person himself as he reveals himself. It expresses that person's character, reputation, dignity, work, power, or his peculiar position in the divine economy. Hence, often the name keeps pace with the person. Abram becomes Abraham. Sarai develops into Sarah. Jacob changes to Israel. Solomon receives the name Jedidiah. Simon is called Cephas, that is, Peter. See Gen. 17:5, 15; 32:28; II Sam. 12:25; John 1:42. Sometimes the old name is not wholly dropped. Sometimes it is.

Now this applies also to the glorious name *Jesus Christ . . . Lord*. It is not just a word or title, a kind of signal for knees to start bowing and for tongues to start shouting. It is not *at* (the mere mention of) the name but *in* the name that great things begin to happen. Phil. 2:9-11 means, accordingly, that by virtue of the power and majesty of Jesus Christ and the recognition of him as Lord every knee will bend and every tongue will proclaim him.[98]

Though *now* the proclamation of Christ's name, the open avowal of his sovereign majesty, is muffled on earth, but echoed forth in heaven, *one day* all creation shall bow to our Lord, as stated beautifully in the words of the Dutch Hymn (translated by Rev. W. Kuipers):

---

[98] That the name is often equivalent to the person himself as he stands revealed is seen in such contexts as: Ps. 8; Matt. 10:22; 24:9; 28:19; Mark 13:13; Luke 21:17; Acts 4:30; 9:15; 10:43; I Cor. 1:10; I John 2:12; 3:23.

"One day all creation shall bow to our Lord;
E'en now, 'mong the angels his name is adored.
May we at his coming, with glorified throng,
Stand singing his praises in heaven's great song:
'Jesus, Jesus, Savior adored,
Of all men and angels forever *the Lord.'* "

Great, indeed, was the reward which Jesus received. But every reward must be to the glory of God, the Father (representing the Trinity). The glory of God is ever the goal, the final purpose, of all things. Hence, Paul, who accordingly loves doxologies and near-doxologies, and who breaks into them again and again (Rom. 9:5; 11:36; 16:27; Eph. 1:3 ff.; 3:20; Phil. 4:20; I Tim. 1:17; 3:16; 6:15, 16; II Tim. 4:18; Titus 2:13, 14), also climaxes the present sentence with the words "to the glory of God the Father." [99] By means of the universal proclamation of Jesus' lordship the glory of God the Father, who raised him to the loftiest heights and gave him the most excellent name, will naturally be enhanced.[100] Cf. John 13:31, 32; 14:13; 17:1. Between the Father and the Son there exists a most intimate love-relationship. When the Son is glorified, the Father is glorified also, and vice versa; and when the Son is rejected the Father is rejected also, and vice versa. (In this connection see N.T.C. on John, Vol. II, p. 372, the diagram.)

Let the Philippians then continue to set their mind on Christ. Let them copy his example. Let them do this because this is the rule of life and because both for Christ and for his followers it is the road to that true glory by which God himself is glorified.

---

12 So then, my beloved, even as y o u have always obeyed, so, not as in my presence only but now much more in my absence, with fear and trembling continue to work out y o u r own salvation; 13 for it is God who is working in y o u both to will and to work for his good pleasure.

---

[99] Of course, these words modify the verb "should confess." Hence, in order to avoid ambiguity I translated as follows, "and that every tongue should confess to the glory of God the Father that Jesus Christ is Lord" (so also the Berkeley Version). A.V., A.R.V., and R.S.V. also avoid ambiguity, *if* due note is taken of the comma after the word *Lord*. Since this glorious lordship of the Anointed Savior is the burden, the main message, of the statement, so filled with thought and emotion, it is probably not incorrect to bring out this emphasis in English by slightly changing the word-order of the original and placing the word *Lord* at the very end. Nevertheless, in order to show that the final purpose of the praise rendered by every creature is God's glory, the word-order of the original may be retained and conveyed in some such manner as the following: "and that every tongue should confess that Jesus Christ is Lord (this confession redounding) to the glory of God the Father" (or, with Goodspeed, "and thus glorify God the Father").
[100] On the concept *glory* see the detailed study in connection with Phil. 1:11, including the footnote there. On *Lord* see N.T.C. on John, Vol. I, p. 103; Vol. II, pp. 234, 235; and N.T.C. on I and II Thessalonians, pp. 40, 41.

14 Practise doing all things without mutterings and argumentations, 15 that y o u may become blameless and guileless, children of God without blemish in the midst of a crooked and perverse generation, among whom y o u are shining as stars in the universe, 16 holding forth the word of life, (which will be) for me something to be proud of with a view to the day of Christ, (as indicating) that I did not run in vain or labor in vain. 17 In fact, even if I am to be poured out as a libation upon the sacrificial offering of y o u r faith, I rejoice, and I rejoice with y o u all; 18 and in the same manner do y o u also rejoice, and rejoice with me.

2:12-18

III. *Shining Lights Producing Mutual Joy*

2:12, 13

A. *Work Out Y o u r Own Salvation*

(1) *The Exhortation*

12. So then, my beloved. This establishes the connection between verses 12-18 and verses 1-11, especially 5-11. In fact, the connection goes back even farther, for there is a close parallel between 2:12 and 1:27 (as will be shown). Very tenderly Paul addresses the Philippians as "my beloved." He means, "Y o u whom Christ loves and I also love, with a love that is deepseated, thorough-going, intelligent, and purposeful."

By saying "So then" or "Therefore," the apostle means:

a. Since Christ Jesus by means of his unrestricted, voluntary obedience gave y o u an example (verse 5-8) ; and

b. since the reward which he received shows that there are great things in store for those who follow this example (verses 9-11) ; and finally,

c. since this highly exalted divine and human Mediator imparts strength from heaven to all who trust in him and yearn so to live as he would have them live (implied in verses 9-11) , *therefore,* etc.

The apostle continues his tactful procedure as follows: **even as y o u have always obeyed.** By and large the members of the Philippian church have always *hearkened* to the demands of *God* as expressed in *the gospel* (cf. Rom. 10:16; II Thess. 1:8), to *Christian teaching and admonition* (Rom. 6:17; II Thess. 3:14). Yet, there was danger. There was a tendency to lean too heavily on Paul, that is, on his physical presence with the church at Philippi. These people were overcome with an emotion bordering on nostalgia when they revived in their memory the events that had transpired when Paul had been personally present with them, enabling them to listen to his very voice, and to go directly to him with their problems. Similarly, at present they can hardly wait until, in God's good pleasure, Paul will be with them again. —Now, in such an attitude there is much that is beautiful and to be appreciated. Yet, it is *not altogether* healthy. The Philippians must learn to lean *completely* on God, not just mostly on God and partly on Paul's physical presence with them. That Paul was keenly aware of this weakness is clear from the fact that he has hinted it once before. Note the aforementioned parallel between 1:27 and 2:12:

1:27	2:12
"Only continue to exercise y o u r citizenship in a manner worthy of the gospel of Christ, that *whether I come and see y o u or am absent*, I may hear of y o u that y o u are standing firm in one spirit," etc.	"So then, my beloved, even as y o u have always obeyed, so, not as in my presence only but now much more in my absence, with fear and trembling continue to work out y o u r own salvation.[101]

The obedience of the Philippians must not be motivated by,[102] and last only as long as, Paul's presence among them. On the contrary, his very absence must impress upon them the fact that *now more than ever* they must take the initiative. *Now especially* they must exert themselves, for *now they are on their own;* not, to be sure, as far as *God* is concerned, but as far as *Paul* is concerned. They must now work out "their own salvation," that is, they must work it out *apart from the assistance of Paul.* Yes, they must *work it out,* that is, carry it to its conclusion, thoroughly digest it, and apply it to day-by-day living. They must strive to produce in their lives all the fruits of the Spirit (the entire long list enumerated in Gal. 5:22, 23!). They must aim at nothing less than spiritual and moral perfection.

In such a context we do not go amiss when we say that *the tense* of the verb indicates that Paul has in mind *continuous, sustained, strenuous effort:* "Continue to work out." Believers are not saved at one stroke. Their salvation is *a process* (Luke 13:23; Acts 2:47; II Cor. 2:15). It is a process in which they themselves, far from remaining passive or dormant, take a very active part. It is a pursuit, a following after, a pressing on, a contest, fight, race (see on Phil. 3:12; also Rom. 14:19; I Cor. 9:24-27; I Tim. 6:12).

Putting forth such a constant and sustained effort is not easy. It is a battle

---

[101] This very comparison clearly shows that the words "not as in my presence only but now much more in my absence" modify "with fear and trembling continue to work out y o u r own salvation," and not "even as y o u have always obeyed." Besides, the negative μή (instead of οὐ, οὐχ) is more natural with limitations of the imperative than with the indicative. Cf. John 13:9; James 1:22. It also stands to reason that Paul, facing a verdict and possible death, would be deeply concerned about the question: How will Christian character and conduct develop among the Philippians if I remain absent? Are there perhaps *even now* certain individuals in that congregation who are taking sinful advantage of my absence? Cf. Phil. 4:2, 3. — Hence, from every point of view — exegetical, grammatical, and psychological — the construction of the sentence which, along with most commentators, I favor must be regarded as the best. This is my answer to R. C. H. Lenski, *op. cit.,* p. 803.
[102] Note: "not *as* in my presence." The retention of the rather difficult "as" probably represents the best reading. As in Rom. 9:32; II Cor. 2:17; and Philemon 14 ὡς indicates inward motivation.

on three fronts, a warfare against the tremendously strong and wily combination of the world, the flesh, and the devil. It will mean making full use of every God-appointed means to defeat the evil and bring out the good within them ("within them" because God placed it there!).

It is one thing to shout, "Do all to the glory of God," but it is quite a different thing to carry this out in practice.

It is one thing to pray "as we have forgiven our debtors," but it is not so easy *really* to forgive.

It is one thing to display a beautiful plaque saying,

CHRIST IS THE HEAD OF THIS HOME

but it is something else again actually to recognize him as Head by submitting every important question to him in prayer and by obeying his every command.

It is one thing to assert very piously, "God's sovereignty is the ultimate principle for faith and practice," but it is far more difficult to submit trustfully to this sovereign will when a dear one is growing gradually weaker and finally dies. Thus one could continue. In fact, so very difficult is the task that is here laid upon the Philippians, that, left to their own resources, they can no more fulfil it than the invalid described in John 5 could get up and walk. Yet Jesus told the latter, "Get up, pick up your mat, and walk." And in substance he tells the Philippians that they must consider *working out their own salvation* to be their life's task. Note: their *salvation,* here with emphasis on that aspect of salvation which is called *sanctification.* (For the rest, see N.T.C. on I Tim. 1:15 for the meaning of the term *Salvation* as used by Paul.)

Because this task is so vital it must be performed "with fear and trembling." This phrase, because of its importance, even precedes the verb which it modifies. We read, "With fear and trembling continue to work out y o u r own salvation."

"With fear and trembling" (cf. I Cor. 2:3;
II Cor. 7:15; Eph. 6:5). Meaning:

NOT in the spirit of:	BUT in the spirit of:
half-heartedness, the divided mind (I Kings 18:21)	wholeheartedness, singleness of purpose (Ps. 119:10, 34)
disrespect and disdain (Acts 17:18)	reverence and awe, *being afraid* to offend God in any way (Gen. 39:9; Heb. 12:28)
trust in self (Matt. 26:33)	trust in God (II Chron. 20:12)
self-righteousness (Luke 18:11)	humility (Luke 18:13).

(2) *The Incentive for heeding it*

13. Such fear and trembling does not spell despair. Quite the contrary. Encouragingly Paul says, as it were, Y o u, Philippians, *must* continue to work out y o u r own salvation, and y o u *can* do it, **for it is God who is working in y o u.** Were it not for the fact that God is working *in* y o u, you Philippians would not be able to work *out* y o u r own salvation. Illustrations:

The toaster cannot produce toast unless it is "connected," so that its nichrome wire is heated by the electricity from the electric power house. The electric iron is useless unless the plug of the iron has been pushed into the wall outlet. There will be no light in the room at night unless electricity flows through the tungsten wire within the light-bulb, each end of this wire being in contact with wires coming from the source of electric energy. The garden-rose cannot gladden human hearts with its beauty and fragrance unless it derives its strength from the sun. Best of all, "As the branch cannot bear fruit of itself unless it abides in the vine, so neither can y o u unless y o u abide in me" (John 15:4).

So here also. Only then can and do the Philippians work out their own salvation when they remain in living contact with their God. It is exactly because God began a good work in them — are they not the "beloved" ones? — and because he who began that good work will also carry it toward completion (Phil. 1:6), that the Philippians, as "co-workers with God" (cf. I Cor. 3:9), can carry this salvation to its conclusion. Not only at the beginning but at every point in the process salvation is from God (John 1:12; 15:5b; I Cor. 15:10; Eph. 2:8; Phil. 1:6, 28, 29; 3:9, 12; especially 4:13). "We are God's workmanship," his creation, his "poem." He has made us what we are. By means of his Spirit working in the hearts of his people (Phil. 1:19), applying to these hearts the means of grace and all the experiences of life, God is the great and constant, the effective Worker, the Energizer,[103] operating in the lives of the Philippians, bringing about in them **both to will and to work.** Note: not only *to work* but even *to will*, that is, to resolve and desire:

> " 'Tis not that I did choose thee,
> For, Lord, that could not be;

---

[103] Paul employs the present participle of the verb ἐνεργέω. He uses this verb with respect to:
a. God (I Cor. 12:6, 11; Gal. 2:8, twice; 3:5; Eph. 1:11, 20; Phil. 2:13, first of two instances; Col. 1:29; cf. also Eph. 3:20 and I Thess. 2:13.
b. the spirit of Satan (Eph. 2:2; cf. II Thess. 2:7).
c. sinful passions (Rom. 7:5).
e. death and life (II Cor. 4:12)
d. comfort (II Cor. 1:6)
f. faith (Gal. 5:6)
g. believers (Phil. 2:13, second of two instances).
The word indicates the effective exercise of power.

> This heart would still refuse thee,
> Hadst thou not chosen me.
> Thou from the sin that stained me
> Hast cleansed and set me free;
> Of old thou didst ordain me,
> That I should live for thee."
>
> (Josiah Conder)

The impotent man whose story is related in John 5 was unable to walk. Yet, at the word of Jesus he gets up, picks up his mat, and starts walking. That which he cannot do in his own strength, he can, must, and does do *in the strength of the Lord.*

As to *willing* and *working,* the facts are exactly as stated in *The Canons of Dort* III and IV, articles 11 and 12: "He infuses new qualities into the will, which though heretofore dead he quickens; from being evil, disobedient, and refractory, he renders it good, obedient, and pliable; actuates and strengthens it, that like a good tree, it may bring forth the fruits of good actions. . . . Whereupon the will thus renewed, is not only actuated and influenced by God, but in consequence of this influence becomes itself active." [104]   Nowhere is the manner in which God operates within the heart of his child, enabling him to will and to work, more beautifully described than in Eph. 3:14-19.

It is comforting that the apostle adds **for his good pleasure.** It is *for the sake of* and *with a view to the execution of* God's good pleasure that God, as the infinite Source of spiritual and moral energy for believers, causes them to work out their own salvation. *"Causes* them," yet without in any way destroying their own responsibility and self-activity. Note, moreover, the word *good pleasure.* Says Dr. H. Bavinck (*The Doctrine of God,* English translation, p. 390), "Grace and salvation are the objects of God's delight; but God does not delight in sin, neither has he pleasure in punishment." This statement is in harmony with Scripture (Lam. 3:33; Ezek. 18:23; 33:11; Hos. 11:8; Eph. 1:5, 7, 9).

2:14-18

B. *Thus Y o u Will Be Shining Lights Producing Mutual Joy*

14-16. Paul has been speaking about the necessity of obedience (verse 12) in the great task of working out salvation. But obedience may be of two kinds: grudging or voluntary. "On the outside I may be sitting down, but

---

[104] How Lenski can speak in this connection of Calvinistic error is not clear to me (*op. cit.,* p. 806). Calvinism, like Paul, maintains both divine sovereignty and human responsibility. Man is neither "a self-starting and self-perpetuating organism" nor "a mechanized automaton."

on the inside I am still standing up," said the boy who after repeated admonitions to sit down and finally "obeyed," fearing that otherwise he might be punished. Such grudging obedience is in reality no obedience at all. Example: rendering hospitality while you pity yourself (cf. I Peter 4:9). True religion is never *merely* external compliance. Hence, Paul continues, **Practise doing all things without mutterings and argumentations.** In the original "all things" heads the command; hence really, "All things practise doing without mutterings and argumentations." All the dictates of God's will must be obeyed cheerfully; in such a manner that *the will* of man does not rebel against them by means of discontented, undertone *grumblings,* nor *his mind* by means of perpetual ingenious disputations. Cf. Exod. 4:1-13; 16:7-9, 12; Eccles. 7:29; Num. 17:5, 10; John 6:41-43, 52; I Cor. 10:10. Paul continues . . . **that y o u may become blameless and guileless,** "blameless" in the judgment of others, and "guileless" (literally "unmixed," or "unadulterated," that is, without any admixture of evil) in y o u r own inner hearts and lives. Further, **children of God without blemish.** Note, "that y o u *may become* children of God." But were they not *even now* children of God? The answer should probably be sought in this direction: One becomes *a child* (τέκνον) *of God* by *regeneration,* for a child of God is one who is *begotten* of God. But this is not the end. *Regeneration* is followed by *sanctification.*[105] Those who by virtue of regeneration (and partial sanctification) *are* children of God must endeavor *to become children of God without fault or blame.* And this **in the midst of a crooked and perverse generation.** The description of the worldly contemporaries and neighbors of the Philippians is borrowed from The Song of Moses (LXX Deut. 32:5). Close parallels are found in Matt. 12:39 ("evil and adulterous generation"); 17:17 ("faithless and perverse generation"); and Acts 2:40 ("crooked generation"). People who are crooked are "morally warped." They cannot be trusted. They have arrived at this terrible condition by having turned and twisted themselves in different directions, but always away from the straight path pointed out by the law of God. They are spiritually perverted or distorted. **Among whom,** continues Paul, **y o u,** by y o u r sanctified, blameless and guileless character, **are shining as stars in the universe.**[106] As the stars

---

[105] There are other explanations. Some deny that Paul is here using τέκνον, pl. —α, in the Johannine sense. But the context, which stresses the process of sanctification, surely reminds one of John 1:12. See N.T.C. on that verse. "A child of God" should strive *to become* (hence also "to become manifest as") "a child of God without blemish."

Some commentators, failing to see how children of God can, in any progressive sense, still *become* children of God, re-arrange the clause so that it would read "that y o u, being children of God, may become blameless and guileless," etc. But this change is neither necessary nor justifiable.

[106] Whether φαίνεσθε is taken as (present, middle) *indicative* or as *imperative* makes little difference as long as the main clause "Practise doing all things without mutterings and misgivings" is imperative. *Indicative* here impresses me as the more

dispel physical darkness so believers banish spiritual and moral darkness. As the former illumine the firmament, so the latter enlighten the hearts and lives of men. Moreover,

> "The spacious firmament on high,
> With all the blue ethereal sky,
> And spangled heavens, a shining frame,
> Their great Original proclaim."
>
> (Addison — *Ode.*
> *The Spacious Firmament on High*)

Similarly also believers, by *being* "the light of the world" (Matt. 5:14, 16; cf. Eph. 5:8; I Thess. 5:5), *are constantly proclaiming* their Maker and Redeemer to a world lost in sin. They perform this glorious missionary-task by **holding forth** [107] **the word of life,** the gospel of salvation, not only

---

natural of the two, especially because the verb occurs in a dependent clause removed so far from the main clause. With Lex. N.T. (A. and G.) I agree that even in the middle voice φαίνεσθε with respect to light and its sources can mean "*are shining*" and need not be translated "*are seen.*" Cf. Isa. 60:2. The transition from *to be seen* to *to shine* is a very natural semantic shift when the verb is used in connection with stars, etc. For φωστήρ, *luminary,* in the sense of *star* see same lexicon. The word κόσμος is used in various senses. See N.T.C. on John, Vol. I, p. 79, footnote 26. Here the meaning *universe* would seem to be the most fitting. Hence, there is much to be said for the rendering, "y o u are shining as stars in the universe" (or perhaps even "in the firmament," see for this possibility The New English Bible, footnote on Phil. 2:15; and H. G. Liddell and R. Scott, *Greek-English Lexicon,* entry κόσμος). Daniel 12:3 is a close thought-parallel.

[107] Lenski, among others, definitely rejects this rendering of ἐπέχοντες. Along with many others, before and after him, he favors *holding* or *holding fast.* Among versions and commentaries the two interpretations are about equally divided. Favoring the rendering *holding* or *holding fast* or something similar (for example, *being attached to*) are Moffatt, R.S.V., Berkeley Version, Dutch (Nieuwe Vertaling), Luther, Bengal, Michael, Kennedy (*Expositor's Greek Testament*), and Robertson, to mention only a few of a much longer list. Favoring the translation *holding forth* or *holding out* (to them) are A.V., A.R.V., (The New English Bible has "proffer"), Weymouth, Goodspeed, Wuest, Amplified New Testament, Dutch (Statenvertaling); Eadie, Alford, Vincent (*International Critical Commentary*), Scott (*The Interpreter's Bible*), Greijdanus, Müller, and many others. (Still others favor "being in the place of," "possessing," etc.)

The most detailed and, as I see it, the most satisfactory discussion on this subject is found in Greijdanus (*Kommentaar op het Nieuwe Testament, Philippensen,* on Phil. 2:16). He favors *holding forth. Both renderings make good sense.* Here in Phil. 2:16, however, the rendering "holding forth" or "holding out (to them)" or "proffering" (offering for acceptance) would seem to be best suited to the context. As for the missionary idea, this is already present in the words, "among whom y o u are shining as stars in the universe." Surely, lives that are shining in the darkness of this world of sin and unbelief are exhibiting to men the power of the gospel in sanctified living. Cf. Matt. 5:16. They do it by *holding out* to them the word of life, just like, according to Homer, who uses the identical verb, red wine was *held out* or *offered* to a person (*The Odyssey* XVI, 442-444). When Lenski states that,

as *preached* but also as *practised.* See John 6:68; Acts 5:20; Eph. 2:1; I John 1:1. Light and life go together. "In him was life. And the life was the light of men." See N.T.C. on John 1:4. It is the life and light of salvation.

Says Paul, Such spiritual shining among men, such holding forth the word of life, is that **(which will be) for me something to be proud of with a view to (the) day of Christ.** If the Philippians so conduct themselves in word and deed, then on the glorious day of Christ's Return (see on Phil. 1:10) the apostle, far from being ashamed, will be able to point with pride to the Philippians, to their life and to their testimony. For him this will be *a reason for exultation* (see on Phil. 1:26). Says Paul, I can then be proud of y o u r accomplishment **(as indicating) that** — looking back from the glorious day to the days of my ministry on earth — **I did not run in vain or labor in vain.** "Not *for empty glory*" did I exert myself so strenuously. Not *for nothing* did I run or labor. Here *running* is a metaphor taken from the foot-race in the stadium. Paul frequently employs such figures. See N.T.C. on the Pastoral Epistles, I Tim. 4:7, 8 and II Tim. 4:7, 8. *Laboring* indicates exerting oneself in exhausting toil. Paul, looking back, would be able to point to fruit upon his heavy missionary toil for Christ. Cf. Phil. 4:1; then also I Cor. 3:12, 13; 4:3-5; II Cor. 1:4; and I Thess. 2:19, 20.

17, 18. Accordingly, if the Philippians will continue to work out their own salvation, shining as stars, holding forth the word of life, then there will be every reason for joy. And this remains true even though sooner or later Paul himself should fall a victim to his labors for Christ. Says Paul, **In fact, even if I am to be poured out** [108] **as a libation upon the sacrificial offering of**

---

so interpreted, "it would be the only instance of this meaning in the New Testament," the answer is as follows:

(1) The meaning *holding,* which he adopts, would indeed be the only instance of this meaning in the New Testament. The only other New Testament passages in which this verb occurs are: Luke 14:7 ("holding out the mind to," "focusing the attention upon," "marking"), Acts 3:5 ("held out his mind to," "focused his attention on," "gave heed to") ; I Tim. 4:16 ("hold out your mind to," "focus your attention on," "look to") and Acts 19:22 ("he held out in Asia — remained in Asia — for a while").

(2) If Paul intended to say, "holding," "holding on to," or "holding fast" the word of life, would he not have made use of the verb κατέχω, just as he does elsewhere? Cf. I Cor. 11:2; 15:2; II Cor. 6:10; and I Thess. 5:21?

[108] The present σπένδομαι must be understood as a vivid reference to the future. Paul is probably thinking of his present imprisonment as "the beginning of the end" for himself, whether that end be climaxed at the close of the present imprisonment or a few years later.

I agree with H. A. A. Kennedy (*The Expositor's Greek Testament*) , who in commenting on this passage states, "Here again unnecessary difficulties have been raised over the question whether Paul or the Philippians are to be regarded as offering the sacrifice. There is no evidence that the apostle wishes to strain the metaphor to the breaking point." The *passive* here as well as in II Tim. 4:6 is natural, the supposition being that the apostle's life is being — or is to be — poured out like a drink-offering.

y o u r faith, I rejoice. The pouring out of Paul's blood is a reason for joy
to him as long as it can be considered *a drink-offering* [109] which crowns *the
sacrificial offering* [110] brought by the Philippians. By this *sacrificial offering*
which the Philippians must bring — and have already begun to bring (see
Phil. 1:29) — is to be understood their Christian life and conduct, springing
from faith. It is *their faith in action in the midst of persecution and trial.*
If that offering is fully presented by the Philippians, then the apostle can
truly rejoice, even in the face of death. He can be happy because it will have
become evident that God has been willing to use him to bring the Philippians to their goal of the fully surrendered life. That surely would be an
honor for Paul personally. He adds, **and I rejoice with y o u all.** He rejoices with them, because they will thus be fully experiencing the joys of
redemption in Christ. **And in the same manner do y o u also rejoice** in the
blessings of redemption, **and rejoice with me,** that is, in my having obtained
the martyr's crown as a result of my labor for y o u and for others like y o u.

So speaks *Paul, the humble cross-bearer,* humble even to the point of rejoicing at the thought that "some day he would be the lesser part of the
sacrifice poured out upon the major part, the Philippians' Christian testimony and service to God" (K. S. Wuest, *Philippians in the Greek New
Testament,* p. 78).

Synthesis of 2:1-18

There is here a stirring appeal with a *fourfold incentive* to Christian living. Has not Christ given them his:
(1) encouragement
(2) love
(3) closeness (Spirit-fellowship)
(4) tender compassion?
Then let them exercise toward one another:
(1) oneness
(2) lowliness (humility)
(3) helpfulness.
That is the *threefold directive.*
In Christ this spirit has been beautifully exemplified. Let them therefore
constantly turn their attention to him. If Christ Jesus humbled himself
so deeply, Philippians should surely be willing to humble themselves in their
own small way. If he became obedient to the extent of death by a cross,
they in their own small way should be obedient to his directives. If he was
rewarded, so will they be rewarded.

---

[109] Whether the underlying figure is the *Jewish* libation, poured out *beside* the altar,
or the *pagan* libation, poured out *over* the sacrifice, makes no difference.
[110] ἐπὶ τῇ θυσίᾳ καὶ λειτουργίᾳ to be understood as *hendiadys.*

From all eternity Christ existed and continues to exist in the form of God. He is God. His deity cannot be diminished or shrunken in any way whatever. Yet, he emptied himself, not of his deity of course, for that were impossible, but of his existence-*in-a-manner*-equal-to-God. By taking on the form of a servant and becoming like human beings, he, in that human nature, became poor that we through his poverty might become rich.

As a reward for this humiliation, and following hard upon it, God the Father raised the Mediator to the loftiest heights, seating him at his right hand in the highest heaven, and bestowing on him the name that is above every name, in order that at his glorious Return all intelligent creatures — angels, men, demons may confess to the glory of God the Father that JESUS CHRIST is LORD.

A few propositions can be safely laid down:

(1) According to the clear teaching of this passage — note "Christ Jesus *existing* in the form of God" — Christ's divine nature is immutable. Note how in this passage *the present durative* stands in sharp contrast with *the aorists* which follow it. Any theory which ascribes to the divine nature mutability and the ability to become temporal and spatial finds no support here. Christ's divine nature will be what it has been from all eternity: fully divine.

(2) Exaltation clearly *follows* humiliation. It was because Christ became obedient even to the extent of death, yes death by a cross, that God raised him to the loftiest heights. The view which teaches that these two states coincided, so that Christ was exalted in his humiliation and humiliated in his exaltation, throws overboard the plain meaning of words, and cannot be regarded as being in accordance with sound principles of exegesis.

(3) Christ's two natures, though united in his one person, are and ever remain clearly distinct. He who exists eternally as God took upon himself the human nature, and now has both. The rejection of the two-nature doctrine is in direct contradiction to the plain teaching of Phil. 2:5-11. Exegesis should never surrender to mere fancy, wild speculation. But even the most careful exegesis will be insufficient if it ignores the real reason why the apostle was led by the Holy Spirit to write this paragraph, namely, that we should pattern ourselves after the spirit of Christ who for our sake was willing to humble himself so deeply!

True, if one so conducts himself, persecution from the side of the kingdom of darkness is in store for him. Paul, accordingly, presents himself as *humble cross-bearer,* willing to be poured out as a libation upon the sacrificial offering of the faith of the Philippians. He urges the addressees: with fear and trembling to continue to work out their own salvation, this all the more in the absence of their leader (Paul). Let their incentive be that there is One who is working within them both to will and to work for his good pleasure. And let them do it from the heart, without complaining. Thus, as stars in the universe they, too, will shine in the midst of a crooked and perverse generation, holding forth the word of life, that is, fulfiling their mission-task, so that Paul can rejoice in them, and this both now and on the day of Christ's Return. "And in the same manner," concludes Paul, "do y o u also rejoice, and rejoice with me."

---

[87] The word ἁρπαγμός, acc. -ον, has given rise to several questions: Should it be taken in the active sense — an act of robbery or usurpation — or in the passive sense — *a prize* to be held on to, a treasure to be clutched? Is it *an action* or is it *a thing?* Several Latin fathers, notably also Augustine, favor the former. Most of the early Greek writers prefer the latter, that is, they interpret the passage to mean that Christ Jesus did *not* regard his existence in a manner equal to God as a prize to be retained at all hazards.

The active sense — robbery —is favored by the A.V. But this meaning is in conflict with *the words that precede* (see Phil. 2:1-4). The apostle has just exhorted the Philippians to be humble and not always to be insisting on their own rights but to be thoughtful of others. Surely, in such a context the idea that Christ *asserted* his rights — "thought it not robbery to be equal with God" — does not fit. Also, the rendering does not do justice to *the words that follow*. The conjunction *but* suggests a direct contrast. This demand is satisfied only when the clause "he emptied himself" is preceded by something like "he did not cling to," or as the text actually reads, "He did not count his existence-in-a-manner-equal-to-God something to cling to." Certainly when a word can have either an active or a passive meaning it is the specific context that decides the issue.

But is not ἁρπαγμός after all an active concept because of its suffix –μος which is an active-ending, in contrast with –μα, which is a result-ending? The answer is: this rule allows for many exceptions. Note the following:

ἐπισιτισμός	(in Luke 9:12) means	food.
θερισμός	(in Luke 10:2) means	harvest or crop.
ἱματισμός	(in John 19:24) means	vestment.
ὑπογραμμός	(in I Peter 2:21) means	writing-copy, hence example.
φραγμός	(in Luke 14:23) means	hedge or fence.
χρηματισμός	(in Rom. 11:4) means	oracle.
ψαλμός	(in I Cor. 14:26) means	psalm.

And as to ἁρπαγμός Eusebius in his Commentary on Luke (vi) uses this very word, and *in the passive sense,* as meaning *prize.*

This, however, brings up another matter. Such a *prize* can be either *res rapta,* that is, *something which one already has in his possession, ostensibly displays, and retains in his grasp,* or (as in the case of Peter's death on a cross) *res rapienda,* that is, *something which one does not yet have in his possession, a prize to be eagerly sought.* But here, too, it is the context in each given case that is decisive. The idea that also here in Phil. 2:6 the futuristic sense *(res rapienda)* should be ascribed to the word ἁρπαγμός is defended by H. A. A. Kennedy *(The Expositor's Greek New Testament,* Vol. III, pp. 436, 437) ; J. H. Michael *(The Moffat New Testament Commentary: Philippians,* pp. 88-89); A. M. Hunter *(Paul and his Predecessors,* pp. 45-51) ; J. Ross *(J Th S,* July, 1909) ; W. Warren *(J Th S,* April, 1911) ; and more recently by J. M. Furness *(J Th S,* Dec., 1957); and D. R. Griffiths, "Harpagmos and heauton ekenōsen in Philippians 2:6, 7" *(Ex T* 69, No. 8, 1958) . With variations as to detail this view may be summarized as follows: Jesus might have used his miraculous powers in such a way as to compel men to worship him as God. He might have reached out for this honor in order to *grab* it. Is not that what, in substance, *"the first Adam"* did (see Gen. 3:4, 5 and cf. Phil. 3:6) ? And was not that the very thing which in the desert of temptation and in fact throughout our Lord's earthly sojourn Satan tempted *"the second Adam"* to do? But Jesus said

"No." Instead of using *force* he showed *obedience*. And on account of his great renunciation and obedience God now highly exalted him and bestowed upon him, as a reward, the name that is above every name (Phil. 2:9-11).

The theory is very interesting, but will not do, and this for the following reasons: (1) To imply that the One who is here described as "existing in the form of God" lacked "existence in a manner equal to God," so that he looked forward to it as a reward is indefensible. Surely, as a starting-point, one must proceed from the idea that he who is the possessor of the divine nature also had the divine glory and authority.

(2) The clearly parallel-passage, II Cor. 8:9, teaches that *Christ gave up the glory which he already had!*

(3) The context, as has been shown, requires the idea that the Philippians must be willing *to sacrifice* certain things in the interests of others.

Summary of Chapter 2

Verses 19-30

Paul, the Thoughtful Administrator

promising to send Timothy to the Philippians as soon as his (Paul's) own case has been decided,
and even now sending Epaphroditus back to them.

2:19-24 The contemplated mission of Timothy.
2:25-30 The authorized return of Epaphroditus.

19 But I hope in the Lord Jesus to send Timothy to y o u soon, so that I also may be heartened by knowing y o u r affairs. 20 For I have no one likeminded who will be genuinely interested in y o u r welfare. 21 For they all look after their own affairs, not those of Jesus Christ. 22 But y o u know his proved worth, how as a child (serves) with (his) father, so he served with me in the gospel. 23 Him, then, I hope to send at once, that is, as soon as I can see (how) my affairs (will turn out). 24 But I trust in the Lord that I myself shall also come soon.

2:19-24

I. The Contemplated Mission of Timothy

19. Paul, the joyful servant of Jesus Christ, the optimistic prisoner, the humble cross-bearer, is also the thoughtful administrator. Even from his prison in Rome he manages in a masterly fashion the spiritual terrain entrusted to his care, so that we marvel at his practical wisdom, gracious consideration of the needs and feelings of others, and delightful unselfishness. Are the Philippians anxious to receive a report about the verdict that is about to be pronounced regarding Paul? As soon as this decision is known, a messenger will be rushed to Philippi with the news. See verse 23. However, the apostle wants the Philippians to know that he is as concerned about them as they are about him. In fact, it is of importance to note that the *first* reason which he mentions for dispatching someone to Philippi is that he, Paul, may be brought up to date in his information concerning *them.* He writes, **But** — though it is possible that my blood will be poured out presently (implied in verses 17 and 18), yet — **I hope in the Lord Jesus to send Timothy to y o u soon.** Although in this letter Paul never entirely dismisses from his mind the possibility of an unfavorable verdict (Phil. 1:20-23; 2:17, 18, 23), yet his expectation of an imminent acquittal and release predominates (Phil. 1:25, 26; 2:19; 2:24; cf. Philem. 22). He is full of hope. This hope is, of course, "in the Lord Jesus" (Phil. 1:8, 14; 2:24; 3:1). It is cherished in complete and humble subjection to him who alone is *Lord,* sovereign Ruler of all, the One with whom the apostle is living in intimate fellowship.

Now for this important mission of imparting information to the Philippians and (as here) obtaining news from them the apostle has selected no one less than Timothy. See on Phil. 1:1. And since hopefully this is to be a mission of good news and encouragement, Timothy will be sent not only *to* them but *for* them, *in their interest.*

Paul continues . . . **so that I also may be heartened by knowing y o u r affairs.** Just as the apostle expects that the Philippians will be heartened by news from him, so he *also* expects to be refreshed in his soul when he receives Timothy's report with reference to them.

Paul does not indicate the place where he, if released, hopes to meet Timothy again when the latter, having performed his task at Philippi, will make his report. Perhaps at Ephesus? See N.T.C. on The Pastoral Epistles, pp. 39, 40.

20, 21. A description of Timothy's unique fitness for his task follows: **For I have no one likeminded who will be genuinely interested in y o u r welfare.** For detailed description of Timothy's life and character see N.T.C. on The Pastoral Epistles, pp. 33-36.

As far as temperament, disposition, and inclination were concerned, and this especially with a view to the present assignment, there was no one who could compare with Timothy.[111] There was no one with a heart like his. His was a fine, sympathetic, amiable spirit. It is as if Paul were saying, "Y o u, Philippians, must not be disappointed if upon my release I cannot *in person* immediately come to see y o u. As soon as ever possible (see verse 23) I will dispatch Timothy. No one is better qualified and more favorably disposed. Already as a child he was an eager student of the sacred writings, a teachable and obedient son (II Tim. 3:15). As he grew up he was highly recommended by those who knew him best (Acts 16:2). Upon his conversion to the Christian faith he became my beloved and faithful child in the Lord (I Cor. 4:17), and a little later my special deputy and fellow-worker (Rom. 16:21), always ready to go wherever I sent him or to be left behind wherever I told him to remain (Rom. 16:21). To top it all, he is *God's* minister in the gospel of Christ (I Thess. 3:2). And do not forget either that from the very founding of y o u r church he has known y o u, and y o u have known him, for not only was he present when y o u r church was established (Acts 16:11-40; I Thess. 2:2) but subsequently he has also visited y o u upon more than one occasion (Acts 19:21, 22; 20:3-6; II Cor. 1:1). He therefore is a *natural.* Yes, y o u can surely bank on it that he will be genuinely interested in y o u r welfare (literally, *in the things concerning y o u).*"

But is it not true that upon his release Paul would like nothing better than to keep Timothy in his own immediate company? Was not Timothy the man whom Paul could least afford to spare? True, but in his mind and heart the apostle has already decided on this personal sacrifice. And this

---

[111] As is indicated by the relative clause ("who will be genuinely interested in y o u r welfare") which refers to Timothy, the word "likeminded" means "in comparison with Timothy," not "in comparison with myself (Paul)."

willingness always to subordinate his own immediate interests to those of the kingdom (see I Cor. 10:33) also explains, at least in part, why the apostle can use such strong language with respect to those who are of an opposite disposition. Surely, the names of others had occurred to him when he had decided that upon the publication of the verdict concerning himself someone must convey the news to Philippi. But a moment of reflection — or perhaps *their* excuses when approached on this subject — had convinced him that *they* were not qualified. Says Paul, **For they all look after their own affairs, not those of Jesus Christ.** Attempts have been made to tone down the sharpness of this judgment. This is hardly warranted. The words are simple and direct, whether read in the original or in translation. With many interpreters I believe, however, that they do not apply to absolutely every gospel-worker who was at this time in any way whatever associated with the apostle, but rather to those only who might be available at this particular juncture, and who might for a moment be regarded as qualified for a mission to Philippi.

The following facts must be borne in mind:

(1) Paul was not thinking of men like Luke and Aristarchus. These, though having been with him in Rome (Col. 4:10, 14; Philem. 24), were now no longer with him. Paul in writing Philippians cannot even send their greetings. The apostle is in the habit of sending his envoys to various stations, wherever they are needed. Thus later also, during his *second and far more severe* Roman imprisonment, he was not selfishly going to try to keep around him as many friends as possible, but was going to send Tychicus to Ephesus and also "Crescens to Galatia and Titus to Dalmatia" (II Tim. 4:10-12). Accordingly, here in Phil. 2:21, apostolic deputies absent on various missions must be subtracted from the number of those whom Paul judges so severely.

(2) The statement "For they all look after their own affairs, not those of Jesus Christ," is, nevertheless, indicative of the keen disappointment which the apostle suffered. Now Phil. 1:15, 17 has already shown that not every gospel-worker in Rome was inspired by the highest motives. And this was not the only disappointment Paul was going to experience in his missionary labors in the great metropolis. For example, Demas, whose name is still mentioned in earlier epistles that belong to this imprisonment (Col. 4:10; Philem. 24), but who is no longer mentioned in Philippians (perhaps because he too was absent on some legitimate mission?), *is going to* prove a bitter disappointment (II Tim. 4:10). And then there is II Tim. 4:16, "At *my first defense* no one was at my side but all deserted me." See N.T.C. on The Pastoral Epistles, pp. 325-330. If this "first defense" is connected with the first imprisonment, as may well be the case, then in II Tim. 4:16 we would have a statement similar to that in the Philippian passage now under consideration. The very people from whom Paul had expected help during

his trial had disappointed him. And so also, the very people whose names had momentarily occurred to Paul when the decision was made to send someone to Philippi, either had offered excuses or upon further reflection were simply dismissed from the apostle's mind as spiritually unqualified because of their previous failures, inability to endure the trial of fire, and lack of *genuine* interest. In the light of such passages as Phil. 1:15, 17; II Tim. 4:10, 16, *we are no longer surprised* to read Phil. 2:21. Paul here graciously withholds the names of those who because of their evident selfishness were unfit for a mission to Philippi.

22. How altogether different was Timothy! Hence, Paul continues in the spirit of verse 20, **But y o u know his proved worth.** Timothy is no novice. To be sure, he is still young, perhaps in his middle thirties. See N.T.C. on I Tim. 4:12. But he is not inexperienced. "The crucible of affliction" was known to him. Yes, the life of this young Christian had been subjected to the searching eyes of God and had stood the test.[112] He had been "approved." Timothy's reliability was by now a well-established fact. "Y o u know," says Paul, **how as a child (serves) with (his) father, so he served with me** [113] **in the gospel.** For the details, showing how the Philippians had become aware of this, see above on verse 20. Timothy's association with Paul was like that of a child with his father, father and son being intensely interested in the same cause. Willingly, enthusiastically, the younger man had subjected himself, in filial attachment, to his spiritual father, for the latter's aim was also his own. Timothy's service was a thoroughly dedicated, spontaneous, loving ministry in the interest of and for the promotion of *the gospel.* See on 1:27. In order that God's truth might be established in the hearts of men — including the Philippians — Timothy had been doing all in his power to lighten Paul's heavy load.[114]

23, 24. After this brief aside on Timothy's virtues the apostle resumes the thought of verse 19, the *sending* of Timothy: **Him, then, I hope to send at once, that is, as soon as I can see (how) my affairs (will turn out). But I trust in the Lord that I myself also shall come soon.** Once the verdict has been pronounced, the Philippians, far from being left in the dark, will be informed by no one less than beloved Timothy, who will carry the news to

---

[112] For the meaning of δοκιμή see on Phil. 1:10; also N.T.C. on I Thess. 2:4; and W. Grundmann, art. and related words, in G. Kittell, Th.W.N.T., II, pp. 258-264.
[113] This is better than *he slaved with me.* See on Phil. 1:1; 2:7.
[114] The idea of some that Paul started to write, "Timothy served me," but changed this to, "Timothy served with me," when it occurred to him that both men were after all servants of Jesus Christ, is probably not the most natural way to account for the structure of the sentence. If allowance is made for "compressed style," so characteristic of New Testament writers, especially of Paul, the sentence as it stands is sufficiently clear.

them without any delay. Will that verdict be condemnation or acquittal? Paul does not know for sure but is rather confident that it will be the latter. In any event his trust in the Lord remains unshaken. The best commentary on this underlying pendulation of thought with emphasis on hope of release and especially on complete trust in the Lord is found in Paul's own words recorded in 1:19-26 and 2:17, 18 (see comments on these verses). Was the apostle released? And did he soon follow Timothy to Philippi? The answer must be that this was actually what happened. See N.T.C. on The Pastoral Epistles, pp. 23-27 for detailed argument.

---

25 But I consider it necessary to send (back) to y o u Epaphroditus, my brother and fellow-worker and fellow-soldier, and y o u r messenger and minister to my need, 26 for he has been longing for y o u all, and he has been distressed because y o u heard that he was sick. 27 And sick he was indeed, on the verge of death. But God had mercy on him, and not only on him but also on me, that I might not have sorrow upon sorrow. 28 Accordingly, I am sending him (back) the more eagerly in order that when y o u see him again y o u may rejoice and I may be less sorrowful. 29 So, extend to him a most joyful welcome in the Lord, and hold such men in honor, 30 because for the work of Christ he came to the brink of death, risking his life that he might supply what was lacking in y o u r service to me.

2:25-30

II. *The Authorized Return of Epaphroditus*

25. Paul, the thoughtful administrator, now turns from Timothy to Epaphroditus. See Introduction, IV. Briefly the facts concerning him were the following:

---

(1) He was *a spiritual leader* in the church at Philippi.

(2) He had been commissioned by that church to bring a bounty to Paul, the prisoner, and to be his constant assistant and attendant.

(3) While engaged in this service he had become dangerously ill.

(4) His friends in Philippi had heard about this illness and had become alarmed, in turn. He learns about their anxiety.

(5) God graciously restores Epaphroditus.

(6) He yearns to return to the church which had delegated him, in order to allay its fears with respect to his health.

(7) Paul, in complete accord, sends him back to Philippi, bespeaks a cordial "Welcome home!" for him, and in all probability makes him the bearer of this letter.

Now *the fact* of Epaphroditus' authorized return, together with a brief

137

description of the man, is found in verse 25; *the reasons for his return* are stated in verses 26-28; and *the manner in which he should be received* is indicated in verses 29, 30.

Says Paul: **But I consider** [115] **it necessary to send (back) to y o u Epaphroditus, my brother and fellow-worker and fellow-soldier, and y o u r messenger and minister to my need.** Epaphroditus! His name [116] means *lovely,*

---

[115] Instead of "I consider" in verse 25 and "I am sending" in verse 28 the original has "I considered" and "I sent." The latter are epistolary aorists written from the point of view of the readers. When Paul's letter is received by them the considering and the sending will belong to the past. Hence, in Greek a past tense is used, where our language, viewing the situation from the point of view of the writer, would use the present.

[116] The name, a rather common one, is related to that of the goddess of love and beauty, Aphrodite. Since in this predominantly heathen community the church was of fairly recent origin the conjecture that Epaphroditus descended from a Greek family *devoted to Aphrodite* may well be correct. The following facts must, however, be borne in mind:

A. (1) As a result of Alexander's conquest with its spread of Hellenistic culture names of Greek-pagan origin had become popular all over the wide-stretching empire.

(2) Jews, too, had adopted the habit of giving their children Greek names, and even Christians did not hesitate to copy and retain these names; just as today Christion parents often do not hesitate to name their children Dennis, Dion, Diana, Isadora, Minerva. They also retain the pagan names of the days of the week.

(3) In such names as Timothy (I Tim. 1:2, honoring God), Theophilus (Luke 1:3, Acts 1:1, loved of God) and Theudas (Acts 5:36, contraction of Theodorus, gift of God) the deity referred to is not definitely indicated. Hence, these lend themselves to Christian interpretation. This holds too for several others, including in a sense even Epaphroditus. See B 2.

B. Names derived from heathen deities abound on the pages of the New Testament. For our present purpose it is necessary to note only the following items of ancient mythology:

Many or all the Olympic deities are reflected in Olympas (Rom. 16:15). Offspring of Cronos and Rhea were the Olympic deities Demeter and Zeus.

Demeter (see also footnote 95), goddess of agriculture, of the fruitful earth, protectress of the social order and marriage (by the Romans identified with Ceres; cf. our "cereals"), finds her echo in Demetrius (Acts 19:24). Zeus (Acts 14:12), chief of the gods, ruler of the heavens (by the Romans identified with Jupiter) returns to us in the name Zenas (Titus 3:13, abbreviation of Zenodorus, given by Zeus), and in Diotrephes (III John 9, nourished by Zeus).

Zeus had several wives and children:

(1) *Offspring of Zeus and Leto:* Apollo and Artemis.

Apollo was considered the god of the sun; later, of healing, music, poetry, prophecy, youthful male beauty. Hence, we have Apollos (Acts 18:24, abbreviation of Apollonius) and Apelles (Rom. 16:10).

The twin-sister of Apollos was Artemis, the goddess of the moon; later, of youth, health, freedom, the dance, the dewy meadows and green forests, especially of the chase, "the virgin-huntress" (by the Romans identified with Diana); whence Artemas (Titus 3:12). Another name for Artemis was Phoebe, the bright and radiant moon-goddess; hence Phoebe (Rom. 16:1).

(2) *Offspring of Zeus and Dione* (but according to others sprung from the seafoam, ἀφρός): Aphrodite (by the Romans identified with Venus).

Epaphroditus and its abbreviation Epaphras are derived from Aphrodite (hence, *devoted to Aphrodite,* the goddess of love; and so *lovely*). Yet though the two

and a lovely person he was! Paul describes him first in his relation to him-self, then in his relation to the church at Philippi. With respect to Paul he is *my brother, fellow-worker, and fellow-soldier.* The words are evidently arranged in an ascending scale. In common with every believer Epaphro-ditus is Paul's *brother,* united with him *in faith.* He is a member of the same spiritual family, with God in Christ as Father. Paul is fond of this word *brother,* for it is a term of affection (cf. 4:1). It is no surprise, there-fore, that in the present letter, written to his dearly-beloved Philippians, the famous prisoner uses it more often than in any other prison-epistle (1:12, 14; 2:25; 3:1, 13, 17; 4:1, 8, 21). But Epaphroditus is even more than Paul's *brother.* He is united with him not only in faith but also *in work,* the work of the gospel; hence, *fellow-worker,* a title given elsewhere to such kingdom-laborers as Apollos, Aquila and Priscilla, Aristarchus, Clement, Mark, Onesimus, Philemon, Timothy, Titus, Tychicus, etc. Finally, Epa-phroditus is united with Paul not only in faith and in work but also *in battle.* He is a *fellow-soldier,* a *companion in arms.* A *worker* must needs be a *warrior,* for in the work of the gospel one encounters many foes: Judais-tic teachers, Greek and Roman mockers, emperor-worshippers, sensualists, the world rulers of this darkness, etc. Accordingly, on the part of every worker there must be prodigious exertion of energy against the foe, and unquestioning obedience to the Captain, in the full assurance of ultimate victory (cf. Philem. 2; II Tim. 2:3, 4; 4:7, 8). How Epaphroditus had ful-filled his commission as a worker and a soldier is explained in verse 30.

In relation to the church of Philippi Epaphroditus is called y o u r *mes-senger and minister to my need.* The word *messenger* is literally *apostle,* but this term is here used in its widest sense,[117] indicating someone who has been delegated by the church to carry out an assignment, *an official representative through whom the church itself speaks and acts.* In the present case the assignment was not only to bring to Paul the gift of the

---

names are the same, the Epaphroditus of Philippians is not the Epaphras of Colos-sians, for the respective contexts (cf. Phil. 2:25 with Col. 1:7) show that these two belong to different cities.

(3) *Offspring of Zeus and Maia:* Hermes (Acts 14:12).
He was the herald and messenger of the gods, the god of roads, commerce, in-vention (by the Romans identified with Mercury); whence Hermas (Rom. 16:14; abbreviation of several names, including Hermodorus, that is, given by Hermes) and Hermogenes (II Tim. 1:15, born of Hermes).
C. Even the lesser deities and supernatural beings are reflected in Biblical personal names. Thus Hymen, the god of marriage, returns to us in Hymenaeus (II Tim. 2:17); Nereus, a lower sea-deity, father of the Nereids or sea-nymphs, in Nereus (Rom. 16:11); and with less certainty Tyche (by the Romans identified with For-tuna), the goddess of fortune, chance, luck, in Tychicus (Acts 20:4), Syntyche (Phil. 4:2), and Eutychus (Acts 20:4, 9). Some find the sea-nymphs in Nymphas (Col. 4:15), but because of a textual-critical problem this is very uncertain.
[117] For the various meanings of the word *apostle* see N.T.C. on The Pastoral Epis-tles, pp. 49-51.

Philippian church but also to serve Paul in whichever way that service might be *needed* (note: minister *to my need;* cf. Phil. 4:16; Acts 20:34; Rom. 12:13) ; for example, as his personal attendant and as his missionary-assistant. Hence, Epaphroditus had been sent both to *bring* a gift and to *be* a gift from the Philippians to Paul. The very word used in the original for *minister,* namely *leitourgos,* indicates that the task of Epaphroditus was viewed as one in which he — and the church of Philippi through him — rendered *official* and *sacred* service, and this not only to Paul but to the cause of the gospel; hence, to God himself. The sending of Epaphroditus, with all that it implied, was a religious act, a true offering or sacrifice! Proof: see Phil. 2:17 (*"sacrificial offering* of y o u r faith") and 2:30, which use the cognate noun *leitourgia;* and also 4:18, which calls the gift which this messenger brought *"a sacrifice,* acceptable, well-pleasing to God." Cf. also Rom. 15:16 and II Cor. 9:12.[118]

Epaphroditus had done whatever he was able to do. He had done it in the right spirit. Let no one criticize this worthy servant when he now returns to his church at Philippi. Let no one say, "How shameful for you to have acted contrary to the charge which we gave you, and to have deserted Paul at the very time when that honored prisoner, who is awaiting a life-or-death verdict needs you most." Says Paul, as it were, "Bear in mind, Philippians, that Epaphroditus is returning to y o u because I myself consider it necessary to send him back to y o u."

26-28. The reasons for the authorized return are now stated. These reasons are three and are closely intertwined. They concern *him* (Epaphroditus) , *y o u* (Philippians) , and *myself* (Paul) :

(1) In order that the ardent wish of *Epaphroditus* may be satisfied (verses 26 and 27) ;

(2) In order that y o u may rejoice (verse 28a) ; and

(3) In order that *I* (Paul) may be less sorrowful (verse 28b) .

Beginning with (1) Paul says, **for he has been longing for y o u all, and he has been distressed because y o u heard that he was sick.** This implies that word of the illness of Epaphroditus had reached Philippi, and that the report of Philippi's resulting alarm had been brought back to Rome. The result for Epaphroditus was twofold:

First of all, he is worried over their worry! Severe distress of mind and

---

[118] As the Greek *leitourgos,* motivated by love for his city and its gods, financed a great drama or fitted out a warship, so the Philippians, impelled by a love for the one true God in Jesus Christ, had sponsored this truly great undertaking, namely, the gathering of a substantial gift for Paul and the sending to Paul of this wonderful bounty and of its even more wonderful bearer. See also N.T.C. on The Pastoral Epistles, p. 225, footnote 113.

heart, profound agony, overwhelms his soul. The word used in the original to express this disturbance (a word of uncertain derivation) is the one that is used in connection with the unspeakable anguish which Jesus experienced in Gethsemane (Matt. 26:37; Mark 14:33).

Secondly, his love for the church that had sent him becomes so overpowering that he yearns to see again the familiar faces of those whose sympathy is so real, and whose anxiety must be removed.

Now this anxiety of the Philippian church cannot be removed by stating that the report concerning the sickness of their beloved leader was unfounded or had been exaggerated. On the contrary; Paul continues: **And sick he was indeed, on the verge of death.**

The question is asked, "But why had not Paul, by means of a miracle or by means of prayer, prevented this illness, or at least quickly healed Epaphroditus, even long before his illness had taken such a grave turn?" The answer must be: first, that even in that charismatic era the apostles could not perform miracles whenever they felt so inclined. *Their* will was subject to *God's* will. And as to prayer, even though this is indeed a mighty means of healing and often leads to recovery, it is no cure-all. It does not operate mechanically like pressing a button. It, too, is ever subject to God's will, which is wiser than man's desiring. And in this all-wise providence of God it has been determined that believers too at times become ill, sometimes gravely ill (Elisha, II Kings 13:14; Hezekiah, II Kings 20:1; Lazarus, John 11:1; Dorcas, Acts 9:37; Paul, Gal. 4:13; Timothy, I Tim. 5:23; Trophimus, II Tim. 4:20; and so also Epaphroditus, Phil. 2:25-27). Yes, they get sick and they even die! The passage, "With his stripes we are healed," does not mean that believers have been exempted from the infirmities of the flesh, from grave illness or from death. But when believers are stricken, theirs is the comfort of such passages as Psalm 23; 27; 42; John 14:1-3; Rom. 8:35-39; Phil. 4:4-7; II Tim. 4:6-8; Heb. 4:16; 12:6, to mention only a few among many references.

Another question is, "What was the nature of Epaphroditus' illness?" Many guesses have been made, but all that is really known is that it was in connection with the work of the Lord and more specifically in connection with his loving attendance upon and assistance to Paul that Epaphroditus had become sick (see verse 30). Was the illness a result of over-exertion? Had he been trying to do too much? Had this wonderful fellow-believer, worker, soldier, after a very difficult and exhausting journey exerted himself to the utmost in the work of attending to Paul's every need, caring for believers in Rome, preaching to everyone willing to listen to the glorious gospel of the Crucified One, and doing all this amid great difficulty and personal danger, in a city whose multitudes paid homage not to Christ but to the emperor? At any rate, he had lost every bit of strength, and at last had been brought to death's very door, so close to it that he could, as it were,

141

touch it. For a while his life, humanly speaking, had been hanging by a thread. But then — in answer, to be sure, to the prayers of many — the experience of the author of Ps. 116 had become his also. Epaphroditus had been graciously restored to health. This surely is implied in the words which now follow: **But God had mercy on him.** God *compassionated, pitied* Epaphroditus! [119] He had mercy on him, **and,** continues Paul, **not only on him but on me also that I might not have sorrow upon sorrow,** that is, sorrow that would have resulted from the death of Epaphroditus added to sorrow because of his grave illness.

God *pitied* both Epaphroditus and Paul! It is comforting to know that the heart of God is filled with *mercy,* that is, with *lovingkindness and active pity.* In Christ he is "touched with the feeling of our infirmities."

"Mindful of our human frailty
Is the God in whom we trust;
He whose years are everlasting,
He remembers we are dust.

"Changeless is Jehovah's mercy
Unto those who fear his name,
From eternity abiding
To eternity the same."

The following are some of the beautiful passages in which this comforting doctrine is set forth or illustrated:[120]

Gen. 39:21; Exod. 3:7; 20:6; Deut. 30:3; 33:27; II Sam. 7:15; 24:14; II Chron. 36:15; Neh. 1:5; Ps. 5:7; 23; 34:6; 36:5, 7; 81:10; 86:5; 89:28-34; 103:14-17; 108:4; 116:1-9; 136; Is. 1:18; 40; 42:3; 53:4-6; 54:7; 55:1-7; 63:7-9; Jer. 12:15; 31:34; Lam. 3:22, 32, 33; Ezek. 33:11; Hos. 11:4, 8; Joel 2:13; Jonah 4:11; Mic. 7:18-20; Nah. 1:7; Zeph. 3:17; Zech. 9:9; Matt. 5:7; 9:13, 27-31, 36; 11:28, 29; 12:7; 14:14; 15:21-28; 17:14-18; 18:27, 33; 20:29-34; 23:23, 37; Mark 1:41; 5:19; 6:34; 10:14, 46-52; Luke 1:46-80; 7:13; 8:54, 55; 10:25-37; 12:32; 14:23; 15:7, 20-24; 16:24; 17:11-19; 18:35-43; 23:34, 43; John 3:16, 17; 10:11-16; 11:5, 35; 14:1-3; 17; 19:25-27; 21:15-17; Acts 2:46, 47; Rom. 5:8-10; 8:26-39; 9:15-18, 23; 11:30-32; I Cor. 7:25, II Cor. 4:1; 6:17, 18; Gal. 2:20; 6:16; Eph. 2:1-10; 3:14-19; Col. 3:12-17; I Thess. 4:17, 18; I Tim. 1:2, 13-16; II Tim. 1:2, 16, 18; 4:8, Titus 2:11; 3:5; Heb. 2:17; 4:14-16; 7:25;

---

[119] The original has, "God *mercied* him," but this does not sound well in English. German: *Gott hat sich über ihn erbarmet;* Swedish: *Gud förbarmade sig över honom;* Dutch: *God heeft zich over hem ontfermd.*
[120] Here in Phil. 2:27 the original has ἠλέησεν; cf. the noun ἔλεος: mercy. See the word-study of this concept in N.T.C. on The Pastoral Epistles, pp. 54-56, including footnote 23 on p. 55 there.

James 2:13; 3:17; 4:5; I Peter 1:3, 18, 19; 2:10; I John 1:9; 3:1-3; II John 3; Jude 2, 21; Rev. 7:9-17; 21:1-7.

This divine tenderness of heart that expresses itself in helpful deeds is beautifully reflected in Paul. To satisfy his faithful helper's ardent yearning and to relieve his deep distress he orders him to return to Philippi. Epaphroditus, now fully recovered, longs to be reunited with the church that had sent him. In all probability he wanted to present himself in person so that all could see that he had regained his health. No doubt he also wished to express his personal thanks to them for the prayers that had been offered and for the interest shown. And we may well believe that above all he was eager to help the Philippians in their continuing difficulties and afflictions (Phil. 1:29, 30; 3:2, 17–19; 4:2). Yet, on the other hand, he fully understood the charge he had received, loved Paul dearly, and would certainly not have left him had not the thoughtful administrator ordered him to do so.

The second reason for sending Epaphroditus back to Philippi is stated as follows: **Accordingly, I am sending him (back) the more eagerly in order that when y o u see him again y o u may rejoice.** Paul is sending his friend home again in order that the membership of the Philippian church, on seeing him again fully recovered, may leap for joy. This affords a glimpse into the inner soul of the great apostle. Easing the mind of his dearly beloved Philippians and imparting to them gladness of heart meant more to him than any personal service he might be able to derive from Epaphroditus.[121]

But although Paul's appreciation of his friend and of the services which he rendered in Rome was genuine, *he himself* is able to rejoice when he reflects on the usefulness of Epaphroditus to the Philippians. Accordingly, the third reason for bidding the valiant helper to return to his own church is stated as follows: **and I may be less sorrowful.** The joy of the Philippians upon the return of Epaphroditus will make Paul's own burden lighter. The great apostle proves himself to be a true imitator of God (cf. Eph. 5:1, 2), who rejoices in the joy of his beloved ones, in fact rejoices over them *with singing* (Zeph. 3:17).

29, 30. The manner in which Epaphroditus should be received by the church of Philippi is stated in these words: **So, extend to him a most joyful welcome in the Lord,** or more literally, "So, receive him in the Lord with all joy." This faithful minister must be received with deep gratitude to the Lord. Certainly, no welcome could be too cordial. And he deserves more than a welcome. Hence, **and hold such men in honor.** Note: *such men,* Epaphroditus and others like him (cf. I Tim. 5:17). When Paul wrote this,

---

121 Sending Epaphroditus back to Philippi was a real sacrifice for Paul. The idea of some, that Epaphroditus had become a burden on the apostle's hands, and that for this reason he wanted to get rid of him, is completely contrary to the entire context.

he could not foresee that at a later date men would twist these words as if a person who in any way had become a martyr for Christ must always be given the privilege of casting the deciding vote in important ecclesiastical matters. The apostle, however, was saying no more than this, namely, that due respect must be shown to those who have proved themselves willing, if necessary, to surrender their lives for Christ. This implies, of course, that weight must be attached to their judgments and opinions, but not *undue* weight. The teaching of the Word must remain the final criterion, and the advice of the entire church must be carefully considered. Returning now to Epaphroditus personally — though as an eminent example of the entire class of loyal, valiant, and self-effacing ministers — Paul states the reason why honor should be accorded to this attendant and assistant, namely, **because for the work of Christ** (see on verse 25) **he came to the brink of death.** Epaphroditus had been in mortal danger, **risking** [122] **his life,** as a gambler will take risks for possible gain.

By saying that for the cause of Christ Epaphroditus had exposed himself to the peril of losing his life, Paul probably had reference to more than the violent illness which seized his loyal friend, bringing him to death's very door. Likely the phrase also points to the danger involved in the delegate's very presence in Rome in the capacity of the constant and intimate attendant and assistant of a prisoner who might be on his way to execution. Peter, in a somewhat analogous situation, denied his Lord! Yes, Epaphroditus risked his life, says Paul, **that he might supply what was lacking in y o u r service to me.** This must not be viewed as a reprimand, as if Paul were in any way dissatisfied with the *sacred, sacrificial service* (see on Phil. 2:17; 2:25; 4:18) which the Philippians had rendered. What he meant was probably this: "Y o u r favors shown to me are deeply appreciated. If there were anything lacking in y o u r kindness toward me, y o u have certainly made up for it by sending me Epaphroditus." [123]

The example of Epaphroditus, who was willing to risk his very life for Christ, was copied by others. Accordingly, in the early church there were societies of men and women who called themselves *the parabolani*, that is, *the riskers or gamblers.* They ministered to the sick and imprisoned, and they saw to it that, if at all possible, martyrs and sometimes even enemies

---

[122] $\pi\alpha\rho\alpha\beta o\lambda\epsilon\upsilon\sigma\dot{\alpha}\mu\epsilon\nu o\varsigma$, aorist participle of $\pi\alpha\rho\alpha\beta o\lambda\epsilon\acute{\upsilon}o\mu\alpha\iota$. The variant $\pi\alpha\rho\alpha\beta o\upsilon\lambda\epsilon\upsilon$-$\sigma\dot{\alpha}\mu\epsilon\nu o\varsigma$ must be regarded as a scribal substitute for the less familiar original. Deissmann (*Light from the Ancient East*, p. 88) cites an example of $\pi\alpha\rho\alpha\beta o\lambda\epsilon\upsilon\sigma\dot{\alpha}\mu\epsilon\nu o\varsigma$ from an inscription at Olbia on the Black Sea, probably of the second century A.D.
[123] Similarly, at a previous occasion Stephanus, Fortunatus, and Achaicus had made up for the *lack* or *deficiency* of the Corinthians. They had done what, because of distance, the Corinthians had not been able to do personally (I Cor. 16:17). That the Philippians had fallen short in their duty toward Paul Phil. 2:30 does not imply any more than Col. 1:24 ("filling up whatever is lacking in the sufferings of Christ") implies that Christ in his own person had not suffered enough.

would receive an honorable burial. Thus in the city of Carthage during the great pestilence of A. D. 252 Cyprian, the bishop, showed remarkable courage. In self-sacrificing fidelity to his flock, and love even for his enemies, he took upon himself the care of the sick, and bade his congregation nurse them and bury the dead. What a contrast with the practice of the heathen who were throwing the corpses out of the plague-stricken city and were running away in terror!

Synthesis of 2:19-30

Paul appears in this section as *thoughtful administrator*, who even from his prison in Rome, under God, in a wise, considerate, and unselfish manner directs the affairs of his extended spiritual domain. In the first subdivision of the present section he says that as soon as he knows how his affairs will turn out he will send Timothy to the Philippians, and this not only with news concerning himself (Paul) but "that I also may be heartened by knowing y o u r affairs." He warmly recommends Timothy, whose unselfish devotion to the cause of Christ contrasts sharply with the attitude of all such other persons who might be considered for this mission. The apostle adds, "But I trust in the Lord that I myself shall also come soon."

In the second paragraph Paul informs the Philippians that he is sending (back) to them the man who was probably the bearer of the letter, namely, Epaphroditus. The latter had been sent to Rome as a gift and with a gift from the church of Philippi. While busily engaged in gospel-work and as Paul's personal attendant he had become grievously ill, having been brought to death's very door, but by God's marvelous mercy he had been completely restored. In returning him to Philippi Paul had a threefold purpose:

(1) To satisfy the wish of Epaphroditus, who desires to go back to the brothers at Philippi in order to remove their alarm.

(2) To gladden the hearts of the Philippians who will rejoice when they see Epaphroditus fully restored.

(3) To rejoice in the joy of the Philippians.

The apostle, who could surely have made good use of the continued services of Epaphroditus in Rome, gladly makes this sacrifice, and, to offset possible criticism on the part of some, emphasizes that this faithful servant of Christ must be given a hearty welcome and that he and others like him should receive the honor which they so richly deserve.

Summary of Chapter 3

Paul, the Indefatigable Idealist

warning against evil workers (the *con*cision) who by placing confidence in flesh seek to establish *their own* righteousness and perfection; as contrasted with God's true servants (the *circum*cision); *for example,* with Paul, who could boast of many external prerogatives, but has rejected them all and relies completely on the righteousness of Christ, in whom he is pressing on to perfection; *exhorting* the Philippians to imitate him, to honor the friends and beware of "the enemies of the cross," sensualists, who set their minds on things of earth, while believers know that *their* home-land is in heaven.

3:1-3   Warning against Judaizers.
3:4-16   Paul's Example as an Argument against the Judaizers.
        3:4-6   I, Paul, the Jew, had the following advantages (these are enumerated).
        3:7-8a   I repudiated these advantages as basis of my righteousness before God.
        3:8b-11 I now rely on another righteousness.
        3:12-16 In Christ I press on to perfection (Paul, the runner).
3:17-21 Warning against Sensualists. The Home-land in Heaven.

CHAPTER III

3 1 For the rest, my brothers, rejoice in the Lord. To write the same things
to y o u is no trouble to me, and for y o u it is a safeguard. 2 Beware of
those dogs, beware of those evil-workers, beware of the *concis*ion. 3 For, it is we
who are the *circum*cision, we who worship by the Spirit of God, and glory in Christ
Jesus, and put no confidence in flesh.

3:1-3

I. *Warning against Judaizers*

1. Paul, the joyful servant of Jesus Christ, the optimistic prisoner, the
humble cross-bearer, the thoughtful administrator, is also the indefatigable
idealist, and in that sense, perfectionist. He seeks perfection *in Christ,* in
whom his soul rejoices. His creed is, "Nothing in myself I bring, only to
thy cross I cling." Redemption in Christ is all-sufficient. When the apostle
hears that the church of Philippi is being harassed by false teachers who
deny this all-sufficiency and trust in ceremonial rites to supplement divine
grace, he is deeply disturbed, and writes: **For the rest,**[124] **my brothers,** —
members of the same spiritual family (see on 1:12 and on 2:25 — **rejoice.**
This is by no means the first time Paul has touched on the exalted theme
of joy (see also 1:4; 2:17, 18; 2:28, 29), but this time he specifically adds
in the Lord, that is, only in union with him, and then solely in the person
and work of the Lord Jesus Christ, not in anything that man might wish
to contribute. This naturally leads the apostle to refer once more to a theme
on which he has dwelt repeatedly; namely, that believers should acknowledge
their oneness in Christ, and should not permit this unity to be undermined
by enemies. It is entirely natural that before returning to this subject he

---

124 The words "for the rest" or "finally" are very appropriate when a letter is gradually drawing to a close (Phil. 4:8; also II Cor. 13:11; I Thess. 4:1; II Thess. 3:1). It
is not true, however, that this expression proves that Paul was about to end the
letter at this very point, for (τὸ) λοιπόν may also simply introduce a new paragraph
in which the apostle proceeds to a subject different from the one he has just now
been discussing, a subject which he regards as very important and which he now
wishes to stress. Besides, if "for the rest" when there are still forty-four more
verses in Philippians disproves the unity of Philippians, would not the same expression followed by forty-six more verses (I Thess. 4:1) disprove the unity of
I Thessalonians?

states: **To write the same things to y o u is no trouble to me, and for y o u it is a safeguard.**

It is *the duty of militant unity in a world of unbelief and hostility* that Paul has set before the church of Philippi previously; first, no doubt, orally, while he was present among them, later in writing. In this selfsame letter to the Philippians he had already written:

"Only continue to exercise y o u r citizenship in a manner worthy of the gospel of Christ, that whether I come and see y o u or am absent, I may hear of y o u that y o u are standing firm in one spirit, with one soul striving side by side for the faith of the gospel and not frightened in anything by the adversaries . . . make full my joy by being of the same mind, having the same love, with souls united setting y o u r minds on unity, doing nothing from selfish ambition or from empty conceit, but in humble-mindedness each counting the other better than himself; each looking not only to his own interests but also to the interests of others. . . . that y o u may become blameless and guileless, children of God without blemish in the midst of a crooked and perverse generation, among whom y o u are shining as stars in the universe, holding forth the word of life . . ." (1:27, 28; 2:2-4; 2:14-16).

Thus he had clearly warned against "the adversaries" and had just as clearly summoned the members of the church *unitedly* to be on their guard against these enemies and to combat them with the only effective weapon, namely, "the word of life." But in view of the fact that these opponents are very shrewd, numerous, and determined, and that he, Paul, is filled with love for the Philippians, he writes that to *him* it is "no trouble," no irksome task, to repeat previous warnings, and that for *them* this is a precaution for their spiritual safety.[125]

---

[125] Other explanations of "to write the same things to y o u" are:

(1) F. W. Beare and others see here an abrupt break in the course of the letter, a complete lack of connection between this chapter and the remainder of the letter. Answer: the unity of the letter has already been defended. See Introduction, VI.

(2) John Calvin represents those who think that the apostle means, "To repeat the same things to you which, while present, I told you." Answer: in view of such passages as Phil. 3:18; II Thess. 2:5, a reference to previous *oral* teaching may indeed be included in the meaning. *Written* admonitions, and these in this very letter, urging believers to take a courageous, united stand against the adversaries, are clear, as has been shown.

(3) H. Alford, etc., regard the expression as referring to the immediately preceding exhortation to rejoice in the Lord. Answer: the words, "for y o u it is safe" (or "a safeguard") are an indication of *danger*, which hardly suits the exhortation to rejoice.

(4) J. B. Lightfoot implies that the expression "to write the same things" is an allusion to admonitions against dissension. He points out that several of these warnings are found in this very letter. Answer: see under the next point (5).

(5) R. C. H. Lenski regards 3:1b to refer to the warning found in Phil. 1:27-30 to stand firm against opponents. Answer: On the whole I agree with Lightfoot and Lenski, and have combined the two views. Paul, as I see it, refers to his previous

And so the "adversaries" of 1:27, 28 appear once more here in Chapter 3, but now explicitly; first *the Judaists* (3:2); then *the sensualists* (3:18, 19).

2. With respect to the Judaists or Judaizers Paul writes, **Beware of those dogs, beware of those evil-workers, beware of the concision.** Note the threefold re-iteration, Beware . . . beware . . . beware! This can be very effective; for example,

"Holy, holy, holy is Jehovah of hosts" (Isa. 6:3);

"The temple of Jehovah, the temple of Jehovah, the temple of Jehovah, is this" (Jer. 7:4);

"Alleluiah! Alleluiah! Alleluiah! Amen" (in the refrain of *Hark! Ten Thousand Harps and Voices*);

"Goodnight! Goodnight! Goodnight!" (*in The Christian's Goodnight*);

all the more effective when, as in "Beware . . . beware . . . beware!" they occur in the form of terse commands or exhortations; compare:

"O land, land, land, hear the word of Jehovah" (Jer. 22:29); or

"Break, break, break" (Tennyson, giving expression, in a beautiful little poem, to the burdensome sense of loss on the death of a beloved one).

Here in Philippians also, the three words are, as it were, blows of the gavel, signaling for attention, in order that the church of Philippi by giving heed may be safeguarded against spiritual and moral loss.

It is clear that the apostle had become profoundly disturbed by continued news from Philippi. It was a wonderful congregation, to be sure (4:1), but danger was threatening. It is entirely possible that just now fresh tidings of a renewed onslaught against the very essence of the gospel of salvation through Christ alone had reached him. At any rate, Paul uses vigorous language to guard against the evil. He speaks of dogs, evil-workers, the concision.

It has been said that his language undergoes a sudden change here; that unexpectedly it turns from tenderly loving address to sharp rebuke and denunciation; and that for this reason the present section must belong to another letter. With this judgment I cannot agree. To be sure, there is here something bordering on fiery vehemence. But an incisive caution against a dangerous foe is not necessarily a sign of lovelessness. On the contrary, the warmer a father's affection for his son, the deeper will be his distress when that son's life is being persistently threatened by shrewd

exhortations that believers take a *united* stand against *the adversaries*. I believe, however, that Lenski has somewhat weakened his case by writing that here in Chapter 3 the apostle has in mind another set of opponents than before. As he sees it, 1:28 refers exclusively to *pagan* opponents; 3:1b, 2, to the *Judaizers*. But in that case would Paul have said, To write *the same things* to y o u?

enemies, and the more earnest will be his warnings. So it is also in the present instance. What Paul writes here in verse 2 is in complete harmony with the tender appellation in verse 1, where he addresses the members of the Philippian church as "my brothers."

Now when Paul describes the opponents as those dogs, those evil-workers, the concision, he has in mind *one* kind of enemy, not three different types. This is clear from the context, which in the present paragraph concerns itself with *one* foe only: the concision over against the circumcision (see 3a). Besides, also in 3b a threefold description is given of *one* type of people, namely, God's true worshipers.

But when Paul speaks about the enemy, whom precisely does he have in mind? That he is thinking of Jews is clear from the use of the term "the concision" and from the entire argument in verses 2-6. But is he thinking of those Jews who persisted in their sullen rejection of the Christ? Or of those Jews who had indeed confessed Jesus but insisted that in order to attain salvation — at least *complete* salvation — it was necessary for all, Gentile as well as Jew, to keep the law of Moses, with special emphasis on circumcision? To save space, I shall from this point on call the first group *Jews,* the second, *Judaizers.* As I see it, it was the latter group he had in mind. The words here used form a striking parallel to Paul's denunciation of Judaizing teachers in Galatians (1:6-9; 3:1; 5:1-12, note especially verse 12 there; 6:12-15) and II Corinthians (11:13, cf. "deceitful workers" there with "evil workers" here). To be sure, the *Jews* had followed Paul on his missionary journeys, in order to contradict his message (Acts 13:50; 14:2, 19; 17:5, 13; 18:12; etc.), but so to some extent had the *Judaizers* (Acts 15:1). The theory that this latter opposition ceased completely after the council of Jerusalem (Acts 15:6-29) cannot be substantiated. Rather the opposite. Else why would it have been necessary for Paul to write Galatians? And is it not true that even the Pastoral Epistles (later than Philippians) combat a heresy consisting of the error of the Judaizers mixed with ingredients of other sinister falsehoods? (See N.T.C. on the Pastoral Epistles.)

When Paul reflects on the fact that the Judaizers are attacking the doctrine of salvation by grace alone and are striving to substitute for it a mixture of divine favor and human merit, with emphasis on the latter, he flings at them the derisive epithet which the Jews were always applying to the Gentiles. *Dogs* he calls them. He is thinking not of pets but of pariahs, large, savage, and ugly. One could see them almost everywhere, prowling about the garbage and the rubbish thrown into the streets. In comparing the Judaizers with these loathsome scavengers Paul has in mind *all,* or more likely *some,* of the following items; certainly item (1).

Are these dogs (1) unclean and filthy (Prov. 26:11; cf. II Peter 2:22; Matt. 7:6; Rev. 22:15)? So are also the Judaizers as to their motives. Do these (2) howl and snarl (Ps. 59:6)? So do also those, uttering loud and angry words against the true doctrine. Are these (3) greedy and shameless (Isa. 56:11)? So are also those, for they would devour the church. Are the former (4) contemptible (II Sam. 9:8; 16:9; II Kings 8:13)? So are also the latter. Other characteristics common to both dogs and Judaizers might be added; such as, (5) insolent, (6) cunning, and (7) roaming. The metaphor was apt.

Workers Paul also calls these men. Yes, church-workers are they. Right inside the church they themselves, as church-members, recognized as such somewhere, are carrying on their work. Missionaries are they, propagandizers! Was there not — and is there not always — a crying need for workers? Cf. Matt. 9:37, 38. But note the modifier: *evil* workers. These men are *wicked* laborers, *malicious* toilers. Cf. "deceitful workers" (II Cor. 11:13) and "workers of iniquity" (Luke 13:27). By no means are they "workers of righteousness." Instead of *helping* the good cause, they actually *harm* it. They draw the attention away from Christ and his accomplished redemption, and fix it upon an outworn ritual, and upon human worth and attainment in insisting upon its perpetuation and application. Here is Satan's demolition crew. It is working very hard to demolish God's beautiful palace of grace and peace.

The scorching parody continues as Paul adds: The *con*cision, that is, the mutilation-party, a name here scornfully given to those who insisted on the cutting away of the foreskin of *the body* only, not also of *the heart*. The apostle contrasts *con*cision with *circum*cision.[126]

What he means when he thus castigates the Judaizers with their emphasis on the outward rite of circumcision, as if the mere rite apart from the inner consecration of the heart were of any value, is set forth by himself in these words: "For he is not a Jew who is one outwardly; neither is that circumcision which is outward in flesh; but he is a Jew who is one inwardly; whose circumcision is that of the heart, in spirit, not in (the) letter; whose praise is not of men but of God" (Rom. 2:28, 29). For circumcision of *heart* cf. Lev. 26:41; Deut. 10:16; 30:6; Jer. 4:4; Ezek. 44:7; of *ear,* Jer. 6:10; and of *lips,* Exod: 6:12, 30. This is *Christian* circumcision (Col. 2:11, 12). On the other hand, the circumcision *merely* of the body, especially when this is performed and insisted upon by those who profess to believe in Jesus as Savior, is worse than useless. It is actually *mutilation,* cutting away, spiritual destruction, for if anyone receives this kind of circumcision, Christ

---

[126] He is fond of this kind of pun; cf., for example, "not busy workers but busybodies" (see N.T.C. on II Thessalonians 3:11). This style-characteristic is found in many languages. Often the real punch of such paronomasia (the use of words similar in sound but different in meaning) is lost in translation. But from the Latin compare the charge of pope against antipope, that the latter was "not consecrated but execrated (accursed)," and from the German note Luther's letter addressed to the pope, calling him, "Your hellishness" instead of "Your holiness."

will profit him not at all (Gal. 5:2; cf. 1:6-8). He will be farther removed from Christ than he ever was before!

3. Beware of such leaders, says Paul, **for it is** not they but **we who are the circumcision.** We Christians out of Jews and Gentiles (Rom. 9:24) are the truly circumcized ones. The Jew is no better than the Gentile (Rom. 3:9). "There is no distinction; for all have sinned and fall short of the glory of God; being justified freely by his grace through the redemption that is in Christ Jesus" (Rom. 3:24). This Jew-Gentile church, the church in which neither circumcision nor uncircumcision amounts to anything, is the Israel of God (Gal. 6:16). All those who belong to this church have Abraham as their father (Gal. 3:9, 29). The middle wall of partition, separating Jew and Gentile, has been completely broken down, never to be rebuilt. Through Christ both have their access in one Spirit unto the Father (Eph. 2:14, 18).

Language could not be clearer. The notion that God even today recognizes two favored groups — on the one hand the church and on the other the Jews — is thoroughly unscriptural. What Paul teaches here is, moreover, entirely in harmony with what is taught elsewhere. Jesus said, "I also have other sheep that do not belong to this fold. Them also I must lead, and they will listen to my voice, and become one flock, one shepherd" (John 10:16). And Peter applies to the church of the New Testament period the very terms which in the old dispensation pertain to the people of Israel. He writes, "But y o u are an elect race, a royal priesthood, a holy nation, a people for (God's) own possession" (I Peter 2:9).

A threefold description is now given of the truly circumcized. Yet, although in this description there are three grammatically parallel elements, items two and three describe essentially the same mark, first positively, then negatively. Hence, there are just two distinctive marks. The first one is: **we who worship by the Spirit of God.**[127] Their *religious worship*[128] is Spirit-guided. It proceeds from personalities renewed and energized by the Holy Spirit. Hence, it is wholly from the heart, and is not hampered by physical considerations. It does not ask, "Is the flesh of the worshipers circumcized or not circumcized?" "Is the place of worship a beautiful cathedral or a simple home?" "Must we worship on Mt. Gerizim or in Jerusalem?" (John 4:19-24).

The second distinctive mark is expressed positively as follows: **and glory in Christ Jesus.** Paul is fond of this word *glorying, boasting,* or *exulting.* He uses it about 35 times (see also on Phil. 1:26), mostly in I and II Corinthians. In all the rest of the New Testament it occurs only twice (James 1:19; 4:16).

---

[127] The textual evidence for this reading is stronger than that on which are based the renderings "which worship God in the spirit" (A.V.) and "who worship God in spirit" (R.S.V.).
[128] See R. C. Trench, *Synonyms of the New Testament* xxxv.

The apostle loves the beautiful Jeremiah passage (Jer. 9:23, 24), and in abbreviated form quotes it both in I Cor. 1:31 and in II Cor. 10:17. Those whose hearts — hence also lips and ears — have been circumcized make their boast in the Lord, in him alone. Such boasters rely entirely on Christ Jesus, the Anointed Savior; on his *person* and *work*. They glory in his *cross*, that is, in his atonement, as the only basis for their salvation. His presence is their consolation. His power provides them with energy to endure persecution and to raise and carry forward into battle the banner of the cross. On his unfailing, sovereign grace they rest for time and for eternity. Let the apostle be his own interpreter: "For I determined not to know anything among y o u but Jesus Christ, and him crucified" (I Cor. 2:2). "But far be it for me to glory, except in the cross of our Lord Jesus Christ, through which the world was crucified to me, and I to the world" (Gal. 6:14).

> "My hope is built on nothing less
> Than Jesus' blood and righteousness;
> I dare not trust the sweetest frame,
> But wholly lean on Jesus' name.
> On Christ, the solid Rock, I stand;
> All other ground is sinking sand."
>
> (Edward Mote)

Negatively, this is expressed as follows: **and put no confidence in flesh.** It stands to reason that if a person is constantly making his boast in Christ Jesus, he will put no confidence in flesh, for what is flesh? In broad terms, *flesh is anything apart from Christ on which one bases his hope for salvation.* In the present context it refers to merely human advantages and attainments, ceremonial, hereditary, legal, and moral in character (note Paul's own explanation in verses 4-6). It is the merely carnal self, viewed as a ground of eternal security.[129] It was on this self that the Judaizers relied. They boasted in mere *flesh*. In fact the term fitted them not only in the broader sense, as explained, but even in a more restricted sense, for they insisted on the circumcision of the literal, physical flesh.

Now the *truly* circumcized place confidence not in flesh but in Christ alone.

Paul had been saying, "For it is we who are the circumcision, we who worship by the Spirit of God, and glory in Christ Jesus, and put no confidence in flesh." Turning now from *we* to *I* he continues:

---

4 though I myself have reason for confidence even in flesh. If anyone else imagines that he has reason for confidence in flesh, I (have) more: 5 circumcized on the eighth day, of the people of Israel, of the tribe of Benjamin, a Hebrew

---

129 For the various meanings of the term *flesh* as used by Paul see on Phil. 1:22, footnote 55. Here in Phil. 3:3 meaning g. applies.

of Hebrews, as to law a Pharisee, 6 as to zeal persecuting the church, as to legal righteousness having become blameless. 7 Nevertheless, such things as once were gains to me these have I counted loss for Christ. 8 Yes, what is more, I certainly do count all things to be sheer loss because of the all-surpassing excellence of knowing Christ Jesus my Lord, for whom I suffered the loss of all these things, and I am still counting them refuse, in order that I may gain Christ, 9 and be found in him, not having a righteousness of my own, legal righteousness, but that (which is) through faith in Christ, the righteousness (which is) from God (and rests) on faith; 10 that I may know him, and the power of his resurrection, and (the) fellowship of his sufferings, becoming increasingly conformed to his death, 11 if only I may attain to the resurrection from the dead.

12 Not that I have already gotten hold or have already been made perfect, but I am pressing on (to see) if I can also take hold of that for which I was laid hold on by Christ Jesus. 13 Brothers, I do not count myself yet to have laid hold, but one thing (I do), forgetting what lies behind (me) and eagerly straining forward to what lies ahead, 14 I am pressing on toward the goal for the prize of the upward call of God in Christ Jesus. 15 Accordingly, let us, as many as are mature, continue to set our mind on this, and if on some minor point y o u are differently minded, that, too God will make plain to y o u. 16 Only, let our conduct be consistent with the level we have attained.

3:4-16

II *Paul's Example as an Argument against the Judaizers*
  A. *I, Paul, the Jew, Had the Following "Advantages"*
    (1) *I, not They* (at least not in the same degree)
    (2) *What My Parents Gave Me*
      a. Circumcision
        "circumcized on the eighth day"
      b, c, d. Noble Birth
        "of the people of Israel"
        "of the tribe of Benjamin"
        "a Hebrew of Hebrews"
    (3) *What I, Through My Own Efforts Attained*
      e. Recognition as a Pharisee
        "as to law a Pharisee"
      f. Zeal
        "as to zeal persecuting the church"
      g. Legal Rectitude
        "as to legal righteousness having become blameless"

3:4-6

  A. *I, Paul, the Jew, Had the Following "Advantages"*
(1) *I, not They (at least not in the same degree)*

4. By means of a telling argument, taken from his own experience, the apostle now presents himself as being, by God's grace, an example (Phil. 3:17) of God's true servants, as contrasted with those who were putting confidence in flesh. He writes, **though I myself have reason for confidence** [130] **even in flesh.** He emphasizes "I myself" (even more than the Judaizers). He cannot very well say, *"We* ourselves," for though the trusting in Christ alone is true of *all* God's genuine servants, yet the particular experience which the apostle is about to relate (in verses 4-7) pertained to himself alone, not literally to all Christians or to all the members of the church at Philippi, in Rome, or anywhere else. When he now writes that he himself *has reason for confidence even in flesh,* he does not mean that, after all, he does regard ceremonial and hereditary advantages and personal attainments to have *saving* value. On the contrary, he means that *if* this were actually the case, then he himself, even more than the Judaizers, would be entitled to such a ground of trust. This is in line with his own explanation, namely, **If anyone else** — he has the Judaizer in mind, of course — **imagines that he has reason for confidence in flesh, I (have) more.** The question might be asked, "But if Paul does not attach any merit for eternity to these Jewish distinctions, why then does he give us this list of special privileges which he, as a Jew, had enjoyed?" Two reasons immediately present themselves. He does this:

a. To answer the possible charge, "Paul is decrying privileges to which he himself cannot lay claim. He minimizes them because he never had them and cannot get them. The grapes are sour." This possible charge is answered in verses 5 and 6.

b. To refute the argument of the Judaizers that there is saving value in these distinctions. The apostle is going to show, from his own experience, that what he had considered gain turned out to be loss. This he does in verses 7-11.

As to a., the apostle shows that if the Judaizers present their list of special advantages, and Paul places his own list next to theirs, he, adopting for the sake of argument their "foolish" line of reasoning, emerges as a winner in this competition. On that basis the apostle has a right to speak, being in every sense an authentic Jew.

It is in that sense that the apostle now presents his credentials. In particulars the list here is on the whole substantially different from that in II Cor. 11:22-33. Yet *the argument* is the same, namely, "If there must be

---

[130] πεποίθησις , acc. *-ν*, not used here in the sense of subjective confidence (as in II Cor. 1:15; Eph. 3:12) but as the context clearly shows, *ground of confidence.* Similarly, in the next line, πεποιθέναι, second perfect active infinitive from πείθω, means (imagines) *to have reason for confidence.* Compare the use of ἐλπίς and χαρά in I Thess. 2:19. The use of words like confidence, hope, joy, for the ground of the feeling is found in many languages.

boasting, I, too, can indulge in it" (II Cor. 11:21). And so we come to Paul's list here in Phil. 3:5, 6, with its seven items.

(2) *What My Parents Gave Me*

5, 6. circumcized on the eighth day. The reason why the apostle mentions circumcision before giving any details with respect to his ancestry is probably that it was this very rite for which the Judaizers contended most of all. "With respect to circumcision I am an eighth-day-er," [131] writes Paul. This was in strict accordance with the law (Gen. 17:12; Lev. 12:3). Isaac was circumcized when he was eight days old (Gen. 21:4); [132] so was Jesus (Luke 2:21). But the same thing could probably not be said for every Judaizer. In all likelihood *some* of these were proselytes from the Gentile world, and as a result had been circumcized not on the eighth day but as adults. In this respect, therefore, Paul excelled them, that is, *if* circumcision according to law was an advantage.

of the people of Israel. His parents did not belong to a mixed stock, like so many people who were living in Palestine at that time, nor had they been grafted into Israel. He was a direct descendant not only of Abraham (the Ishmaelites were also Abraham's offspring), nor only of Abraham and Isaac (the Edomites could claim as much), but of Abraham, Isaac, *and Jacob.* It was to Jacob, after his wrestling with God, that God himself had given the new and significant name *Israel* (Gen. 32:28). Of this very *Israel* Paul was a descendant. He belonged therefore to the chosen people, the people of the covenant, the specially privileged people (Exod. 19:5, 6; Num. 23:9; Ps. 147:19, 20; Amos 3:2; Rom. 3:1, 2; 9:4, 5). Were the Judaizers able truthfully to claim such purity of descent for every one of their party?

of the tribe of Benjamin. Why does Paul mention this? According to several commentators, for reasons such as the following: the Benjamites were Israel's élite, its highest aristocracy. Did not the tribe always have the place of honor in Israel's line of battle? (Judg. 5:14; Hos. 5:8) This tribe, moreover, produced "seven hundred picked men lefthanded; every one could sling stones at a hairbreadth, and not miss" (Judg. 20:16); also "mighty men of valor, archers" (I Chron. 8:40). These interpreters add that Israel's first king was a Benjamite (I Sam. 9:1, 2). According to J. B. Lightfoot, in Acts 13:21 it is "with marked emphasis" that Paul himself refers to King Saul.

---

[131] Cf. for the Greek idiom "for he is a fourth-day-er" (or "fourth-day man"), that is, "for he (Lazarus) has been dead four days" (John 11:39). In such cases the ordinal is used with persons.
[132] Ishmael and the Ishmaelites at the age of thirteen (cf. Gen. 17:25).

Had not the apostle received his Hebrew name from this very king? [133] It is also said that the tribe of Benjamin was unique among all the tribes of Israel in always remaining loyal to the Davidic dynasty. A very noble, a most illustrious tribe, this tribe of Benjamin!

I fear, however, that this oft displayed picture is somewhat off balance, that this representation suffers from lack of careful exegesis. Is it correct to say that Judg. 5:14 and Hos. 5:8, in their respective contexts, prove that this tribe always held the place of honor in Israel's line of battle? It is doubtful, to say the least, whether Paul, in referring with pride to his descent from Benjamin, was thinking of Ehud and the other "southpaws" (Judg. 3:15; 20:16); or of the archers, for that matter. As to Israel's first king, he was hardly a person of whom a deeply religious Jew could be particularly proud (see I Sam. 15:10, 11, 23; 28:15-19).[134] I believe that Lightfoot is wrong in his interpretation of Acts 13:21, and that Lenski is right when he states that no motive of pride actuated Paul in making mention of King Saul. And finally, as to this tribe's unswerving loyalty to David, fact is that after Saul's death Benjamin yielded rather reluctantly to David (read II Sam. 2 and 3). And at the disruption of the kingdom it was indeed the *one* tribe of *Judah* but by no means the entire tribe of Benjamin that followed the house of David (see I Kings 11:32; 12:20).

Not only is the lavish praise bestowed on Benjamin somewhat out of line with history and exegesis, but other well-established and recorded facts with reference to this tribe are being conveniently ignored. Left unmentioned, for example, is the fact that it was precisely in this very tribe of Benjamin that a great atrocity had been committed, described in some detail (Judg. 19:22-26). When the other tribes demanded punishment for the wrongdoers, this was refused, with, as result, dire retribution for the guilty tribe (Judg. 20:35). Then there was the rape at Shiloh! (Judg. 21:20, 21). Surely, there must be a more honorable solution to the wife-shortage problem than the horrible expedient adopted by the tribe of Benjamin, upon the advice — let this be added in the interest of complete objectivity — of the other tribes. Finally, there was Shimei, who cursed and threw stones at God's anointed, David. This profane fellow, too, was a Benjamite (II Sam. 16:5-14). He repented, at least outwardly (II Sam. 19:16-20). Subsequently, however, he failed to keep his oath to Jehovah, and was slain (I Kings 2:36-46).

Since then it is a fact that the tribe of Benjamin presents such a mixture of light and shadow, virtue and vice, with the latter frequently predominating, why did Paul, in his pre-Christian state to which he here refers (and in a

---

[133] For a discussion of the apostle's names see N.T.C. on I and II Thessalonians, pp. 38, 39.
[134] David, in II Sam. 1:23, is being very magnanimous.

sense even later, Rom. 11:1), take such pride in being a Benjamite? The probable answer is as follows: *Israel,* as a theocratic people, was the recipient of God's special promises. Hence, the more convincingly Paul would be able to prove the proposition, "I am, indeed, an Israelite," the more inescapable would be the conclusion, "Therefore I am a specially privileged person." Now of all the tribes none was more Israelitish than Benjamin.

Whether or not the circumstance that Benjamin was the only son of Israel who was born in the land of promise (Gen. 35:16-20) has any particular bearing here would be hard to establish. But the following facts surely are significant. First, in common with Joseph but in distinction from the other patriarchs, Benjamin was not only a son of Israel but also of Israel's most beloved wife, Rachel (Gen. 35:17, 18). And secondly, of these two favored sons (Joseph and Benjamin) it was Benjamin alone (be it only *part* of his tribe) who, together with Judah, after the disruption formed *Israel Reconstituted* (I Kings 12:21); after the return from the captivity, *Israel Restored* (Ezra 4:1); [135] and who in connection with the plot of Haman, was God's chief agent in bringing forth *Israel Delivered* (see Book of Esther). Moreover, in thinking of the tribe of Benjamin it would be unfair to mention Shimei and then to leave out that other Benjamite, Mordecai. It was he who encouraged Esther to perform a great deed of faith and courage, and who gave us that marvelous saying, "For if you keep altogether silent at such a time as this, then relief and deliverance will rise for the Jews from another quarter, but you and your father's house will perish. And who knows whether you have not come to the kingdom for such a time as this?" (Esther 4:14).

The conclusion then is this: *if* indeed there were saving value, merit for eternity, in the special distinction of being an Israelite, then Paul was entitled to it, for, *being a Benjamite,* he surely was a most authentic Israelite. Could the Judaizers make an equally strong case for themselves? Yes, Paul was "of the tribe of Benjamin," and therefore:

a Hebrew of Hebrews. Paul was, indeed, a Hebrew, that is, an Israelite.[136] He was in fact "a Hebrew of Hebrews," that is, "purest of the pure." The

---

[135] Not all of those who returned belonged to Judah and Benjamin, but these two tribes formed the nucleus. See my *Bible Survey,* pp. 119, 120.

[136] Paul himself uses the terms *Hebrews, Israelites,* and *seed of Abraham* synonymously (II Cor. 11:22). The Old Testament uses the term *Hebrew* in a broader and in a more restricted sense. Long before Israel (Jacob) was born, there were Hebrews; e.g., Abraham (Gen. 14:13; cf. 40:15; 43:32). According to some, Abraham was a Hebrew because he was a descendant of Eber (Gen. 10:21, 24, 25). Others are of the opinion that the noun *Hebrew* is related to a verb meaning *to cross over.* On that theory the Hebrews are the people from across the Euphrates (cf. Josh. 24:2). In a more restricted sense the Hebrews are the descendants of Israel (Exod. 1:15; 2:6, 11, 13; 3:18; 21:2; Deut. 15:12; I Sam. 4:6, 9).

idiom stresses *at least* [137] the purity of his lineage: Hebrew son of Hebrew parents; hence, *definitely* a Hebrew, a Hebrew if there ever was one! In this way he emphasizes what was already implied in the preceding. He is proving this *one* point.

(3) *What I, Through My Own Efforts, Attained*

as to law a Pharisee. With reference to the law of Moses Paul had chosen to become a Pharisee. Was he not a son of Pharisees (Acts 23:6)? [138] And here he reflects how in his pre-Christian period he prided himself in this fact, namely, in his position and honor as a Pharisee. He had advanced in the religion of the Jews beyond many of his own age among his countrymen and had been exceedingly zealous for the traditions of his ancestors (Gal. 1:14). "After the strictest sect of our religion I lived, a Pharisee," he himself declared (Acts 26:5).

But how could a Jew ever take pride in being a Pharisee? Did not Jesus describe the Pharisees in language which plainly states or else implies that they were snobs and peacocks (Matt. 6:2, 16; 23:5-7), hair-splitters and fools (Matt. 23:16-22), serpents and the offspring of vipers (Matt. 23:33), cheats and hypocrites (Matt. 23:3, 13, 15, 23, 25, 27, 29)? Did they not make one think of green-eyed monsters (cf. Matt. 27:18)?

All this is true, but not all Pharisees were equally bad. Pharisaism, moreover, in its origin was not nearly as bad as it became later on. This religious party originated during the inter-testamentary period as a reaction to the excesses of those careless and indifferent Jews who had imbibed the Hellenistic spirit in its unsavory aspects. So the Pharisees or Separatists had withdrawn themselves from these worldly persons. They abstained also from politics and placed great stress on religious purity. They accepted the entire Torah, the doctrines of the immortality of the soul, the resurrection of the body, and the existence of angels. They were neither chauvinists like the Zealots, nor radicals like the Sadducees, nor politicians like the Herodians. Their high regard for the law of God deserves admiration. It explains Paul's pre-Christian pride expressed in the words "as to law a

---

[137] Many are of the opinion that the phrase "a Hebrew of Hebrews" *also* calls attention to the fact that the apostle was a Jew not only by race but also by language and customs. They think that the distinction (see Acts. 6:1) between Hellenists (Greek-speaking Jews) and Hebrews (Aramaic-speaking Jews) applies here. Paul, then, is not a Hellenist but a Hebrew as were his parents. He spoke Aramaic fluently (Acts 21:40; 22:2), was trained by a Hebrew teacher in Jerusalem (Acts 22:3), often quotes from the Hebrew Old Testament, etc. The possibility that the apostle had this additional idea in mind when he called himself "a Hebrew of the Hebrews" must be granted. Yet, with the early Greek commentators I believe that the explanation I have given is probably all that is required in the present context. See also H. A. A. Kennedy, *The Epistle to the Philippians,* in The Expositor's Greek Testament, vol. III, p. 451.
[138] Or, according to another reading, *of a Pharisee.*

Pharisee." They made their great mistake when they began to attach high value to the entire system of legalistic interpretations which the scribes superimposed upon the law, burying the law itself under the load of their traditions (cf. Mark 7:13), and when they began to think that by means of their own strict adherence to the law, so interpreted, they could bring about the coming of the Messiah and secure for themselves entrance into the kingdom of heaven. Of course, the attempt to achieve all this was far too great a strain on human nature. Hence, it is no wonder that many of them became hypocrites, some worse than others; also self-righteous, looking down with disdain upon the mere riffraff, "this rabble that does not know the law" (see N.T.C. on John 7:49). Now Paul must have been one of the better Pharisees (cf. Acts 26:9), but deluded nevertheless.

as to zeal persecuting the church. Paul had been one of the most bitter haters of the early Christians. In his zeal for the law, as misinterpreted by the scribes and Pharisees (Matt. 23:23), he had breathed threatening and slaughter against the disciples of the Lord, that is, the "Church" in its ecumenical sense, carrying out his program of molestation "even to foreign cities," "putting in chains and committing to prisons both men and women" (Acts 9:1, 2; 22:1-5; 26:9-15; I Cor. 15:9). If persecuting zeal could ever have opened the gates of heaven, Paul would have walked right in! Here, too, his "advantage" over the Judaizers was great. *They* merely proselyted. *He* had been a persecutor even "unto the death."

as to legal righteousness having become blameless. So strict had Paul been in his outward observance of the Old Testament law, as interpreted by the Jewish religious leaders, that in the pursuit of this legal rectitude he had become *blameless* (cf. Phil. 2:15), that is, in *human* judgment. His outward conduct had been irreproachable. Could the Judaists claim the same with respect to themselves? Or was Matt. 23:3, 4 also applicable, to some extent, to *them*?

3:7, 8a

B. *I Repudiated These Advantages As Basis of My Righteousness before God*

7, 8a. In the two preceding verses Paul has enumerated his superior advantages as a genuine Israelite, of noble birth, orthodox in his belief, and scrupulous in his conduct. By means of these advantages the apostle, in his pre-conversion period, had been "bleeding to climb to God." But had it not been a case of

"Gaining a foothold bit by bit
Then slipping back and losing it"?

160

Worse even, for never at all had there been any *real* progress, no matter how hard he, Paul the Pharisee, had labored to establish his own righteousness. But on the way to Damascus to persecute Christians the great event occurred which changed his entire life. Christ, as it were, came down the stairs to him (read the gripping account in Acts 9:1-31; 22:1-21; 26:1-23). In a moment Paul saw himself as he really was, a deluded, self-righteous, damnable sinner. Then and there he embraced the One whom until now he had been persecuting with might and main. He became "a new creature." In his mind and heart he experienced a complete turn-about, a sudden and dramatic reversal of all values. The cause which with every means at his disposal and with all the zeal of heart and will he had been trying to wipe out now became very dear to him. And also, those things which to *Paul, the Pharisee,* had seemed very precious *became* at this moment — and ever after *remained* — useless to *Paul, the sinner, saved by grace;* and not merely *useless* but definitely *harmful.* Writes Paul, **Nevertheless, such things as once were gains to me these have I counted loss.** Not that any of these things which he enumerated in verses 5 and 6, and other things like them, were bad in themselves. Quite the contrary. To receive the sign of the covenant is not bad in itself. It is, in fact, a blessing. And was it not a blessing to belong to that people to which the oracles of God had been entrusted? Orthodoxy, too, is in itself a good thing. So is zeal, and so certainly also is irreproachable conduct. Paul himself elsewhere informs us that he considers such things as these to be blessings (Rom. 3:1, 2; 9:1-5; cf. 11:1). They are blessings because they can be of inestimable value if properly used, namely, as a preparation for the reception of the gospel. But when these same privileges begin to be viewed as a basis for self-satisfaction and self-glorification, when they are regarded as a ticket to heaven, they are changed into their opposites. All these separate *gains* become *one huge loss.* This is Paul's deliberate, considered judgment. He considered the gains, and counted [139] them loss. And in that judgment he persisted, as is implied in the tense of the Greek verb. On his balance-sheet those things which once were included, one by one, in the column of *assets* have now been transferred to the column of *liabilities,* and have been entered as *one gigantic liability.* Note that the plusses have not become a zero (0), but have become even less than zero, that is, one colossal MINUS (−). "For what will it profit a man if he gains the whole world and forfeits his life?" (Matt. 16:26; cf. Mark 8:36).

---

[139] Compare "I have counted" (perfect tense) here with "he did not count" (aorist) in 2:6. The verb indicates arriving at a sure judgment based on careful weighing of facts. Cf. Phil. 2:3. The similarity between 3:7 and 2:6 is striking. Christ *"did not count* his existence-in-a-manner-equal-to-God something to cling to, but *emptied* himself." This *counting* and this *emptying* is reflected in Paul, who, by *having counted* things that were gain to him to be loss for Christ, *emptied* himself of "all things" (Phil. 3:8) that he might gain Christ.

The word *loss* which Paul uses here in verses 7 and 8, and nowhere else in his epistles, occurs in only one other New Testament chapter, Acts 27 (verses 10 and 21), in the story of The Voyage Dangerous. And it is exactly that same chapter which also indicates how *gain* may become *loss*. The cargo on that ship bound for Italy represented potential *gain* for the merchants, for the owner of the ship, and for hungry people. Yet, had not this wheat been thrown into the sea (Acts 27:38), *loss,* not only of the ship but even of all those on board, might well have been the result. Thus also, the advantage of being born in a Christian home and having received a wonderful Christian home-training, becomes a disadvantage when it is viewed as a basis upon which to build one's hope for eternity. The same holds with respect to money, the charming look, a college education, physical strength, etc. All such helps may become hindrances. The stepping-stones will be turned into stumbling blocks, if wrongly used.

When the question is asked, "Why was it that, in Paul's considered judgment, these gains had become a loss?" the answer is **for Christ,** that is, for the sake of Christ; for, had Paul been unwilling to renounce his former estimate of these privileges and achievements, they would have deprived him of Christ, the one real gain (see verse 8).

Paul continues, in a sentence that is almost untranslatable,[140] **Yes, what is more, I certainly do count all things to be sheer loss because of the all-surpassing excellence of knowing Christ Jesus my Lord.**

In verse 8 Paul strengthens his previous statement, and this in two ways. First, he underscores what was implied in the preceding, namely, that what he counted loss at the moment of his conversion he is still counting to be loss. It is as if he were saying, "On this subject no Judaizer will ever be able to change my mind." Secondly, he now affirms that he considers not only the things mentioned in verses 5 and 6 to be a liability, a detriment, but also all other things that could stand in the way of fully accepting Christ and his righteousness. We may think of such matters as making too much of earthly possessions, delight in intimate fellowship with former anti-

---

[140] The sentence begins with the piling up of particles: ἀλλὰ μενοῦν γε καὶ. As in every language, when the heart is deeply stirred and when thoughts crowd the mind, the utterance becomes compressed, and words are left out. See N.T.C. on John 5:31 with respect to Abbreviated Style. A word for word, literal, rendering, so that the English sentence would start as follows, *"But, indeed, therefore, at least, even,"* would make little sense. By inserting a word here and there, an attempt could be made to get into our sentence everything that is in the original; somewhat as follows, *"But, indeed* (that is not all), *therefore* (I affirm) *at least even* (this, that) I do count all things to be loss because of the all-surpassing excellence of knowing Christ Jesus my Lord." Not only would this be rather clumsy but perhaps even unwarranted: it is a question whether, for example γε is translatable at all. It could be equivalent (in English) to a tone of voice rather than an actual word. The manner in which I have rendered the sentence is, accordingly, not literal but, I trust, natural.

Christian friends, anticipation centered on even more brilliant prospects as a Pharisee, etc. All such matters and many more are nothing but sheer loss, and this *because of* — hence also *in comparison with* — the all-surpass-ingness,[141] that is, the all-surpassing excellence or value, of "knowing Christ Jesus[142] . . . Lord." On the way to Damascus Paul had learned to know Jesus. Although there had been ample preparation for this knowledge — such as, Paul's acquaintance with the Old Testament, the testimonies he had heard from the lips of the martyrs, their behavior under fire —, when it broke in upon the soul, the experience was sudden and dramatic. Prophecy and testimony began to take on meaning now. It was an unforgettable experience, that meeting with the exalted Christ, while, a moment before, the apostle had still been breathing threatening and slaughter against Christ's Church, hence against this very Christ himself! Yes, he now *saw and heard* the actual Jesus, about whom he had been told so much. And he saw and heard him now as *Christ Jesus . . . Lord,* the name above every name (see on 2:9-11). And at the same time he here and now began to understand something of the condescending pity and tenderness of Christ's great and merciful heart, a love poured out upon *him,* even upon *Paul, the bitter persecutor!*

All this had occurred about thirty years ago. And during the period that intervened between the "Great Experience" and the writing of the present epistle to the Philippians, the joy of knowing, with a knowledge of both mind and heart (see on verse 10), *Christ Jesus . . . Lord* had been growing con-stantly, so that it outshone everything in beauty and desirability. Hence, Paul inserts a little word which makes "that beautiful name, that wonder-ful name, that matchless name" of Jesus even more adorable. He says "Christ Jesus *my* Lord." What this appropriating *my* implies is better explained by Paul himself. Read Phil. 1:21; 4:13; Rom. 7:24, 25; II Cor. 12:8-10; Gal. 1:15, 16; 2:20; 6:14; Eph. 5:1, 2; Col. 3:1-4:6; I Tim. 1:5, 16; II Tim. 1:12; 4:7, 8. According to these passages Christ Jesus is much more than Paul's Example and Friend. He is his Life, Lover, Strength, Boast, Rock, Re-warder, and especially as here, his Anointed Savior and Sovereign.

As before the rising sun the stars fade out, and as in the presence of the pearl of great price all other gems lose their luster, so fellowship with "Christ Jesus my Lord" eclipses all else. And it is Christ himself of whom

---

141 τὸ ὑπερέχον, the neuter of the present participle of ὑπερέχω (see also Phil. 2:3; 4:7; Rom. 13:1; I Peter 2:13). For other substantivized neuters in Paul see Rom. 2:4; 8:3; 9:22; I Cor. 1:25. The word *super-ness,* that is, *all-surpassing greatness* is one of a list of super-combinations used by the apostle. See N.T.C. on the Pastoral Epistles, p. 75. In Phil. 4:7 we have another.
142 Literally, "of the knowledge of Christ Jesus," etc. As is clear from verse 10, "that I may know him," the apostle is thinking of Christ Jesus not as the subject but as the object; hence, to avoid ambiguity, the translation "knowing Christ Jesus" com-mends itself.

Paul is thinking, not this or that matter about Christ. Paul is in complete agreement with the poet who said, (not *"What"* but) *"Whom* have I in heaven but thee? And there is none on earth that I desire besides thee" (Ps. 73:25). The apostle continues, **for whom I suffered the loss of all these things.**[143] It was for the sake of his Lord and Savior that Paul had lost whatever was at one time very dear to him: pride of tradition, of ancestry, of orthodoxy, of outward conformity with the law, and of whatever else there had been on which he had formerly depended as gateways to the heavenly city. Moreover his attitude of having willingly suffered this loss has not changed at all. So he continues, **and I am still counting them refuse.** What the Judaizers prize so very highly, the apostle considers to be nothing but *refuse,* something that is fit only to be thrown to the *dogs.*[144] The apostle is very consistent. Had he not, just a moment ago (see 3:2), called these dangerous enemies *dogs?* Paul, then, considers all these inherited privileges and human attainments, *considered as merits,* to be something that must be discarded as worthless leavings, abominable trash.

3:8b-11

C. *I Now Rely on Another Righteousness*
(1) It is Christ's
(2) It is not merited by works performed by man, law-works
(3) It is appropriated by faith
(4) It comes from God
(5) It results in a striving after spiritual perfection

(1) *It is Christ's*

8b, 9a. "I am still counting them refuse," says Paul, **in order that I may gain Christ and be found in him.**[145] Paul wishes to make Christ more and

---

[143] τὰ πάντα in the summarizing sense, as in II Cor. 4:15; Col. 3:8; hence, "all these things."

[144] This, in fact, may be the very derivation of the word σκύβαλον, pl. -α. By some it is said to be derived from τὸ τοῖς κυσὶ βαλλόμενον (what is thrown to the dogs). Others, however, connect it with σκῶρ, dung. Though M.M. gives the preference to the meaning *dung* here in Phil. 3:8, which may be correct, the connotation *refuse* is well attested. Cf. Ecclesiasticus 27:4, "When a sieve is shaken the refuse remains"; Josephus, *Jewish War* V. 571, "they ate the refuse therefrom;" and Philo, *The Sacrifice of Abel and Cain* 109, "The chaff and husk and other refuse are scattered."

[145] The simplest and most natural construction here would seem to be that which makes κερδήσω καὶ εὑρεθῶ dependent on the nearest preceding verb, the second ἡγοῦμαι of verse 8, present middle indicative. The words κερδήσω καὶ εὑρεθῶ then state the purpose or motive of this continued act of counting all these things to be mere refuse, that purpose or motive being "that I may gain Christ and be found in Him." Now gaining Christ is indeed a life-long activity. More and more fully does

more fully his own. As long as one keeps clinging, even in the slightest degree, to his own righteousness, he cannot fully enjoy Christ's. The two simply do not go together. The one must be fully given up before the other can be fully appropriated. It is Paul's great aim that in the observation of all his fellow-believers he may be *found* to be completely *in him*, that is, in union with Christ. For the meaning of "in Christ" see also on Phil. 1:1. Here in Phil. 3 this "in him" relationship is described as to its forensic side in verse 9, and as to its practical side in verse 10. The "in him" relationship means that Christ's righteousness is imputed to the sinner, so that it is reckoned as his own. This implies redemption from the claims of Satan (Rom. 8:31, 33), reconciliation with God (II Cor. 5:18-21), forgiveness of sins (Eph. 1:7), hence, the state of being in conformity with the law of God (Rom. 8:1-4).

Now when Paul states that he is counting everything to be refuse in order that he may gain Christ and may be found in him, this sacrifice with the purpose of capturing the one, real prize must not be interpreted in a selfish, mercenary sense. It must, of course, be interpreted in the light of such passages as Rom. 11:36 and I Cor. 10:31. It is the glory of God that Paul has in mind, not just his own selfish benefit. To be sure, he is not forgetting himself. His is, in fact, seeking to promote his own welfare, which is altogether right and proper. But this ideal is never separated from the highest possible objective. The two go together. Hence, Paul is not like a man who sells an article in order to make a huge profit for himself, to be used entirely on himself. He is not like a fisherman using bait in order to catch a big fish, to be proudly displayed. Nor even like a chess-player who "sacrifices" Knight and Queen in order to checkmate his opponent's King, for the simple pleasure of winning the game. No, the apostle is more like a sea-captain who in time of war, *for patriotic reasons* jettisons his cargo, thereby lightening his ship so that it will have the speed needed to overtake and capture the enemy's vessel that contains a far more precious treasure. Even better, he is like a young man, heir to a going concern, who cheerfully gives up this inheritance in order that he may prepare himself for the ideal of his life: that of *rendering service to the Lord* in the work of the ministry, whether at home or abroad. Cf. Mark 10:21.

(2) *It is not merited by works performed by man, law-works*

Christ become united with the believer, and the believer with Christ. The fact that the *aorist* subjunctive is used to indicate this purpose or motive does not in any way cancel the duration of the process. *The aorist simply states the fact*, without indicating the time-element, whether long or short. It is simply "the flashlight picture." Also, since the aorist is properly indefinite as to time, and the subjunctive "is future in relation to the speaker," the interpretation which, along with many others, I give of this passage does not contradict grammar. See Gram. N.T., pp. 848, 849, 1380. Hence, I cannot accept Lenski's reasoning on p. 846 ff. of his Commentary.

9b. Says Paul, **not having a righteousness of my own, legal righteousness** (or: *a righteousness proceeding from law*). The apostle's meaning is: not in any sense can the righteousness that counts before God be regarded as based on my own accomplishments in conformity with the Old Testament law. *Sin earns wages* (Rom. 6:23). This return is *paid* to those who *deserve* it. But *God's righteousness is given to the undeserving.* God justifies the ungodly. Christ died for the ungodly (Rom. 4:5; 5:6; Titus 3:5).

(3) It is appropriated by faith

Not righteousness proceeding from law, says Paul, **but that (which is) through faith in Christ.** Faith is the appropriating agent, the hand extended to receive God's free gift. Since the only righteousness that has any value before God is Christ's righteousness *imputed* to the sinner as God's free gift to the undeserving, it stands to reason that the only possible way to obtain this righteousness is to *accept* it (one *accepts,* one does not *earn,* a gift!) by simple faith, that is, by appropriating confidence in the Giver; hence also in his word. God's Anointed is himself the object of this childlike trust (Rom. 1:16, 17; 3:21, 22; Gal. 2:20; 3:22; cf. Hab. 2:4; John 3:16).

(4) It comes from God

The faith-appropriation is repeated for the sake of emphasis, but first one more element is added: the divine origin of this righteousness. Hence, **the righteousness (which is) from God (and rests) on faith.** This righteousness is provided by God and avails before God (Rom. 3:24, 25; 8:3; II Cor. 5:19). Its possession and enjoyment rests on, is conditioned on, faith, faith possessed and exercised by man, to be sure (John 3:16), and for which man is fully responsible, but given, nurtured, and rewarded by God (Eph. 2:8).

(5) It results in a striving after spiritual perfection

10. Paul continues, **that I may know him.** Here he resumes the thought of verse 8 ("the all-surpassing excellence of knowing Christ Jesus, my Lord"), but also links his words to the immediately preceding idea of *the righteousness (which is) from God (and rests) on faith.* The progress of thought here is altogether natural. The experience of every person who has been brought out of the darkness into God's marvelous light, and has felt in his heart the glory of Christ's pardoning love is that he will sing:

> "More about Jesus would I know,
> More of his grace to others show;
> More of his saving fulness see,
> More of his love who died for me.

> "More, more about Jesus,
> More, more about Jesus,

166

More of his saving fulness see,
More of his love who died for me."
(E. E. Hewitt)

Thus the *faith-appropriation* of "the righteousness (which is) from God" and *contemplation* upon this fact implies, calls forth, the ardent yearning, that I may get to know Christ better and better.[146]   And, considering the matter from God's side, we can say that when God justifies his child he also sends forth his sanctifying Spirit into the heart.   Hence, from the divine side the link between righteousness *imputed* and righteousness *imparted* is the Holy Spirit; from the human side — ever dependent upon the divine — the link is the gratitude of faith.

Now "that I may know him" refers to a knowledge not only of the *mind* but also of the *heart*.   (See also a similar use of *know* in John 17:3; Gal. 4:9; I John 2:18, 29; 4:8.)   Though the first should never be excluded, the emphasis here is on the second.   See N.T.C. on John 7:17, 18, for details on the inter-relation of the various elements of Christian experience.   The apostle, being *an indefatigable idealist,* and in that sense *perfectionist,* wants to gain as full an understanding of Christ's person and love as possible.   He is not satisfied with anything short of perfection.   When he expresses his yearning *to know* Christ, he has in mind not only or even mainly the learning of certain facts about Christ but also and especially the sharing of certain experiences with him, as is clearly indicated by the rest of verse 10 and by verse 11.   He wishes to become entirely "wrapped up" in Christ, so that Jesus will be "all the world" to him.[147]   One gains such *experiential knowledge* by wide-awake attendance at public worship and proper use of the

---

[146] The articular second aorist infinitive τοῦ γνῶναι may, therefore, be called an *explanatory* infinitive, or also an infinitive of *contemplated result* or *purpose*. It sets forth what is the result and purpose of embracing the righteousness of Christ, by a living faith, what is *implied* in this act.   My interpretation here differs but slightly from that which would connect the infinitive with the entire thought of verses 8b and 9.   Least satisfactory, as I see it, is the explanation of those who leapfrog the second ἡγοῦμαι of verse 8, and, ignoring what lies in between, connect τοῦ γνῶναι with ἐζημιώθην, so that the thought would be "I suffered the loss of all things . . . that I might get to know Christ."   My objection is this: Paul clearly is here no longer speaking about his experience on the way to Damascus but of his *present* yearning to get to know Christ better and better right along, in order to reach spiritual perfection in him, as is clear not only from the immediately preceding context but also from verses 11-14.

[147] The word used in the original for *that I may know* is a form of γινώσκω. See N.T.C. on John 1:10, 11, 31; 3:11; 8:28, 55; 16:30; 21:17, for distinction between γινώσκω and οἶδα.

Besides, the concept *knowledge* as referred to by Paul in verses 8 and 10 was probably also influenced by the use of the related word in the Old Testament where *to know* Jehovah means *to revere* him, *to be consecrated* to him (Prov. 1:7; Isa. 11:2; Hab. 2:14).   It is a distinctly *personal, intimate, practical, religious* knowledge that Paul has in mind.

sacraments (Heb. 10:25; cf. Matt. 18:20, 28:19; Luke 22:14-20; I Cor. 11:17-24) ; by showing kindness to all, practising the forgiving spirit, above all love; by learning to be thankful; by studying the Word of Christ both devotionally and exegetically so that it dwells in the heart; by singing psalms, hymns, and spiritual songs to the glory of God, and continuing steadfastly in prayer; and thus by redeeming the time as *a witness of Christ to all men* (Col. 3:12-17; 4:2-6) .

To show what this knowledge of Christ implies Paul continues: **and the power of his resurrection.** He longs for an ever-increasing supply of the power that proceeds from the risen and exalted Savior. That resurrected Savior, *by dint of his very resurrection,* assures Paul, through the Spirit, *of justification* (Rom. 4:25; 8:1, 16; I Cor. 15:17) ; for when the Father raised the Son he thereby proved that he had accepted the ransom paid by Christ (Matt. 20:28; Acts 20:28; I Peter 1:18) as full satisfaction for Paul's sin.

It was that same resurrected Christ who sent his Spirit into Paul's heart for the purpose of *sanctification.* Christ's life in heaven is ever the cause of Paul's new life (John 14:19) . Paul desires a growing supply of this cleansing power, this *dynamite* that destroys sin and makes room for *personal holiness and for effective witness-bearing!*

Finally, this resurrected Christ also seals Paul's *glorification* and this with respect not only to the soul but also to the body, and not only for one person separately but for Paul together with all the saints. (Rom. 8:11; I Cor. 15; Phil. 3:21; II Tim. 4:8) .

Now when the life of the risen Christ has entered into the heart of the believer and makes itself more and more manifest in his entire conduct, the inevitable result will be a sharing in Christ's *sufferings.* Hence, the apostle continues, **and (the) fellowship of his sufferings.** Paul yearns to participate more and more fully in the reproaches and afflictions of his Lord and Savior. He wants to "fill up whatever is lacking in the sufferings of Christ for his body, the Church" (Col. 1:24) . Not as if Christ's atonement were incomplete (Heb. 10:14) . But though the atonement left nothing to be desired, suffering *for the sake of Christ and his cause* (Rom. 8:17; II Cor. 11:24-28; 12:10) continues. Such suffering is a privilege (for detailed proof see on Phil. 1:29) . It implies beatings, stonings, hunger, thirst, cold, nakedness, etc., endured in the work or being *a witness for Christ to all men* (Acts 9:15, 16; 22:15) . It includes also the experience of the hatefulness and hurt of one's own sins, the sins that caused the Savior to suffer such indescribable agonies (Rom. 7:9-25) . Hence, the desire to participate in the sufferings of Christ is part of the intense longing and striving for complete holiness, as is clear also from the words which follow immediately: **becoming increasingly conformed to his death.** This, as the apostle himself explains in a closely parallel passage (Rom. 6:4-11), means to become *dead to sin.* It implies death to selfishness; hence, eagerness to be a blessing to others, as was Christ in his death. Thus a person becomes *conformed* to Christ's death.

Union with Christ implies that all of Christ's redemptive experiences are duplicated unredemptively in the believer. The Christian, accordingly, suffered with Christ (Rom. 8:17), was crucified with him (Rom. 6:6), died with him (Rom. 6:8; II Tim. 2:11), was buried with him (Rom. 6:4; Col. 2:12), made alive with him (Col. 2:13), raised with him (Col. 2:12; 3:1), made joint-heirs with him (Rom. 8:17), is glorified with him (Rom. 8:17), enthroned with him (Col. 3:1; Rev. 20:4), and reigns with him (II Tim. 2:12; Rev. 20:4).

11. However, one should be careful to avoid the conclusion that these experiences are all *literally* reflected in the life and death of believers. Failure to note this important point has given rise to errors in exegesis both here and in connection with verse 11. Thus, when the apostle yearns to become increasingly conformed to Christ's death, this has been interpreted to mean that he longed for death by crucifixion or at least for death as a martyr. But why not allow the apostle himself to clarify the meaning? When with a believing heart the Christian appropriates the saving value of Christ's death, he dies to sin, for the guilt of his sin is removed, and its power over him is gradually reduced and at death completely annihilated by the work of the Holy Spirit. Rejecting sin and selfishness he throws himself into the work of being a means in God's hand to open men's eyes, that they may turn from darkness to light, and from the power of Satan to God (Rom. 6:4-11; Acts 26:18). It is in that sense that the believer experiences fellowship with Christ's sufferings and becomes conformed to his death.[148]

Similarly, when it is stated that the believer was crucified with Christ or was buried with him or raised with him, these expressions cannot be taken *literally* to mean that Christ's followers suffered physical death by crucifixion, that their bodies were interred, or that they have already been physically raised. The immediate context and parallel passages must be permitted to explain the meaning. And this also holds with respect to the next statement, in which Paul expresses his intense longing thus: **if only I may attain to the resurrection from the dead.** What is meant by this *out-resurrection out of the dead* (thus literally)? In the light both of the preceding and following contexts, these words give expression to Paul's intense longing and striving

---

[148] Entering into the fellowship of Christ's suffering and becoming conformed to his death by dying unto sin and selfishness and thus becoming, like Christ in his death, a blessing to others, is beautifully illustrated by M. C. Tenney in his book *Philippians, The Gospel At Work,* Grand Rapids, Michigan, 1956, pp. 77, 78. Not for a moment does the apostle forget his great missionary task, his exalted calling, as is evident not only from verses 12-14 of the present chapter, but also from Phil. 1:12-14, 18; 2:15, 16.

to be raised completely above sin and selfishness, so that he can be a most effective agent for the salvation of men to the glory of God. Cf. Rom. 6:4, 5, 11; 7:24; I Cor. 9:22-24. *This is his aim even now.* However, absolute, spiritual perfection for the entire person will not be fully attained until Christ's brilliant Return, when in both soul and body Paul will glorify God in Christ forevermore, and will delight in all the blessings of fellowship *with him and with all the saints* in the new heaven and earth. This will be the gracious reward, the prize, given to all who aim for perfection even now. Such is the apostle's teaching not only here but everywhere (see verses 12-14, 20, 21 of the present chapter; also I Cor. 15:50-58; I Thess. 3:11-13; 5:23; II Tim. 1:12; 4:7, 8; Titus 2:13, 14.[149]

When Paul, with reference to this *out-resurrection out of the dead* writes, "If only I may attain," he is not expressing distrust in the power or love of God nor doubt as to his own salvation. Paul often rejoices in assurance of salvation (Rom. 6:5, 8; 7:25; 8:16, 17, 35-39. In this assurance he was strengthened as the years went by (I Tim. 1:15-17; II Tim. 1:12; 4:7, 8). But he wrote it in the spirit of *deep humility* and commendable distrust *in self.* The words also imply *earnest striving.* They show us Paul, the Idealist, who applies to himself the rule that he imposes on others (Phil. 2:12, 13).

It is in this same humble spirit that in verses 12-14 Paul enlarges on the theme, "In Christ I press on to perfection."

3:12-16

D. *In Christ I Press on to Perfection*
Paul, the Runner
His

    (1) *Frame of Mind*
    (2) *Exertion*
    (3) *Goal*
    (4) *Reward*

(1) *Frame of Mind*

12. Paul's intense yearning and striving for spiritual perfection is expressed now under the symbolism of the familiar foot-race.[150] In order to grasp the apostle's meaning the underlying figure must be borne in mind at every point. Picture then the ancient Greek stadium with its course for foot-races and tiers of seats for the spectators. At Athens the length of the course was one-eighth of an old Roman mile; hence, about 607 feet in our measurement. The one at Ephesus was somewhat longer. The purpose of the race was to

---

[149] Because of its length this footnote has been placed at the end of the chapter, page 185.
[150] See N.T.C. on I Tim. 4:7, 8; II Tim. 4:7, 8. Cf. I Cor. 9:24; Phil. 2:16; Heb. 12:1. Other references that come in for consideration in this connection are: Acts 13:25; 20:24; Rom. 9:16; Gal. 2:2; 5:7; II Thess. 3:1.

reach the goal opposite the entrance, or to run up and back, and this once or even twice. Near the entrance the contestants, stripped for the race, have been assigned their places on a stone threshold. In fact, several of the old stadia show what is left of rows of stone blocks at either end of the track. These blocks contain grooves to give the sprinter's feet a firm hold for a quick take-off. Here the contestants stand, body bent forward, one hand lightly touching the threshold, awaiting the signal: the letting down of a cord that has been stretched in front of them. At the signal they leap forward.

When the question is asked, "Will this contestant succeed?" the answer is, "Much will depend on his frame of mind." If he tells himself, "I'm a sure winner, no matter what I do," he will probably undergo the experience of the hare, in the fable, *The Hare and the Tortoise*. While the tortoise was plodding steadily on, the hare took a nap, and on awakening discovered, too late, that his opponent had already reached the goal!

The same holds in the spiritual race. Here, too, much depends on the frame of mind. Paul completely rejects the idea that even now the race is as good as won. Says he, **Not that** [151] **I have already gotten hold or have already been made perfect.** Paul was a firm believer in the doctrine of election "before the foundation of the world" (Eph. 1:4), and accordingly also, as has been pointed out, in the possibility of assurance of salvation. But not in election apart from human responsibility, in salvation apart from human effort, or in assurance without constant recourse to the promises. Even though he had already sacrificed everything in his service for the Lord, he is certain of one thing, namely, that he has not yet completely gotten hold of the spiritual and moral resurrection that lifts one out from among those who are dead in sin; in other words, he is sure that he has not yet been made *perfect*. In principle, yes! But in full measure, no! Far from it! The struggle against sin, fear, and doubt is not yet over. The fact, moreover, that believers do not attain this perfection in the present life is the teaching of Scripture throughout (Ps. 51:1-5; Matt. 6:12; 23:75; Luke 18:13; Rom. 7:14-24; James 3:2; I John 1:8). Paul continues, placing the positive over against the negative, as he often does, **but I am pressing on (to see) if I can also lay hold on that for which** [152] **I was laid hold on by Christ Jesus.** Paul is *pursuing* with the purpose of *overtaking and laying hold on.*[153] Has

---

[151] Rejecting a possible misunderstanding; cf. Phil. 4:11, 17; II Cor. 3:5; 7:9; II Thess. 3:9.

[152] ἐφ' ᾧ either "on that for which" (cf. Luke 5:25) or "for this reason that" (or simply "because"). The difference is minor. In either case the apostle is saying that had not Christ Jesus laid hold on him, he would never be able to lay hold on Christ Jesus, that is, on perfection in him.

[153] For the idea of *pressing on* or *pursuing, keeping up the chase, eagerly seeking or running after* see N.T.C. on I Tim. 6:11; II Tim. 2:22; cf. I Cor. 14:1. For the combination *pursue — overtake* (or *firmly lay hold on, capture*) see Exod. 15:9 (LXX); Rom. 9:30. Interesting in the present connection (pursuing *one* definite

he not been laid hold on by Christ Jesus? When Paul was on his way to Damascus had not the exalted Lord and Savior commissioned him to a definite task? See Acts 9:1-19, especially verse 15; also 22:15, 21; 26:15-18. Encouraged and enabled by this very fact, namely, that it was Christ Jesus who *has laid a firm hold* on him, so as to *possess* him completely, the apostle is now pressing on in hot pursuit of the objective assigned to him. Cf. Phil. 2:12, 13; 4:13; II Thess. 2:13. He continues,

13. Brothers, I do not count myself yet to have laid hold. This is no superfluous repetition of a confession of imperfection. On the contrary, something is added now. The very word that introduces the sentence — namely, *brothers,* a word of endearment and also in this case of deep concern (see on 1:12) — shows that the apostle is deeply moved. Far more clearly than before, he is now intimating that the church at Philippi is being vexed by people who imagine that *they* have laid hold on perfection. These errorists probably based this claim on the fact that, as they saw it, they had not only accepted Jesus as their Savior but were also scrupulous in their adherence to Judaistic rites (see above, on verses 1-3). The apostle summarily rejects their claims by saying, as it were, "Such has not been *my* experience. Legal rectitude, slavery to outworn ordinances, hindered me instead of helping me. Moreover, as a believer in Christ alone, I for one am still far removed from the goal of spiritual perfection. Whatever any one else may claim, *I* have not yet laid hold on it."

This, however, does not mean that Paul is indolent or despairing. On the contrary, he refuses to acquiesce in sin. As a runner in the race he stresses his *exertion.*

(2) Exertion

Paul writes, **But one thing (I do).** The runner in the race practises *persistent concentration* on one, and only one, objective, namely, to press on toward the goal for the prize. He permits nothing to divert him from his course. His aim is definite, well-defined.

So it is also with Paul. On reading his epistles one is amazed by this unity of purpose which characterizes the apostle's entire life after conversion. Paul aimed at gaining Christ and perfection in him, a perfection not only of uninterruptible assurance but also of loving consecration: "Teach me to love thee as thy angels love, *one holy passion* filling all my frame."

> "Lord Jesus, I long to be perfectly whole;
> I want thee forever to live in my soul,
> Break down every idol, cast out every foe,

---

object and not permitting oneself to be sidetracked or distracted) is Ecclesiasticus 11:10, "My son, do not busy yourself with many matters. If you *pursue,* you will not *overtake.*" Cf. also Herodotus IX. 58, "They (the enemies) must be *pursued* until they are *overtaken.*" On the verb see also N.T.C. on John 1:5.

Now wash me, and I shall be whiter than snow.
Whiter than snow, yes, whiter than snow;
Now wash me, and I shall be whiter than snow."

(J. Nicholson)

Such concentration is absolutely necessary. In everyday life distractions are often disastrous. Excitement about an impending trip to Asia distracts a motorist. The result: a serious accident. Similarly, in the spiritual realm worldly cares, the false glamor of wealth, and all kinds of evil desires enter in to choke the word of the gospel (Mark 4:19). Over-emphasis on sports, clothes, physical charm, etc., prevents the runner from reaching the spiritual goal. Real, undivided concentration is a matter of ceaseless effort on man's part. It is at the same time the product of the operation of grace in the heart. It is the answer to the prayer, "*Unite* my heart to fear thy name" (Ps. 86:11).

Such concentration presents its requirements. The first is *mental oblitera-tion* of that part of the course which the runner has already covered. Paul says, **forgetting what lies behind (me)**. The runner does not look back. He knows that if he does, he will lose his speed, his direction, and finally the race itself. Looking back while running ahead is always very dangerous.

So it is also spiritually. Here too looking back is forbidden. Remember Lot's wife (Luke 17:32). Now when Paul says that he forgets what lies behind, he refers to a type of forgetting which is no mere, passive *oblivion*. It is active *obliteration,* so that when any thought of merits, piled up in the past, would occur to Paul, he immediately banished it from his mind. This is not Nirvana. It is not the state resulting from drinking the waters of Lethe. It is a constant, deliberate *discarding* of any thought of *past attainments.*[154]

The second indispensable requisite of effective concentration is *unwavering progression*. Hence, Paul continues, **and eagerly straining forward to what lies ahead**. The verb used in the original is very graphic. It pictures the runner straining every nerve and muscle as he keeps on running with all his might toward the goal, his hand stretched out as if to grasp it.

No less necessary is unwavering progression in the spiritual sphere. But if it be true that Paul on this side of the grave never reaches ethical-spiritual perfection — the perfection of *condition,* that is, holy living, and of constant,

---

[154] ἐπιλανθανόμενος, present participle, durative. Just what is Paul forgetting or discarding: his pre-Christian experiences or his previous progress as a Christian? If a choice must be made, the context (see especially verses 7 and 8) would seem to favor the former; logic, consistent application of the figure of the Christian race, the latter. But is it necessary to make a choice? Is it not possible that Paul is simply stating that, in his race for perfection, he refuses to become absorbed in past attainments of whatever kind; in other words, that in order to win the race one should, with eyes fixed on the goal, advance steadily toward it?

never-interrupted, full assurance of his *state* —, then why strive so eagerly for it? Is not the apostle foolish when he strives with such constancy and ardor to reach a goal which he knows he cannot fully attain in this life? The answer is twofold:

a. Although a person cannot actually reach this objective here and now, he can, indeed, make progress toward it. This matter of ethical-spiritual perfection is by no means an all-or-nothing proposition. As Paul himself teaches everywhere, there is such a thing as *making progress* in sanctification. The line of progress may indeed be zig-zag, but this does not rule out the possibility of real progress. In fact, such advancement, such gradual development when the seed of true religion has been implanted in the heart, must be considered normal (Mark 4:28; Phil. 1:6, 9, 26; 4:17; then Eph. 4:12, 13; Col. 1:9-11; I Thess. 3:12; 4:1, 10; II Thess. 1:3; I Tim. 4:15; II Tim. 2:1).

b. Such spiritual perfection in Christ, considered as God's gracious *gift*, is actually *granted* only to those who *strive* for it! The *prize* is given to those who *press on* toward the *goal* (verse 14; cf. II Tim. 4:7, 8).

Concentration, obliteration, progression, accordingly, are the key-words of that spiritual *exertion* which results in *perfection.* It is by these means that one presses on toward the goal.

(3) Goal

14. So Paul continues, **I am pressing on toward the goal.** By derivation, the word translated *goal* is that on which one fixes his eyes. Throughout the race the sight of that pillar at the end of the track encouraged the contestant to redouble his exertions. He was ever running goal-ward, that is, *in accordance with* [155] the line from his eyes to the goal.

In the spiritual race that goal is Christ, that is, ethical-spiritual perfection in him (see Phil. 3:8, 12). With all his heart the apostle desired to be completely raised above sin. He sought eagerly to promote the glory of God by every tool at his disposal, particularly by being a witness to all men (Acts 22:15, 21; 26:16-18), that he might by all means save some (I Cor. 9:22).

(4) Reward

Never does the runner forget the prize (I Cor. 9:24, 25; II Tim. 4:8; Heb. 12:2). Hence, Paul continues, **for the prize of the upward call of God in Christ Jesus.** At the end of the race the successful runner was summoned from the floor of the stadium to the judge's seat to receive the prize. This prize was a wreath of leaves. At Athens after the time of Solon the Olympic victor also received the sum of 500 *drachmai.* Moreover, he was allowed to eat at public expense, and was given a front-row seat at the theater.

Probably some of these facts were in the background of Paul's thinking when he stated that he was pressing on toward the goal for the prize of the

---

[155] Note κατὰ σκοπὸν διώκω.

upward call of God in Christ Jesus. However, *underlying figure* and *spiritual meaning* do not completely correspond here — do they ever? —, for though *the prize* in both cases is awarded at the end of the race, the *upward call* of which the apostle is here speaking was issued already at his *conversion,* hence not only at the *end* of the race. Here as elsewhere in Paul there is *the effective gospel call.* It is the *heavenward* call, the *holy* calling, a calling to holiness of life. Thus God is summoning Paul upward continually. See N.T.C. on II Thess. 1:11, p. 162, footnote 162 there; also N.T.C. on II Tim. 1:9. Nevertheless, *the prize* which corresponds to this call, and is given to those in whom this call has performed its work, is awarded when the race is over and has been won. Then Paul, too, together with all the saints, is called upward to meet the Lord in the air and to remain forever with him in the new heaven and earth (I Thess. 4:17). It is only *in Christ Jesus* that this upward call, this holy calling, is possible. Without him it could neither have been given nor obeyed. Apart from his atoning sacrifice the glorious prize to which the call leads the way could never be awarded.

Is there a real difference between *goal* and *prize?* In a sense they are the same. Both indicate *Christ, perfection in him.* Nevertheless, *goal* and *prize* represent different aspects of the same perfection; as follows,

a. When this perfection is called *goal,* it is viewed as the object of human striving. When it is called *prize* it is viewed as the gift of God's sovereign grace. God imparts everlasting life to those who accept Christ by living faith (John 3:16). He imparts perfection to those who strive to attain it. Though it is true that this believing and this striving are from start to finish completely dependent on God's grace, nevertheless it is *we* who must embrace Christ and salvation in him. It is *we* who must strive to enter in. God does not do this believing and striving for us!

b. The *goal* rivets the attention on the race that *is being run* or *was run;* the *prize* upon the glory that *will begin* in the new heaven and earth. Thus, bringing sinners to Christ, and doing this with *perfect* devotion, pertains to the *goal. Perfect* fellowship with these saved ones on and after the day of the great consummation pertains to the *prize.* Hence, it is correct to distinguish between goal and prize, as Paul also does both here and, by implication, in II Tim. 4:7, 8.

With this glorious prize in mind — namely, the blessings of everlasting life; such as *perfect* wisdom, joy, holiness, peace, fellowship, all enjoyed *to the glory of God,* in a marvelously restored universe, and in the company of Christ and of all the saints — Paul is pressing on toward the goal.

15, 16. Now, in the earthly race the prize is perishable; in the heavenly, imperishable (I Cor. 9:25). In the former only *one* could win (I Cor. 9:24); in the latter *all* who love Christ's appearing win (II Tim. 4:8). They win the prize by being minded as is Paul, and by conduct in harmony with this disposition. Hence, Paul continues, **Accordingly, let us, as many as are mature, continue to set our mind on this.** Do we, the Philippians along with ourselves, desire the prize? Then let us — note tactful use of *us* here! — set our mind on the objective as just described; that is, fully realizing that we are still far from the goal of ultimate moral-spiritual perfection, let us earnestly and continually endeavor to reach this goal. Are we not *mature?* [156] Let us then leave behind any childish notions of reaching perfection by means of rigid law-observance, and let it be our disposition *in Christ* to seek ever higher ground:

> "I'm pressing on the upward way,
> New heights I'm gaining every day;
> Still praying as I onward bound,
> Lord, plant my feet on higher ground.
> Lord, lift me up and let me stand,
> By faith, on heaven's table-land,
> A higher plane than I have found;
> Lord, plant my feet on higher ground."
>
> (J. Oatman)

But while this rule is excellent and necessary, its exact application to all phases of life is not always immediately clear. Hence, Paul continues, **and if on some minor point y o u are differently minded, that, too, God will**

---

[156] Of all the explanations offered to explain τέλειος, pl. –οι, as here used, the one which regards it as meaning *mature, full-grown,* here with respect to knowledge of the way of salvation, would seem to be the best. The frequency with which the apostle uses the term in that sense is striking. Probable meanings as used by Paul:

Rom. 12:2:   *perfect* (will of God)
I Cor. 2:6:   *the mature, the full-grown,* as contrasted with *babes* (I Cor. 3:1)
I Cor. 13:10:   *the total, wholeness,* as contrasted with that which is "in part" (I Cor. 13:9)
I Cor. 14:20:   *mature, grown up, of full age:* "in malice babes, in mind grown-up"
Eph. 4:13:   *full-grown* man, *mature* manhood
Col. 1:28:   *perfect* or *mature*
Col. 4:12:   *mature, ripe, complete*
(Cf. also Heb. 5:14, "Solid food is for *full-grown* men.")
Meanings a. "full-grown" and b. "spiritually perfect" (without any defect and filled with positive goodness) sometimes coincide: the full-grown man is the one who has reached "the measure of the stature of the fullness of Christ." Cf. also Col. 4:12.
The question whether the use of τέλειοι here in verse 15 in connection with the same word implied in the verbal form used in verse 12 presents a play on words cannot be answered definitely. Lenski denies it. Many others are of the opposite opinion to which I also lean. If a play on words — rather frequent in Paul — is intended, then the full meaning is probably as follows: Judaizers may regard themselves as being τέλειοι (perfect), but it is *we* who are the real τέλειοι (mature individuals), for the τέλειοι are exactly the ones who in full awareness of their own imperfection reach for the goal.

make plain to y o u. If the Philippians will adhere to the rule as laid down, then if with respect to this or that minor point of application their views should be defective, God, through his Spirit, will unveil to their hearts and minds the truth also regarding such a matter. Cf. Ps. 25:14; Matt. 7:7; Luke 19:26; John 7:17; 16:13. Emphasizing this same thought, the apostle continues, **Only, let our conduct be consistent with the level we have attained.** Or, more literally, "Only, to what we have attained, with the same let us keep in line." The rule [157] has been established. The principle — namely, "We are still far from perfect, but in Christ we should strive to become perfect" — has been enunciated and exemplified. Let our lives be regulated by the consistent application of this principle. It must never be surrendered.[158]

True religion, then, is a matter not of precept upon precept but of basic principles. These are few but very important. If by the light of God's special revelation these principles are consistently applied, then all the rest will follow. God will not refuse to give further light to him who walks by the light already given.

---

17 Brothers, join in being imitators of me, and watch closely those who are walking according to the example that we have set y o u. 18 For many are pursuing a walk of life, of whom I told y o u often and now tell y o u even weeping (that they are) the enemies of the cross of Christ; 19 whose end is destruction, whose god is their belly, and whose glory is in their shame, who set their mind on earthly things. 20 For our homeland is in heaven, from which we also are eagerly awaiting, as Savior, the Lord Jesus Christ, 21 who will refashion our lowly body so that it will have a form like his own glorious body, (and who will do this) by the exertion of that power which enables him to subject even all things to himself.

3:17-21

III. *Warning against Sensualists. The Homeland in Heaven*

A new paragraph begins here. Warnings continue, but now against a foe described in terms that differ from those used in verse 2 above. Not about dogs, evil workers, the concision does Paul speak now but about men whom he considers as "the enemies of the cross of Christ, whose end is destruction, whose god is their belly, whose glory is in their shame, who set their mind on earthly things." It is well before entering upon a detailed exegesis to answer the question, "Who are these dangerous errorists?"

---

[157] The better text does not have "by that same rule." Nevertheless, that is the idea; cf. Gal. 6:16.
[158] Note use of present active infinitive στοιχεῖν with imperative connotation, here as also in Rom. 12:15.

In harmony with very many interpreters [159] I am firmly convinced that they are *sensualists, men who catered to the flesh, gluttonous, grossly immoral people,* all this though they pretended to be Christians. Reasons for accepting this view:

(1) This would seem to be the most natural explanation of the term "whose god is their belly." It is the interpretation that immediately occurs to the mind.[160] Only the most compelling reason should be permitted to cause one to surrender it. No such reason has been given.

(2) This view is strengthened by some of the other descriptive phrases that occur here; especially, "whose glory is in their shame, who set their mind on earthly things."

(3) This explanation is also in harmony with Pauline language elsewhere. In Romans the apostle warns against those who said, "Let us do evil that good may come" (Rom. 3:8), and "Let us continue in sin that grace may abound" (Rom. 6:1). It can hardly be doubted that these were the very individuals who in Rom. 16:18 are described as "serving not our Lord Christ but *their belly,*" language very similar to that found here in Phil. 3:19.

(4) The transition from a warning against *legalists* (Phil. 3:2) to one against *libertines* (verses 17-21) is, after all, rather natural. We find it also in Galatians (cf. Gal. 5:1 with 5:13). Sinful human nature is prone to jump from one extreme into another. Hardly has it become clear to a person that he should not be "entangled again in the yoke of (Judaistic) bondage" when he begins to use his new-found freedom as "an opportunity for the flesh."

(5) In a parallel passage Peter warns against similar loose individuals, men who forget that the believers' homeland is in heaven, and that, acccordingly, the followers of Jesus are sojourners and pilgrims here below (cf. Phil. 3:19, 20 with I Peter 2:11). Peter clearly implies that these seducers indulge in "fleshly lusts which war against the soul." There is, therefore, every reason to interpret the passage in Philippians similarly.

Other views as to the identity of the errorists against whom Paul warns here are discussed in a footnote.[161]

---

[159] Alford, Barclay, Barnes, Braune (in Lange's "Commentary on the Holy Scriptures"), Beare, Ellicott, Erdman, Johnstone, Kennedy (in "The Expositor's Greek Testament"), Laurin, Lightfoot, Meyer, Michael (in "The Moffatt New Testament Commentary"), Rainy (in "The Expositor's Bible"), The Amplified New Testament.

[160] Similar language is used by Eupolis, 5th century B.C. Athenian comic poet; by Athenaeus who wrote *Banquet of the Learned;* by Euripedes (*Cyclops* 335); and by Xenophon (*Mem.* I.vi.8: note how he uses "slavery to the belly" in close connection with "incontinence").

[161] Such views are as follows:

(1) The people against whom Paul issues his warning here in Phil. 3:17-21 are *the heathen* (B. Weiss, A. Rilliet).

Objection: Would Paul have written, "of whom I told y o u often and now tell y o u even in tears"; in other words, would he have been so deeply disturbed if he had heard a report that *heathen* were guilty of the sin here described? The

17. Deeply moved by what he is about to write, Paul addresses the Philippians with the endearing word **Brothers** (see on 1:12; cf. 1:14; 3:1, 13; 4:1, 8, 21). He continues, **join in being imitators of me.** Should not brothers show that they belong to the same spiritual family, and are, therefore, really *brothers?* Should not their attitude of heart, speech, and conduct remind one of the same model? "Let me be that model," says Paul, as it were, and this in self-renunciation over against self-complacency; in humble, Christ-centered trust instead of arrogant self-esteem; in idealism versus indolence (Phil. 3:7-14); and thus also in spirituality as contrasted with sensuality, that is, in heavenly-mindedness as opposed to worldly-mindedness (verses 18-21).

But is selection of himself as an example consistent with Christian humility? Answer:

(1) Before pointing to himself as an example, the apostle had reminded the Philippians of *Christ* as the chief example (Phil. 2:5-8). Accordingly, they knew that what Paul meant was simply this, "Be imitators of me, as I also am of Christ" (I Cor. 11:1).

(2) The apostle was not placing himself on a pedestal, as if he were perfect, but, quite the contrary, was urging his friends *to strive after perfection,* in the full realization that they were still far removed from the ideal, as was he himself.

(3) Surrounded by immorality on the part both of pagans and of nominal Christians (see verses 18 and 19), these Philippians needed a concrete example of Christian devotion, a picture-lesson. The apostle had every right to point to himself as such an example.

---

apostle certainly knew that! Is it not far more likely that immorality practised by those who professed to be Christians caused him to weep so profusely?

(2) The persons against whom the warning is issued may have been *either* Judaistic legalists *or* Epicurean libertines (Martin, Robertson, Vincent).

Objection: I admire caution in exegesis. However, in the present instance I believe we can be certain, as I have tried to prove.

(3) The Judaizers are meant, just as in verse 2 (Barth, Greijdanus, Lenski, Müller in "The New International Commentary").

Objection: When it is said that the Judaizers made the belly their god *by demanding only kosher food,* and that their glory was in their shame because they gloried *in their circumcized flesh,* that is, *in their private parts,* proof should have been given to show that such interpretations are in line with New Testament usage. The proposition that strictness in the observance of dietary regulations would be tantamount to making a god of one's belly, so that, for example, Paul himself before his conversion was guilty of this sin, is in need of proof. And as to the word αἰσχύνη (shame), nowhere else in the New Testament does this word as such refer concretely and specifically to a person's private parts (Luke 14:9 *disgrace;* II Cor. 4:2, associated with *craftiness;* Heb. 12:2, *disgrace, ignominy;* Jude 13, *shameful deeds* cast up like seafoam; Rev. 3:18, *shameful nakedness*).

But does not the description "the enemies of the cross of Christ" fit the Judaizers? It certainly does, but it is an equally correct characterization of the sensualists!

Surely, far stronger arguments will have to be submitted before the majority of commentators can become convinced that when Paul warned against men whose god was their belly he was referring to Judaizers with their rigorous food laws!

(4) The justifiable character of his exhortation becomes even more clearly evident when it is seen in the light of what immediately follows, showing that when Paul urged the Philippians to imitate him, he was not thinking of himself *alone* but of *himself in company with others,* such as Timothy (Phil. 2:19-24) and Epaphroditus (2:25-30). Note the pronoun *we* instead of *I* in the continuation: **and watch closely those who are walking according to the example that we have set y o u.** Instead of fixing y o u r attention upon individuals who have confused Christian liberty with license, focus it upon those who are safe guides of Christian conduct. Let them be y o u r *example* (see N.T.C. on I Thess. 1:7).

18, 19. The apostle supports his urgent appeal by continuing, deeply moved, **For many are pursuing a walk of life, of whom I told y o u often and now tell y o u even weeping (that they are) the enemies of the cross of Christ.** The wicked life of these persons who wished to be regarded as Christians belied the confession of their lips. They deceived themselves, exerted a most sinister influence upon those who listened to them, kept unbelievers from becoming truly converted, and dishonored God. They may have been traveling "missionaries." They were *numerous* — note the word *many* —, from which, however, it does not follow that they constituted a considerable proportion of the membership of the *Philippian church.* If that had been the case, the apostle could not have praised this church in such glowing terms (see Phil. 4:1). Nevertheless, they were a real menace. Paul, while present among the Philippians, had often warned against this class of deceivers. He considers them not just enemies but *the* (note the definite article here) enemies of the cross of Christ. If *the friends* of the cross are those who show in their lives that they have caught the spirit of the cross, namely, that of *self-denial* (Matt. 20:28; Luke 9:23; Rom. 15:3; Phil. 2:5-8), then surely *the enemies* of the cross are those who manifest the very opposite attitude, namely, that of *self-indulgence.* *The friends* of the cross do not love the world. In fact, the world is crucified to them, and they to the world, and this because they glory in the cross (Gal. 6:14; cf. 5:24). *The enemies* of the cross love the world and the things that are in the world (I John 2:15). They set their minds on earthly things (Phil. 3:19).

  Because of his great love for the Philippians the apostle actually *weeps* when he reflects on the fact that these enemies of the cross are trying to seduce the members of the first church established in Europe. He weeps as did Mary of Bethany because of her brother's death (John 11:31, 33; see N.T.C. on John 11:35), and as did Mary Magdalene on the morning of Christ's resurrection (John 20:11). One of the secrets of Paul's success as a missionary was his genuine, personal interest in those whom the Lord had committed to his spiritual care. Because his love for them was so real and tender, his heart was stirred to its very depths when danger threatened them.

Besides, the apostle was not only a man of penetrating insight and rugged determination but also of profound, surging emotion.

Paul's Deeply Emotional Nature

Various phases of the apostle's intensely emotional personality are exhibited in the book of Acts and in the epistles. Here was a truly *great* soul! What he did he did with all his might, never in a merely detached manner. Having formerly persecuted the followers of Jesus, after his conversion Sorrow, hearty and profound, walked with him (I Cor. 15:9; I Tim. 1:15). That to such a bitter persecutor Christ had revealed himself as a loving Savior baffled him. He just could not get over it (Eph. 3:8; I Tim. 1:16). It caused his heart to overflow with lasting, humble gratitude! For this and for other reasons his epistles are full of magnificent doxologies (Rom. 9:5; 11:36; 16:27; Eph. 1:3; 3:20; Phil. 4:20; I Tim. 1:17; 6:15; II Tim. 4:18) which are the spontaneous utterances of the man who wrote, "For the love of Christ constrains us" (II Cor. 5:14). Having been "laid hold on" by Christ, the apostle in turn was eager to burn himself out for the salvation of others (I Cor. 9:22; 10:33; II Cor. 12:15). His heart ached intensely because so many of his own people (Israelites) were not saved (Rom. 9:1-3; 10:1). Anxiety for all his churches pressed upon him daily (II Cor. 11:28). How fervent and touching were his prayers for them (Eph. 3:14-19; I Thess. 3:9-13). How he loved them, so that he could write, "We were gentle in the midst of y o u as a nurse cherishes her own children. So, being affectionately desirious of y o u, we gladly shared with y o u not only the gospel of God but also our own souls . . . For now we really live if y o u stand fast in the Lord" (I Thess. 2:7, 8; 3:8). How earnest were his pleadings (II Cor. 5:20; Gal. 4:19, 20; Eph. 4:1), and how tactful! Though for their own good he was able to rebuke the wayward very sharply (Gal. 1:6-9; 3:1-4), even this was a manifestation of the love of his great, throbbing heart. Is it any wonder that, when occasion demanded it, out of the eyes of a man with such an ebullient spirit and loving heart there welled forth fountains of tears (Acts 20:19, 31), so that not only here in Phil. 3:18 but also in II Cor. 2:4 these are mentioned? And is it at all surprising that, on the other hand, on one occasion the tears of his friends, because of his imminent departure and the afflictions in store for him, well-nigh broke his heart (Acts 21:13)? Truly Paul's *weeping* when he writes about the enemies of the cross of Christ is as glorious as is the *joy, joy, joy* that sings its way through this marvelous epistle!

Speaking about these enemies of the cross of Christ Paul continues, **whose end is destruction.** This is their appointed destiny, for God has ordained that "their end shall be according to their works" (II Cor. 11:15). This end is the *fruit* of their wicked lives (Rom. 6:21). It is the *wages* earned by their sin (Rom. 6:23). *Destruction,* however, is by no means the same as

181

annihilation. It does not mean that they will cease to exist. On the contrary, it means *everlasting punishment* (Matt. 25:46), for this destruction is an *everlasting* destruction (II Thess. 1:9).[162] This destruction *begins* even in the present life, but is climaxed after death. Paul continues, **whose god is their belly** (cf. Rom. 16:18). Instead of striving to keep their physical appetites under control (Rom. 8:13; I Cor. 9:27), realizing that our bodies are the Holy Spirit's temple, in which God should be glorified (I Cor. 6:19, 20), these people surrendered themselves to gluttony and licentiousness. They worshipped their sensual nature. In this they were prompted, no doubt, by causes such as the following: immoral background (cf. I Peter 1:18), wicked pagan surroundings, licentious incipient gnosticism (see N.T.C. on I Tim. 4:3), perversion of the doctrine of grace (Rom. 3:8; 6:1), and, last but not least, evil lusts within the heart (James 1:14). The apostle further characterizes them as those **whose glory is in their shame:** Their pride was in that of which they should have been ashamed. Not only did they carry out their wicked designs, but they even boasted about them. They were the persons **who set their minds on earthly things.** Being carnal, "after the flesh," they pondered the things of the flesh (Rom. 8:5). Now the mind of the flesh is *"enmity* against God" (Rom. 8:7), and these people were *"the enemies* of the cross of Christ." In a parallel passage the apostle shows us what these *earthly things* were on which these people set their minds, namely, immorality, indecency, lust, evil desire, greed, evil temper, furious rage, malice, cursing, filthy talk (Col. 3:2, 5, 8).

20, 21. Such conduct would certainly be ill-fitting for *the citizens of the kingdom of heaven,* Paul implies, as he continues, **For** [163] *our* [164] **homeland is in heaven.** Do citizens of Philippi think of Rome as their native land to which they belong, in whose tribal records they are enrolled, whose dress they wear, whose language they speak, by whose laws they are governed, whose protection they enjoy, and whose emperor they worship as their Savior? In a sense far more sublime and real these *Christians* dwelling in Philippi must realize that *their homeland* or *commonwealth* [165] has its fixed location in heaven. It was heaven that gave them birth, for they are born from above. Their names are inscribed on heaven's register. Their lives are being governed from heaven and in accordance with heavenly standards. Their rights are secured in heaven. Their interests are being promoted there. To heaven their thoughts and prayers ascend and their hopes aspire.

---

[162] See W. Hendriksen, *The Bible on the Life Hereafter,* pp. 195-199.

[163] The idea for which the conjunction γάρ states the reason must often be inferred from the context. So also in this instance. See L.N.T. (A. and G.) entry γάρ, under 1, e., p. 151.

[164] Note position of ἡμῶν at the very beginning of the sentence.

[165] On the term πολίτευμα, *Gemeinwesen* or *Heimat (commonwealth* or *homeland),* see Hermann Strathmann's article in Th.W.N.T., Vol. 6, p. 535.

Many of their friends, members of the fellowship, are there even now, and they themselves, the citizens of the heavenly kingdom who are still on earth, will follow shortly. Yes, in heaven their inheritance awaits them. Their heavenly mansions are being prepared. See such passages as John 3:3; 14:1-4; Rom. 8:17; Eph. 2:6; Col. 3:1-3; Heb. 4:14-16; 6:19, 20; 7:25; 12:22-24; I Peter 1:4, 5; Rev. 7:9-17. Yes, Jerusalem that is above is their mother (Gal. 4:26). They are fellow-citizens with the saints and of the household of God (Eph. 2:19). On this earth they are strangers, sojourners, and pilgrims (Heb. 11:13; I Peter 2:11). "They desire a better country, that is, a heavenly one. Therefore God is not ashamed to be called their God, for he has prepared for them a city" (Heb. 11:16). Above all, in heaven dwells their *Head,* and they are *the Body;* so infinitely close is their relation to heaven! And this Head is, indeed, Savior. In fact, he is the only, the real Savior, who is coming again to deliver them from all their enemies and to draw them as closely as possible to his own bosom. Hence, Paul continues, **from which** [166] **we also are eagerly awaiting as Savior, the Lord Jesus Christ.**

The hope of Christ's Return has sanctifying power: "every one who has this hope set on him purifies himself even as he is pure" (I John 3:3). If a person makes a god of his belly and sets his mind on earthly things, how can he ever expect to be welcomed by the spotlessly holy and infinitely glorious Christ at his brilliant advent? This surely is the reason — at least one of the chief reasons — why the coming of Christ is here mentioned.

Believers *are eagerly awaiting* [167] their Lord. Theirs in not the attitude of the men of Laodicea, that of lukewarmness (Rev. 3:14-22); nor the attitude of some people in Thessalonica, that of nervousness (II Thess. 2:1, 2); but rather the attitude of the Smyrniots, that of faithfulness. The latter, while looking forward to the crown of life, remained faithful unto death (Rev. 2: 8-11). The citizens of the kingdom of heaven, looking *away from* all sinful pleasures, *eagerly* yearn *to welcome* their Savior, the Lord Jesus Christ. They await his manifestation in glory (I Cor. 1:7; Col. 3:4). It is a waiting *in faith* (Gal. 5:5), with *patient endurance* (Rom. 8:25), and *unto salvation* (Heb. 9:28). In a sense, the entire creation is eagerly looking forward for this great event, when from its present corruption and futility it shall be delivered, being transferred into the sphere of the glorious liberty of the children of God (Rom. 8:21).

Note that believers are yearning for *the Lord Jesus Christ* (see on Phil. 2:10) in his capacity as *Savior.* Even as Judge he will still be *their* Savior. The word Savior is also applied to Christ in Eph. 5:23; II Tim. 1:10; Titus

---

166 The flexible character of Greek grammar certainly makes it possible for ἐξ οὗ to refer adverbially to οὐρανοῖς, plural. The latter noun, though plural in form, must frequently be regarded as singular in connotation.
167 See Walter Grundmann's article on δέχομαι and cognates in Th.W.N.T., Vol. II, p. 49 ff., especially p. 55.

1:4; 2:13; 3:6. In fact, in Titus 2:13 Jesus is called "our great God and Savior." Not this or that heathen deity nor the Roman emperor but the Lord Jesus Christ is the real Savior whom believers are eagerly expecting. As their Savior he will deliver them from the final results of sin, will completely vindicate them and their cause, and will bestow upon them the glorious inheritance of the saints in the light, in a marvelously rejuvenated universe.

Though the glories of the intermediate state, that is, the happiness that will be the believer's portion during the interval between death and bodily resurrection, are not absent from the mind of the apostle (see Phil. 1:21, 23), nevertheless, he does not fall into the error into which we are so prone to become ensnared, namely, that of emphasizing the intermediate state at the expense of the Lord's advent! Will not the latter glory — in which *all* the saints of *all* the ages will take part, and in which Christ will be vindicated before *all* the world — be even greater than the former?

Paul continues, **who will refashion our lowly body so that it will have a form like his own glorious body.** By many Greek pagans the body was viewed as a prison from which at death the soul will be delivered. The body was intrinsically "vile." To Paul, however, that body was a temple, even the sanctuary of the Holy Spirit (I Cor. 6:19). To be sure, right now, as a result of the entrance of sin, it is "the body of our *humiliation*" (cf. cognate verb in Phil. 2:8, "he *humbled* himself"). As such it is exposed to sin's curse in the form of weakness, suffering, sickness, ugliness, futility, death, but at his coming the Savior — who is a *complete* Savior — will refashion it in such a manner that this new outward *fashion* or *appearance* will truly reflect the new and lasting inner *form*,[168] for it will have a *form* like the glorious body of the ascended Lord. We shall be "conformed to the image of his (the Father's) Son" (Rom. 8:29). We shall "bear the image of the heavenly" (I Cor. 15:49). "When he will be manifested, we shall be like him, for we shall see him even as he is" (I John 3:2). The nature of this great change is detailed in I Cor. 15:42-44, 50-58.

The question occurs, however, "But how will this be possible?" What about those martyrs who were devoured by lions? What about those who were burned alive? Yes, what about millions of others, particles of whose dead and decaying bodies, through various stages of disintegration, finally enter into other living bodies? An answer that would be completely "satisfying" to the mind of man — the mind darkened by sin! — is not available. One outstanding fact remains, however. That fact is the almightly power of One who could not be held even by death. Hence, the apostle concludes this exalted paragraph by saying **(and who will do this) by the exertion —** or **exercise — of that power which enables him to subject even all things to himself.** Marvelous is the *energy* of Christ's *dynamite*, that is, of his

---

[168] As to distinction between *fashion* and *form* see on Phil. 2:5-8.

PHILIPPIANS

Synthesis of Chapter 3

For this see the Summary at the beginning of the chapter.

Seed-thoughts of Chapter 3

(1) Christian joy can be cultivated (verse 1).

(2) Even Paul repeated himself, *when necessary* (verse 1).

(3) *Meekness* does not mean *weakness*. The maxim "See no evil" is in need of explanation and perhaps qualification (verse 2).

(4) No *demerit* is so great and harmful as *self-merit* (verse 3).

(5) The Christian has not truly *arrived* until he arrives in glory: "If only I may attain" is the language of the truly saved man. The believer is the enemy of the *status quo* (verses 4-14).

(6) Though justification is a once-for-all affair, the believer desires an ever richer assurance of having obtained this great blessing. Absolute perfection also in this respect is not reached in the here and now. He who spoke the words of Ps. 27:1 also spoke those of I Sam. 27:1. He who praised God by those of I Kings 18:36, 37, also uttered the lamentation found in I Kings 19:4, 10. And then there is the need of sanctification in all other respects (verses 8b-14).

(7) Every Christian is a true perfectionist or idealist (verses 8b-14).

(8) "We love him because he first loved us." We take hold on him because he first took hold of us (verse 12).

(9) Divine preservation implies human perseverance (verses 12-14).

(10) Not only mulling over past failures but also gloating over past "successes" is an enemy of spiritual progress (verse 13).

(11) Those who major on minors, forgetting the real goal of the Christian life, are immature (verse 15).

(12) Be consistent (verse 16).

(13) The sensualist is not a Christian (verses 17-19).

(14) Not the intermediate state but the state of final glory in the new heaven and earth, together with all the saints, at Christ's Return, should be most strongly emphasized in preaching and in meditation (verses 20, 21).

Summary of Chapter 4

Verses 1-9

Paul, the Tactful Pastor

in general, exhorting the brothers at Philippi to remain firm; and in particular, entreating Euodia and Syntyche to be of the same mind, and Syzygus to help these gospel-women;

urging the Philippians to rejoice in the Lord, to be big-hearted to all, and instead of worrying to bring everything to God in prayer that brings peace; finally, admonishing the addressees to meditate only on praiseworthy things, practising these in imitation of Paul and with promise of rich reward.

4:1-3 Exhortations: to all, Remain firm; to two women, Live in harmony; to Syzygus, Help these women.

4:4-7 The secret of true blessedness: Rejoice, Be big-hearted, Instead of worrying pray.

4:8, 9 Summary of Christian Duty: proper meditation, proper action.

CHAPTER IV

4 1 So then, my brothers, beloved and longed for, my joy and crown, so stand fast in the Lord, beloved.

2 I entreat Eudia and I entreat Syntyche to be of the same mind in the Lord. 3 Yes, I request you also, Syzygus (Yoke-fellow), in deed as well as in name,[169] lend these women a hand, for they strove side by side with me in the gospel, along with Clement and the rest of my fellow-workers, whose names (are) in the book of life.

4:1-3

I. *Various Exhortations: General and Specific*

1. Here we are face to face with *Paul, the tactful pastor.* The opening words of the chapter, **So then,** clearly indicate that there is the closest connection with what precedes. That connection may be stated as follows: Because the believers' homeland is in heaven and not on earth, and because a glorious inheritance awaits them at Christ's Return, when even their bodies will be made to resemble Christ's body both outwardly and inwardly, let nothing sway them from their firm foundation. Let them always remain steadfast and sure, so that these glories may be theirs indeed.

Very touching is the manner in which the tactful pastor addresses his charges. Note: **my brothers** — just as in 3:1 —, **beloved,** with a love that is deep-seated, self-sacrificing, thorough, intelligent, and purposeful, a love in which the entire personality takes part,[170] **and longed for,** "with the deeply-felt affection of Christ Jesus" (see on Phil. 1:7, 8), **my joy and crown.** The Philippians are the joy of the apostle's heart because the fruits of the Holy Spirit are clearly evident in their lives. Hence, he praises them again and again, and thanks God for them (Phil. 1:3-7, 29, 30; 2:12, 17; 4:10, 14-20). For the same reason they are also his *crown,* his *adorning-wreath* or *festive garland.* This is true, in a sense, even now but will become even more clearly evident at the coming of the Lord, when it will become manifest to all that these are the fruits of Paul's missionary labors, showing that he did not run in vain or labor in vain (Phil. 2:16). The passage should

---

169 Or simply, *genuine Syzygus* (Yoke-fellow).
170 For the meaning of the cognate verb ἀγαπάω see detailed discussion in N.T.C. on the Gospel of John, Vol. II, pp. 494-500, footnote 306.

be compared with similar language in I Thess. 2:19, 20. It is evident from these words that this was, indeed, a fine congregation, and that the heart of the prisoner went out to them. He pours out his affection upon them, without any attempt to hold back. His exhortation to them all is: **So stand fast in the Lord, beloved.** In view of their high calling, the blessings they have already received, and the inheritance that awaits them (Phil. 1:6; 3:20, 21), let them remain ever firm and steadfast, over against hostile pagans, merely nominal Christians such as legalists and libertines, and the promptings of their own sinful hearts. Let them do so by the continued exercise of their faith in the Lord Jesus Christ.

2. After such an endearing introduction addressed to each and to all, the needed admonition intended for two individuals cannot seem harsh: **I entreat Euodia** — the name means *prosperous journey* — **and I entreat Syntyche** —meaning *fortunate* [171] — **to be of the same mind in the Lord.** Here once again as so often before (Phil. 1:27, 28; 2:2-4; 2:14-16; 3:1) the apostle stresses the idea of militant *unity* in a world of unbelief and hostility. This time, however, the admonition is given a *particular* application.

With respect to Euodia and Syntyche the following facts only can be safely affirmed:

(1) They were, at this writing, and had been for some time, members of the church at Philippi.

(2) When the church was founded and/or at a later visit of Paul to Philippi, they had been the apostle's fellow-workers, and as such had co-operated harmoniously and enthusiastically with each other and with Paul and his companions (verse 3).

(3) An important disagreement, related to kingdom-work, had arisen between them, which called forth this apostolic admonition.

(4) They are still the object of Paul's high regard and deep-rooted, Christian love. They are Christians!

Views which are highly speculative and fanciful are the following:

(1) One of them was Lydia (Acts 16:14, 15).

(2) The two names represent the Jewish and the Gentile section of the church at Philippi (F. C. Baur and the Tübingen School).

(3) The two are the Philippian jailer and his wife. Objection: "these *women*," verse 3.

Paul tenderly *pleads with* — as it were, *calls to his side* — *each* of these women, begging each to return to a harmonious disposition so as to work together as a team. Note the tactful repetition of the verb. The apostle does not say "I entreat Euodia and Syntyche," but, as if to emphasize his tender solicitude and high regard *for each*, he says, "I entreat Euodia and

---

[171] See on Phil. 2:25, footnote 116 under C.

I entreat Syntyche." A wonderful hint for pastors here! Let Euodia and let Syntyche reflect on the fact that their Lord has been — and still is — very gracious to them, and that their present open disharmony does not further his cause. The result of this pious reflection will be that "in the Lord" — praying together and leaning hard on him — they will again become of the same mind.

3. Paul now enlists the aid of another member of the church at Philippi, namely, Syzygus, in order that he may help these women to compose their difference: **Yes, I request you also, Syzygus (Yoke-fellow) in deed as well as in name, lend these women a hand.** Literally, the original has here, "Yes, I request you also, genuine Syzygus." In all probability, however, the apostle is making use here of a play on a name, for Syzygus means Yoke-fellow, a person who pulls well in a harness for two, and Paul is saying that Syzygus was true to his name. A similar pun occurs in Philem. 11: "Onesimus (Useful) who once was *useless* to you but now is *useful* to you and to me." It is safe to infer that Syzygus, about whom we have no further information, was one of Paul's comrades or associates in the work of the gospel. When this letter was written he was a prominent member of the church at Philippi, a man of influence who was highly esteemed by his people. Like the apostle himself, he must have been a man of extraordinary tact. Otherwise Paul would not have requested him to lend a hand in restoring harmony between two women.[172]

Speaking of these women Paul continues, **For they** [173] **strove side by side with me in the gospel.** These women deserve to be assisted. They were, after all, *noble* women. Well does the apostle remember the time when they *contended at his side* (for the verb, see on Phil. 1:27) against a common foe and in the gospel-cause. Eagerly they had worked together, and this not only with Paul but also, says the apostle, **along with Clement,** not otherwise known,[174] **and the rest of my fellow-workers, whose names (are) in the book**

---

[172] The reading as proper name is preferable. Other views as to the identity of this individual:
(1) "true yoke-fellow," not a proper name, merely descriptive. Objections: a. This is out of line with the other proper names here mentioned: Euodia, Syntyche, Clement. b. Nowhere else does Paul call his fellow-workers by the name *yokefellows*.
(2) Lydia. Objection: the adjective γνήσιε is vocative, sing., *masc.*
(3) Paul's wife. Objection: same as above, as well as other objections.
(4) Timothy. Objection: he was one of the senders of the letter (see on Phil. 1:1).
(5) Epaphroditus. Objection: he was in all probability the man who carried and delivered the letter. For the apostle to address him in the body of this letter would have been very unnatural.
(6) Other guesses, equally unnatural, or in some cases even more so: Silas, Luke, Christ!
[173] αἵτινες: inasmuch as they, etc.
[174] That he is to be identified with Clement of Rome is mere fancy.

of life. Why are not these other fellow-workers mentioned by name? Were there too many to mention? Is the apostle unable at this moment to recall all their names? Or is he implying that some had already died and their names had been forgotten? At any rate their names were known to God! They are in *the book of life.* "When earthly citizens die, their names are erased from the records; the names of the spiritual conquerors will never be blotted out; their glorious life will endure. Christ himself will publicly acknowledge them as his very own! He will do this before the Father and before his angels. Cf. Matt. 10:32; Luke 12:8, 9." [175] With respect to this *book of life* see also Exod. 32:32; Ps. 69:28; Dan. 12:1; Mal. 3:16, 17; Luke 10:20; Rev. 3:5; 13:8; 17:8; 20:12, 15; 21:27; 22:19.

---

4 Rejoice in the Lord always; again I will say, Rejoice. 5 Let y o u r big-heartedness be known to everybody. The Lord (is) at hand. 6 In nothing be anxious, but in everything by prayer and supplication with thanksgiving let y o u r petitions be made known before God. 7 And the peace of God that surpasses all understanding will keep guard over y o u r hearts and y o u r thoughts in Christ Jesus.

4:4-7

II. *The Secret of True Blessedness*

4:4-6

A. *What to Do to Obtain It*

(1) Let joy reign *within*

4. Once again, as so often before, the apostle stresses the duty of rejoicing. He says, **Rejoice in the Lord always; again I will say, Rejoice.** The exhortation is repeated, probably because on the surface it seems so unreasonable to rejoice *in obedience to a command,* and perhaps even more unreasonable to rejoice *always,* under all circumstances no matter how trying. Can one truly rejoice when the memory of past sins vexes the soul, when dear ones are suffering, when one is being persecuted, facing possible death? But there is Paul, who does, indeed, remember his past sins (Phil. 3:6; cf. Gal. 1:13; I Cor. 15:9), whose friends are really suffering (Phil. 1:29, 30), who is even now a prisoner facing possible death; yet, who rejoices and tells others to do likewise! It is evident from this that circumstances alone do not determine the condition of heart and mind. A Christian can be joyful *within* when *without* all is dark and dreary. He rejoices *in the Lord,* that

[175] Quoted from my book *More Than Conquerors,* p. 92.

is, because of his oneness with Christ, the fruit of whose Spirit is *joy* (Gal. 5:22). This is reasonable, for in and through Christ all things — also those that seem most unfavorable — work together for good (Rom. 8:28).

It was not unreasonable for Paul *to exhort* the Philippians to rejoice, for the disposition of joy can be and should be cultivated. This can be done, as the apostle indicates in the context (see verse 8), by meditating on the proper subjects, that is, by taking account of the things that should stand out in our consciousness. For Paul such reasons for joy, the joy unspeakable and full of glory, were the following: that he was a saved individual whose purpose was in his entire person to magnify Christ (1:19, 20); that this Savior, in whose cross, crown, and coming again he glories (2:5-11; 3:20, 21; 4:5), was able and willing to supply his every need (4:11-13, 19, 20); that others, too, were being saved (1:6; 2:17, 18), the apostle himself being used by God for this glorious purpose; that he had many friends and helpers in the gospel-cause, who together formed a glorious *fellowship* in the Lord (1:5; 2:19-30; 4:1, 10); that God was causing all things, even bonds, to work together for good (1:12-18; cf. Rom. 8:28), so that even death is gain when life is Christ (1:21, 23); and that at all times he has freedom of access to the throne of grace (4:6). Let the Philippians meditate on these things and rejoice, yes rejoice *always*.

5a. (2) Let big-heartedness be shown *all around*.

A Christian should cultivate an outgoing personality. The secret of his happiness is not confined within the walls of his own meditation and reflection. He cannot be truly happy without striving to be a blessing to others. Hence, Paul continues, **Let y o u r big-heartedness be known to everybody.** For *big-heartedness* one may substitute any of the following: forbearance, yieldedness, geniality, kindliness, gentleness, sweet reasonableness, considerateness, charitableness, mildness, magnanimity, generosity. All of these qualities are combined in the adjective-noun that is used in the original. Taken together they show the real meaning. When each of these would-be-English-equivalents is taken by itself alone, it becomes clear that there is not a single word in the English language that fully expresses the meaning of the original.[176]

The lesson which Paul teaches is that true blessedness cannot be obtained by the person who rigorously insists on whatever he regards as his just due. The Christian is the man who reasons that it is far better to *suffer* wrong than to *inflict* wrong (I Cor. 6:7). Sweet reasonableness is an essential ingredient of true happiness. Now such big-heartedness, such forbearance, the patient willingness to yield wherever yielding is possible without violating any real principle, must be shown *to all,* not only to fellow-believers.

---

[176] For the adjective ἐπιεικής see I Tim. 3:3; Titus 3:2; James 3:17; I Peter 2:18; for the noun ἐπιείκεια see Acts 24:4; II Cor. 10:1.

This Christian magnanimity probably stands in very close connection with the comfort which the Christian derives from the coming of the Lord, which coming has already been mentioned (Phil. 3:20, 21) and is about to be mentioned once more (4:5b, "the Lord is at hand"). The idea seems to be: since Christ's coming is near, when all the promises made to God's people will become realities, believers, in spite of being persecuted, can certainly afford to be mild and charitable in their relation to others.[177]

5b, 6. (3) Let there be no worry but prayerful trusting in God *above.*

Joy *within,* big-heartedness *all around,* and now prayerful trusting in God *above.* Says Paul, **The Lord (is) at hand.** In view of the immediate context (3:20, 21) the meaning is probably not, "The Lord is always nearby or present," (cf. Ps. 145:18) but rather, "The Lord is coming very soon." This, of course, is strictly true with respect to every believer. If the Lord arrives from heaven before the believer dies, then no one surely will be able to doubt that this coming was, indeed, *at hand.* But if the death of the believer occurs before the day of Christ's coming, then two facts remain true both for the believer's own consciousness and according to the clear teaching of Scripture: a. The believer's life-span here on earth was very, very brief. In fact, it amounted to a mere breath (Ps. 39:5; 90:10; 103:15, 16); and b. the interval between the entrance of his soul into heaven and the Lord's second coming was but "a little season" (Rev. 6:11), for in heaven he was geared to a different kind of time-scale.[178] Hence, take it either way, Paul had every right to say, "The Lord (is) at hand." Whatever happens in history is a preparation for this coming, which, as has been shown, will in either case be *soon.* This does not mean that the apostle excludes the possibility that *by earthly reckoning* there could still be an interval of many years before the Lord's arrival. He is not setting any dates (see I Thess. 5:1-3; II Thess. 2:1-3). In view of the fact that no one knows the day and the hour when Jesus will return (Matt. 24:36), it behooves every one to be ready, working, watching at all times (Matt. 25:1-13). At the coming of the Lord all wrongs will be righted, and the believer will stand in the presence of his Lord, fully vindicated. Hence, let him not make too much of disappointments, or unduly trouble himself about the future. So Paul continues, **In nothing be anxious** or "stop being anxious about anything." (See also N.T.C. on John 14:1-4.) There is such a thing as *kindly concern,* that is, *genuine interest* in the welfare of others. The verb (used in Phil. 4:6, and here rendered "be anxious") can elsewhere have a favorable meaning, as it does, in fact, in this very epistle (2:20): Timothy *was genuinely interested* in the welfare of the Philippians. Often, however, it indicates

---

[177] Thus also H. Preisker, article ἐπιείκεια, ἐπιεικής, Th.W.N.T., Vol. II, pp. 585-587.
[178] See my book *The Bible and the Life Hereafter,* Chapter 14, "Is There Time in Heaven?" pp. 70-74.

to be unduly concerned about, to be filled with anxiety, to worry. Such worry may be about food or drink or clothes or one's life-span or the future or words to be spoken in self-defense or even about "many things" (Matt. 6:25-28, 34; 10:19; Luke 10:41; 12:11). The cure for worry is prayer. Hence, the apostle continues, **but in everything by prayer and supplication with thanksgiving let y o u r petitions be made known before God.**

The cure for worry is not *inaction.* If one wishes to plant a garden, build a house, make a sermon, or do anything else, he cannot attain his objective by prayer *alone.* There must be careful planning. There must be *reflection* leading to *action.* Paul is not forgetting this. In fact, the *reflection* is stressed in verse 8, the *action* in verse 9. On the other hand, however, it is also true that reflection and action without prayer would be futile. In fact so very important is prayer to the Christian that it is mentioned first of all (verse 6b).

Neither is the cure for worry *apathy.* God never tells us to suppress every desire. On the contrary, he says, "Open your mouth wide, and I will fill it" (Ps. 81:10). Proper desires should be cultivated, not killed.

The proper antidote for anxiety is *the outpouring of the heart to God.* Here questions occur:

a. *In connection with what situations or circumstances should this take place?*

Answer: "in everything." Note the sharp contrast: *"In nothing* be anxious but *in everything* . . . let y o u r petitions be made known before God." Because of the specific context here, *the emphasis* is, nevertheless, on all such circumstances which might otherwise cause one to worry: "Cast all y o u r anxiety upon him, because he cares for y o u" (I Peter 5:7). The outpouring of the heart to God should, of course, not be *restricted* to this.

> "Sweet hour of prayer, sweet hour of prayer,
>   That calls me from a world of care,
>   And bids me at My Father's throne.
>   Make all my wants and wishes known!"
>   (W. W. Walford)

b. *In what frame of mind should this be done?*

Answer: *with reverence and true devotion.* That is implied in the words, "by prayer." *Prayer* is any form of reverent address directed to God.

c. *What is the nature of this activity?*

Answer: *it amounts to supplication.* Note: "and supplication." By this is meant the humble cry for the fulfilment of needs that are keenly felt.[179]

---

[179] προσευχή is the more general term; δέησις the more particular. The two words occur together also in Eph. 6:18; I Tim. 2:1; 5:5. The former is always addressed to God; the latter to either God or man. See R. C. Trench, *Synonyms of the New Testament,* paragraph li. Also N.T.C. on I Tim. 2:1.

d. *What is the condition of acceptance?*

Answer: that this be done "with thanksgiving." This implies humility, submission to God's will, knowing that this will is always best. There must be grateful acknowledgement for: a. past favors, b. present blessings, and c. firmly-grounded assurances for the future. Paul begins nearly every one of his epistles with an outpouring of thanksgiving to God. Throughout his writings he again and again insists on the necessity of giving thanks (Rom. 1:21; 14:6; II Cor. 1:11; 4:15; 9:11, 12; Eph. 5:20; Col. 3:15; etc.). Prayer without thanksgiving is like a bird without wings: such a prayer cannot rise to heaven, can find no acceptance with God.

e. *What are the contents?*

Answer: not vague generalities. The prayer, "Lord, bless all that awaiteth thy blessing" may be proper at times but can be overdone. It is easy to resort to it when one has nothing definite to ask. Paul says, "Let y o u r *petitions* be made known before God." There must be *definite, specific requests* (I John 5:15). That is also clear from the example given us in what is commonly called "The Lord's Prayer" (Matt. 6:9-13). Note also the preposition *before,* in "before God." One enters into the very presence of God, realizing that nothing is too great for his power to accomplish nor too small for his love to be concerned about. Is he not our Father who in Christ loves us with an infinite love?

4:7

B. *The Result*

7. Now if joy in the Lord reigns *within* the heart, if magnanimity is shown *all around* to everybody with whom one comes into contact, and if there be constant prayer to God *above,* the result will be *peace.* Paul begins the next sentence by saying, **And the peace of God that surpasses all understanding.** This sweet peace originates in God who himself possesses it in his own being. He is glad to impart it to his children. It is, therefore, "the gift of God's love." He not only gives it; he also maintains it at every step. Hence, it has every right to be called "the peace *of* God." It is founded on grace. It is merited for believers by Christ (see John 14:27; 16:33; 20:19, 21, 26). Paul speaks of this peace in every one of his letters, often at the opening and at the close, sometimes also in the body of the epistle. In Philippians Paul mentions it, as almost always, immediately after *grace* (in I and II Timothy *mercy* is interposed between *grace* and *peace*). See on Phil. 1:2. Peace is the smile of God reflected in the soul of the believer. It is the heart's calm after Calvary's storm. It is the firm conviction that he who spared not his own Son will surely also, along with him, freely give us all things (Rom. 8:32). "Thou wilt keep him in perfect peace, whose mind is stayed on thee, because he trusts in thee" (Isa. 26:3). In the present context it is the God-given reward resulting from *joy*ful reflection on God's bounties, *magnanimity* toward the neighbor, and trustful *prayer* to God.

This peace *passes all understanding*. With respect to this modifier an interpretation favored by many is this: "God's gift of peace will do far more for us than will any clever planning or calculating on our part. In that sense *peace* surpasses our *understanding*." Objections, which I share with many, are the following:

(1) This interpretation takes the word *understanding* in a too limited sense.

(2) The parallel, Eph. 3:19, is clear. In that passage the love of Christ is said to surpass knowledge in the sense that, try as they may, believers will never succeed in measuring it in all its breadth, length, height, and depth (Eph. 3:18). Surely, if the passage about Christ's love means that this love is *unfathomable*, why should not the passage about God's *peace* have the same meaning?

By nature man is as totally unable to comprehend this wonderful peace as is a blind man to appreciate a glorious sunset (I. Cor. 2:14). And even the believer will never be able fully to grasp the beauty of this Christ-centered gift that surpasses in value all other gifts of God to man. One reason why it is justly esteemed to be very, very precious is that it **will keep guard over y o u r hearts and y o u r thoughts in Christ Jesus**. The Philippians were used to the sight of Roman sentinels standing guard. Thus also, only far more so, God's peace will mount guard at the door of heart and thought. It will prevent carking care from corroding the heart, which is the mainspring of life (Prov. 4:23), the root of thinking (Rom. 1:21), willing (I Cor. 7:37), and feeling (Phil. 1:7; see on that passage). It will also prevent unworthy reasonings from entering thought-life. Thus, if any one should tell the believer that God does not exist and that everlasting life is a mere dream, he would get nowhere, for at that very moment the child of God would be experiencing within himself the realities which the infidel is trying to reason out of existence. The man of trust and prayer has entered that impregnable citadel from which no one can dislodge him; and the name of that fortress is *Christ Jesus* (note: "in Christ Jesus").

---

8 For the rest, brothers, whatever things are true, whatever things (are) honorable, whatever things (are) just, whatever things (are) pure, whatever things (are) lovely, whatever things (are) of good report; if (there be) any virtue and if (there be) any praise, be thinking about these things. 9 The things which y o u not only learned and received but also heard and saw in me, these things put into constant practice; and the God of peace will be with y o u.

4:8, 9

III. *Summary of Christian Duty*

A. *Proper Meditation*

8. For the rest — see on 3:1 — **brothers** — see on 1:12 — **whatever things
are true.** Many are of the opinion that the apostle is here copying a paragraph from a pagan book on morality or from this or that Manual of Discipline circulated by an Essenic sect. Objections:

(1) The definitely Christian character of this exhortation is clear from the reference to *the peace of God* which precedes it and *the God of peace* which follows it.

(2) It is also clear from the fact that the apostle states that *these things* have been heard and seen *in himself.* Surely, the Philippians had seen *Christian* virtues displayed in Paul!

(3) Wherever possible, words used by Paul in any passage should be interpreted in the light of their true parallels in Scripture, especially in Paul's own letters.

Note the six occurrences of *whatever*, followed by two instances of *any.* Believers should exhibit not just this or that trait of Christian character but "all the graces in choral order and festal array" (Johnstone).

The apostle tells the Philippians to meditate on whatever things are *true.* Truth stands over against falsehood (Eph. 4:25). It has its norm in God (Rom. 3:4), goes hand in hand with goodness, righteousness, and holiness (Eph. 4:24; 5:9) and is climaxed in gospel-truth (Eph. 1:13; 4:21; Col. 1:5, 6). Truth belongs to the armor of the Christian soldier (Eph. 6:14).

Paul adds, **whatever things (are) honorable.** In his speech and in his entire behavior believers should be dignified, serious. Proper *motives, manners,* and *morals* are very important. In an environment then as now characterized by *frivolity* whatever things are honorable surely merit *earnest consideration.* See also I Tim. 2:2; 3:4; Titus 2:2, 7; 3:8.

So also **whatever things (are) just.** Having received from God *righteousness* both of imputation and impartation, believers should think righteous thoughts. They should, in their mind, gratefully meditate on God's righteous acts (Rev. 15:3), appreciate righteousness in others, and should plan righteous words and deeds. Masters, for example, should take account of what is fair and square in dealing with their servants. They should realize that they, too, have an Employer in heaven (Col. 4:1). In all his planning, let the Christian ask himself, "Is this in harmony with God's will and law?"

Next, **whatever things (are) pure.** The Philippians, because of their background and surroundings (both *pagan,* cf. Eph. 5:8, and *antinomian,* cf. Phil. 3:18, 19) were being constantly tempted by that which was *unchaste.* Let them therefore fill their minds with whatever is pure and holy. See also II Cor. 11:2; I Tim. 5:22; Titus 2:5. Cf. James 3:17; I John 3:3. *Let them overcome evil with good* (Rom. 12:21). A wonderful direction also for the present day!

Whatever things (are) lovely follows immediately. The word *lovely*, though occurring only in this one instance in the New Testament, is rather common in epitaphs. That which is *lovely, amiable, pleasing,* breathes love and evokes love. Let believers meditate and take into account all such things.

Whatever things (are) of good report (only occurrence of this adjective in New Testament, but see cognate noun in II Cor. 6:8) closes this list of six whatever's. These things are *well-sounding, appealing.* Even upon non-Christians they may make a good impression. The main consideration is, however, that in their inner essence they are actually worthy of creating that impression.

Paul summarizes: **If (there be) any virtue and if (there be) any praise, be thinking about these things.** Nothing that is really worthwhile for believers to ponder and take into consideration is omitted from this summarizing phrase. Anything at all that is a matter of moral and spiritual excellence, so that it is the proper object of praise, is the right pasture for the Christian mind to graze in. *Nothing* that is of a contrary nature is the right food for his thought. It is hardly necessary to repeat that the *virtue* of which the apostle speaks is the fruit which grows on the tree of *salvation.* The trunk of this tree is *faith,* and its roots are imbedded in the soil of God's sovereign, saving *grace* (Eph. 2:8-10; II Peter 1:5). To be sure, the believer is not at all blind to the fact that "there remain in man, since the fall, the glimmerings of natural light, whereby he retains some knowledge of God, of natural things, and of the difference between good and evil, and shows some regard for virtue and for good outward behavior" (Canons of Dort III and IV, article 4). In a sense even sinners *do good* (Luke 6:33), and even publicans *love* (Matt. 5:46). To deny this, in the interest of this or that theological presupposition, would be to fly in the face of the clear teaching of Scripture and the facts of everyday observation and experience. But surely when Paul told the Philippians to be constantly thinking about anything that is virtuous and worthy of praise, he, great idealist that he was, could not have been satisfied with anything that was less than goodness in the highest, spiritual sense (that which proceeds from faith, is done according to God's law, and to his glory).

This follows also from the continuation:

B. *Proper Action*

9. The things which y o u not only learned and received but also heard and saw in me these things put into constant practice. It becomes very clear now that the *thinking* or *meditation* of which the apostle spoke in the preceding passage was not of an abstractly theoretical character. It was thinking *with a purpose,* and that purpose lies in the sphere of *action.* This is also the teaching of The Sermon on the Mount and of Christ's parables (Matt. 7:24; 13:23; Luke 8:15). True believers *hear.* They meditate until they *understand.* Then they *act* upon it, putting it into *constant practice,* thereby showing that their house was built upon a rock.

The *learning and receiving* of which the apostle speaks here in verse 9 represents one idea; the *hearing and seeing* the other. Paul and others had taught the Philippians the matters summarized in verse 8, and they had accepted them. But the apostle had also exemplified these virtues in his own daily conduct. The Philippians had heard about this from various sources and by the mouth of ever so many messengers. Even by means of the present letter they are hearing about it, and Epaphroditus will surely fill in the details. Moreover, both on his first visit and on subsequent stopovers they have seen these graces displayed in Paul. Hence, the apostle had a right to say, "Brothers, join in being imitators of me" (Phil. 3:17).

The result of such constant Christian practice is stated in the words, **And the God of peace will be with y o u.** The expression *the God of peace* here in verse 9 complements and brings to a climax the phrase *the peace of God* of verse 7. Not only will the Philippians who obey these instructions receive God's most wonderful gift; they will also have as their constant Helper and Friend the Giver himself!

Synthesis of 4:1-9

Exhortations (general and specific) to remain firm and live in unity, an *answer* to the question how true blessedness can be obtained, and a *summary* of Christian duty: these thoughts fill the present section.

In a world of unbelief and hostility believers should continue to take a definite stand for their convictions. Theirs should be the attitude of militant unity. Very tactfully and lovingly Paul admonishes two women of the congregation to settle their dispute and live in harmony. While he administers a veiled rebuke, he yet praises them for their earnest and co-operative effort in days gone by. In fact, he even honors them by mentioning them in one breath with other then-famous gospel-workers. He appoints Syzygus — Yoke-fellow is his name and a true Yoke-fellow he is! — to lend them a hand in arriving at the ideal of true, Christian unity.

He points out that the secret of true blessedness consists in permitting spiritual joy to reign *within,* showing magnanimity *all around,* and trustfully bringing every need to the attention of God *above.* Such taking hold on God must be *reverent* (it must be true *praying*), *humble (supplicating),* *thankful* (no prayer is complete without *thanksgiving*), and *definite* (making definite *petitions* or *requests*). Result: God's peace incomprehensible in its grandeur, will stand guard at the door of the believers' hearts and thoughts, preventing the entrance of fears and doubts.

The summary of Christian duty may be expressed in this one thought that in all their thinking with a view to future deeds believers should strive to overcome evil with good; that is, that which is true, honorable, just, pure, lovely, and of good report must crowd out whatever is base. Let virtue conquer vice! Reward: not only the peace of God but the God of peace will be with them.

Summary of Chapter 4

Verses 10-23

Paul, the Grateful Recipient

rejoicing in the generosity of the Philippians, and testifying that he has learned the secret of contentment and of readiness for every task;

resuming and completing his expression of appreciation for the generosity which the Philippians have shown both in the more recent and in the more distant past;

confessing his faith in God who will supply every need, and ascribing glory to him; and

concluding his letter with words of greeting and benediction.

4:10-13   Thank-y o u note begun; testimony: the secret learned.
4:14-18   Thank y o u note resumed and completed.
4:19, 20 Assurance of God's loving care, Doxology.
4:21-23   Conclusion.

10 Now I rejoice in the Lord greatly that now at length y o u caused
y o u r concern for my welfare to bloom afresh; a matter with reference to which
y o u were indeed concerned, but y o u lacked opportunity. 11 Not that I mention
(this) because of want; for I have learned in whatever circumstances I am to be
content. 12 I know what it means to live in straitened circumstances, and I also
know what it means to have plenty; in any and all circumstances I have learned the
secret, both to be filled and to be hungry, both to have plenty and to be in want.
13 I can do all things through him who infuses strength into me.

4:10-13

I. *Thank-y o u Note Begun. Testimony: the Secret Learned*

10. One of Paul's purposes in writing Philippians was to give written expression to his gratitude for the gift received (see Introduction, IV). Says
C. R. Erdman in his Exposition on Philippians, p. 131, "This message of
thanks is a rare blending of affection, of dignity, of delicacy, with a certain
under undertone of gentle pleasantry. It is an embodiment of ideal Christian courtesy." [180]   It begins as follows, **Now I rejoice** [181] **in the Lord greatly
that now at length** [182] **y o u caused y o u r concern for my welfare to bloom
afresh.** [183]   To be sure, there had been this concern, this interest, all along,
just as throughout the winter-season the tree that seems to be dead is actually
alive. But just as in spring-time the tree puts forth fresh shoots, thereby
proving that it is alive, so also the Philippians' interest in Paul had at last
found a way *to express and demonstrate* itself concretely. "In the Lord,"
that is, motivated by the highest possible considerations as being in the
closest union with his Lord, Paul not only rejoices but, in consideration of

---

[180] The question as to Paul's attitude toward accepting remuneration or gifts for
gospel-work has been discussed under ten points in N.T.C. on I and II Thessalonians, pp. 66, 67.
[181] Thus to be rendered if ἐχάρην is an *epistolary* aorist. Something can be said,
however, in favor of the rendering, "I rejoiced," simple *historical* aorist, going back
to the moment when Paul, after a terrible voyage (see Acts 27), had arrived in
Rome, and then, at some later time, was heartened by the visit of Epaphroditus
bringing not only the gift itself but, bound up with it, also the assurance that his
dear friends in Philippi had by no means forgotten him, and, on the whole, were
standing firm in their faith. It is, however, impossible to say definitely whether
this aorist is a direct reference to the past or is epistolary, and this point is surely
of very minor interest, as in either case the apostle must have *rejoiced greatly*
whenever he thought of the Philippians and their gift.
[182] ἤδη ποτὲ as in Rom. 1:10. Not "because of late" (Berkeley Version).
[183] This, it would seem to me, makes better sense than to interpret ἀνεθάλετε intransitively, "Y o u revived with respect to y o u r concern for me." Transitive
meaning also in LXX; e.g., Ezek. 17:24.

203

the *implications* of this gift, even rejoices *greatly*. The apostle guards against misinterpretation by continuing, **a matter with reference to which** [184] **y o u were indeed concerned, but y o u lacked opportunity.** The "matter" of which Paul speaks was, of course, that pertaining to his *welfare*. As soon as the news of Paul's imprisonment had become known in Philippi the desire had sprung up "to do something" to help him. But at first no favorable opportunity had presented itself. It may have been that no messenger had been immediately available, or that for some reason or other it had been impossible to collect the gift from the various members. These are only two out of many possibilities. At any rate, for a while opportunity to send the gift had been lacking. As soon as this situation changed, the Philippians had acted with characteristic enthusiasm and devotion.

11. Paul had been exuberant in his praise. He had said, "I rejoice *greatly*." Here, too, misinterpretation was possible. The question might be asked, "Is not this a weakness in Paul, to go into such raptures over merely *earthly goods*, as if he were a child who had just received a new toy? Or were his remarks to be taken as an expression of dire want, a kind of complaint with the implication, Please send me another gift soon?" To prevent any inferences of this nature the apostle continues, **Not that** [185] **I mention (this) because of want; for I have learned in whatever circumstances I am to be content.** Meaning: "The satisfaction of a material need must not be construed as being either the real reason for or the measure of my joy. On the contrary, regardless of outward circumstances, I would still be satisfied. My conversion-experience, and also my subsequent trials for the sake of Christ and his gospel, have taught me a lesson. The path which I traveled led me ever closer to Christ, to his love, and to his power, yes to Christ and *contentment* in him. That very contentment is riches to me."

12. It is to be noted that this *contentment* or soul-sufficiency (see on I Tim. 6:6) is derived not from any resources which the soul has *in itself*. Paul is no vain boaster who exclaims, "I am the Captain of my soul." He is no Stoic who, *trusting in his own resources*, and supposedly unmoved by either joy or grief, endeavors with all his might to submit without complaining to unavoidable necessity. The apostle is no statue. He is a man of flesh and blood. He knows both joys and sorrows, yet is content. But his contentment has its cause in One other than himself. The real Source or Fountain of Paul's soul-sufficiency is mentioned in verse 13. And that Fountain never runs dry, no matter what may be *the circumstances*. With reference to the latter Paul continues, **I know what it means to live in straitened circumstances, and I also know what it means to have plenty. In any and all**

---

[184] Of the various ways in which ἐφ' ᾧ can be rendered this yields the best sense.
[185] See on 3:12.

circumstances I have learned the secret, both to be filled and to be hungry, both to have plenty and to be in want.

Paul *has learned the secret* (a verb used only here in the New Testament and related to *mystery*).[186] He has been thoroughly *initiated* into it by the experiences of life applied to the heart by the Holy Spirit. To those who fear him God reveals this mystery (Ps. 25:14). Those who reject Christ cannot understand how it is possible for a Christian to remain calm in adversity, humble in prosperity.

The words in the present passage which require some elucidation are the following:

to live in straitened circumstances

Again and again Paul had been "brought low," same verb as used with reference to Christ in Phil. 2:8, the Christ who *humbled* himself. That the apostle indeed knew what it meant to be reduced to such straitened circumstances is clear from the following passages: Acts 14:19; 16:22-25; 17:13; 18:12; 20:3; Chapters 21-27; II Cor. 4:11; 6:4, 5; 11:27, 33. He knew what was meant by hunger, thirst, fasting, cold, nakedness, physical suffering, mental torture, persecution, etc.

to be hungry

Hunger and thirst are often mentioned together (Rom. 12:20; I Cor. 4:11; II Cor. 11:27; and cf. for spiritual yearning, Matt. 5:6). In glory there will be neither hunger nor thirst (Rev. 7:16), and this because of Christ's submission to these afflictions for his own children (Luke 4:2).

to be in want

The apostle had often *fallen behind*. He had suffered from *lack* of such comforts as many other people would have considered necessities. He had *come short*. Yet, none of these things had deprived him of his contentment.

Over against the expressions indicating poverty and affliction are those referring to riches and glory:

to have plenty

Before his conversion Paul has been a prominent Pharisee. The future looked bright and promising. Paul had had plenty, and this in more ways than one. Yet, he had lacked the greatest boon of all: Christ-centered peace of soul. But even after his conversion there had been moments of refreshment when even physically he had experienced what it meant, in a sense, to have plenty (Acts 16:15, 40; 16:33, 34; 20:11; 28:2; Phil. 4:15, 16, 18), and now no longer apart from but in connection with peace of soul. Now, to carry oneself properly in the midst of plenty is no easy matter (Prov. 30:8;

---

[186] On the verb μυέω see Bornkamm, Th.W.N.T., Vol. 4, p. 834. It is not necessary to suppose that the word was "borrowed from the mystery-cults." Nor is it at all certain that Paul's frequent use of the cognate noun *mystery* has been taken over from these cults. To Paul a mystery is a truth which, had it not been for special divine revelation, would not have been known.

Mark 10:23-25). As the adage has it, "In order to carry a full cup one must have a steady hand." Paul, however, by the grace of the Holy Spirit had been schooled to abundance as well as to want.

to be filled

This word, though used at first with respect to the feeding and fattening of animals (of which meaning there is an echo in the clause: "all the birds *gorged themselves* with their flesh," Rev. 19:21), and applied to men chiefly by the Comic poets, was gradually losing its depreciatory sense and is here simply used as a synonym for *to have plenty.*

13. Paul, then, is saying that *in every particular circumstance as well as in all circumstances generally* he has learned the secret of contentment. The cause that accounts for this soul-sufficiency, that is, the Person who taught and is constantly teaching him this secret, is indicated in the words, **I can do all things in him** [187] **who infuses strength into me.** Surely, a wonderful testimony! Whatever needs to be done Paul can do, for he is *in Christ* (Phil. 3:9), being by the indwelling presence of Christ's Spirit and by Spirit-wrought faith in vital union and intimate fellowship with his Lord and Savior. Christ's grace is sufficient for him and his power rests on him (II Cor. 12:9). This wonderful Helper is standing by him (II Tim. 4:17) as the great Enabler (I Tim. 1:12). The Lord is for Paul the Fountain of Wisdom, encouragement, and energy, actually infusing strength into him for every need. It is for that reason that the apostle is even able to say, "Wherefore I take pleasure in infirmities, in insults, in distresses, in persecutions and frustrations, for when I am weak, then I am strong" (II Cor. 12:10).

---

14 Nevertheless, y o u did nobly in sharing my affliction. 15 Moreover, y o u Philippians yourselves also know that in the early days of the gospel, when I departed from Macedonia, not even a single church entered into partnership with me in an account of expenditures and receipts except y o u only; 16 for even when I was in Thessalonica y o u once and again sent me something to alleviate my need. 17 Not that I seek the gift, but I seek the fruit which increases to y o u r credit. 18 But I have received payment in full and am enjoying abundance. I am amply supplied, having received from Epaphroditus the gifts (that came) from y o u, a fragrant odor, a sacrifice acceptable, well-pleasing to God.

4:14-18

II. *Thank-y o u Note Resumed and Completed*

The Thank-y o u note is now resumed (from verse 10) and completed. The apostle indicates the relation of the gift to:

---

[187] The reading Χριστῷ at the end of the sentence is wanting in the best manuscripts. It was probably added for the sake of clarity, influenced by such passages as II Cor. 12:9, 10; I Tim. 1:12; II Tim. 4:17.

(1) *himself the recipient:* it relieved his need and brought joy to his heart (verses 10, 14-16, 18a).

(2) *the givers:* it enriched them (verse 17).

(3) *God:* it was well-pleasing to him (verse 18b).

14. Paul is careful not to leave the impression that the gift had been superfluous and that he did not appreciate it. On the contrary, he indicates that he was definitely pleased with it. Hence, he says, **Nevertheless, y o u did nobly in sharing my affliction.** It was, says Paul as it were, *a noble, a beautiful deed,* like that of Mary of Bethany (Mark 14:6). Had the Philippians not been true sympathizers, so that they felt Paul's affliction as if it were their very own, they would not have performed their generous deed. The gift indicated that they had made common cause with Paul's affliction, were true sharers in it. Truly, the *fellowship* (see on Phil. 1:5) was operating beautifully!

15, 16. Paul continues, **Moreover, y o u Philippians yourselves also know that in the early days of the gospel, when I departed from Macedonia, not even a single church entered into partnership with me in an account of expenditures and receipts but y o u only.** Paul gratefully acknowledges the fact that the present gift was the continuation of a series of gifts. He mentions something well-known to both the Philippians and himself, namely, that when the Philippian church was *in its infancy,* having just been established — this was at least a decade ago — then already, in those early days of gospel-proclamation in their region, they, and *they alone,* had entered into partnership with himself in (and here follows a business-term) *an account of expenditures and receipts,* that is, an account in which the Philippians were the givers, Paul the receiver. Defining the occasion more exactly as to time, the apostle says that this generosity had been shown in connection with his departure from Macedonia (in which Philippi and nearby Thessalonica were located), a rather sudden departure, as Acts 17:14 indicates. The friends in Philippi had heard about Paul's troubles in Thessalonica and had immediately rushed to his aid in a material way, enabling him to continue his work elsewhere (in Achaia: Athens and Corinth; cf. II Cor. 11:8, 9). Nor was this all, **for even when I was in Thessalonica y o u once and again sent me something to alleviate my need.** This help which had been given during Paul's work in Thessalonica naturally even preceded his departure from Macedonia. So young a church, that of Philippi, yet so prompt and spontaneous in extending help! Truly the stamp of Luke's and Lydia's commendable generosity was upon this congregation! See Introduction, III.

17. Paul's fear of being misunderstood when he speaks about receiving gifts appears again and again, no doubt because his enemies were constantly misconstruing his motives (II Cor. 11:7; 12:14; I Thess. 2:3, 5, 8). If he accepted a gift or if his enemies suspected that he did, they were ready to charge him with selfishness, greed; if he did not, they accused him of making a show of his humility. Yet, in the final analysis it was not the gift but the giver that was the object of Paul's concern. Hence, he says, **Not that I seek the gift, but I seek the fruit which increases to y o u r account.** Note again the business-term *account.* The gift was really *an investment* entered *as a credit* on *the account* of the Philippians, an investment which is increasingly paying them rich dividends. These *dividends* or *fruits* in the lives of his friends are the object of Paul's concern. In this letter he has already mentioned fruits (Phil. 1:11), and he does so also elsewhere (Rom. 1:13; 7:4; Gal. 5:22, 23; Eph. 5:9; Col. 1:6). Right giving always enriches the giver. "The liberal soul will be made fat" (Prov. 11:25). "He who pities the poor lends to the Lord" (Prov. 19:17). "Blessed are the merciful, for they will obtain mercy" (Matt. 5:7). "God loves a cheerful giver" (II Cor. 9:7). And cf. also Luke 21:1-4. Among the fruits that are harvested by such givers may be mentioned the following: a good conscience, assurance of salvation, enriched fellowship with other believers, a broadened outlook into the needs and interests of the church universal, increased joy and love (both of these imparted and received), a higher degree of glory in heaven, Judgment Day praise.

18. In all probability commercial phraseology is continued in the words, **But I have received payment in full and am enjoying abundance.** According to the evidence supplied by papyri and ostraca the term *apecho* (ἀπέχω) here used has the meaning "I have received." The technical sense is, "This is my receipt." A. Deissmann (*Light From the Ancient East*, fourth edition, pp. 111, 112, 331) also informs us that in receipts *apecho* is frequently (as also here in Phil. 4:18) combined with *panta* (πάντα), meaning *everything* that was owed, *full payment.* In a more or less humorous manner, therefore, the apostle is here saying, "I have received full payment, and even more" (or "and am affluent," thus Erdman). He continues, **I am amply supplied, having received from Epaphroditus the gifts (that came) from y o u.** Just what was included in those gifts we are not told. Possibilities: money to cover expenses, reading material, clothes (cf. II Tim. 4:13 for the last two items for which Paul asks at a later occasion). On Epaphroditus see Phil. 2:25-30. The finest thing that can be said about these gifts is this: they are described as a **fragrant odor, a sacrifice acceptable, wellpleasing to God.** Higher praise even Paul could not have bestowed upon the givers. The gifts are "an odor of a sweet smell," "an offering presented to God, welcome and very pleasing to him." They are comparable to the thank-offering of Abel (Gen. 4:4), of Noah (Gen. 8:21), of the Israelites when in the proper frame of mind they brought whole-burnt-offerings (Lev.

1:9, 13, 17), and of believers generally in dedicating their lives to God
(II Cor. 2:15, 16), as did also Christ, but he in a unique manner (Eph. 5:2).
Whether or not an offering is really acceptable and well-pleasing to God
(cf. Rom. 12:1) depends on the motive of the one who brings it (Gen. 4:1-15;
Heb. 11:4).

> "Not what we give but what we share,
> For the gift without the giver is bare."
> (Lowell)

The apostle credits the givers with the proper spirit, that is, the attitude of
faith, love, and gratitude. He acknowledges that their deed was not merely
an act of sympathy shown to a friend in need but a genuine offering presented to God to promote his cause, and thus to Paul as God's representative! That made the deed so grand and beautiful!

---

19 And my God will gloriously supply every need of y o u r s according to
his riches in Christ Jesus. 20 Now to our God and Father (be) the glory forever
and ever. Amen.

4:19, 20

III. Assurance of God's Loving Care. Doxology

A. Assurance of God's Loving Care

19. Approaching the end of his epistle Paul now assures the addressees
that God will supply their every need: **And my God will gloriously supply
every need of y o u r s according to his riches in Christ Jesus.** Had not God's
care rested in a marvelous manner upon the apostle himself, during this
very imprisonment? Note Paul's later testimony regarding this care: "But
the Lord stood by my side and gave me strength in order that through me
the message might be fully heralded, and all the Gentiles might hear it.
And I was rescued out of (the) mouth of (the) lion" (II Tim. 4:17). So
also this same compassion would bless the Philippians. Touching is the
expression *"my* God." See on Phil. 1:3. It was the God who meant so very,
very much to Paul. This God will not fulfill *every wish* but will supply
every need! He will do this "in glory," which in the sense of *gloriously*
must in all probability be construed as modifying the verb *supply;* hence,
"God will gloriously supply." Paul is not primarily thinking of what God
will do for believers when they have entered the glory of heaven, but what
he will do for them in this earthly realm of needs, as they present these needs
to him. These he will fulfill not merely *out of* his riches (as a millionaire
might do when he donates a trifling sum to a good cause, subtracting the
amount from his vast possessions) but *according to* his riches, so that the

209

gift is actually *in proportion to* God's infinite resources! Of course, this loving care, this glorious help in need, is based on the merits of Christ Jesus. "How vast the benefits divine which we *in Christ* possess" (cf. Rom. 8:32). It is only because believers are in vital union with him that they receive all these bounties.

The assurance of this manifestation of God's *very special providence* [188] does not mean that the Philippians would now be justified in becoming lazy, disregarding or even rejecting every means and avenue of caring for themselves. "God's word does not advocate fanaticism, nor does it say that one should throw his pocketbook into the nearest river and then announce that he is going to live by faith" (Tenney). To be sure, God was taking care of Paul, but one of the ways in which he was providing for him was the gift from Philippi which Paul here acknowledges.

Among the many passages in which this tender and loving care of God for his children in the *here* and *now* is described, passages which have given comfort to God's people in many generations, are also the following: Gen. 28:15; 50:20; Exod. 33:14; Deut. 2:7; 32:7-14; 33:27; Josh. 1:9; I Sam. 7:12; I Kings 17:6, 16; II Chron. 20:17; Ps. 18:35; 23; 31:19; 91; 121; Isa. 25:4, 32:2; 40:11; 41:10; 43:1, 2; 46:3, 4; Joel 2:21-27; Mal. 3:10; Matt. 6:32; 14:20; 23:37; Luke 6:38; 12:7; 22:35; John 10:27, 28; 17:11; Rom. 8:28, 31-39; II Tim. 1:12; 4:18; I Peter 5:7.

4:20

B. *Doxology*

20. For Paul doctrine is never a dry matter. Whenever it occupies his mind it also fills his heart with praise. Hence, reflecting on this marvelous care which God bestows on his children he exclaims, **Now to our God and Father (be) the glory forever and ever. Amen.** Note *"our* God and Father,"* through Christ, of course. To this God who in his Son is the Father *of all believers* Paul ascribes *adoration*. See on Phil. 1:11 for detailed word-study of the concept *glory*. The ardent yearning of the apostle's heart is that all God's redeemed children will do their utmost to give *never-ending* praises unto their God, praises "for the ages of the ages," that is, *forever and ever*. The solemn Amen, a word of affirmation or confirmation, underscores the fact that the doxology is not merely a matter of the lips or of the "pen" but is the spontaneous utterance of the heart redeemed by grace. Paul's epistles

---

[188] I am here using the familiar terminology favored by those theologians who distinguish between God's *general providence* over all his creatures, including even plants and animals; his *special* providence over all his rational creatures, including all men, both believers and unbelievers; and his *very special providence* of which believers are the objects. See L. Berkhof, *Systematic Theology*, p. 168.

abound in doxologies. For this see above, on Phil. 3:18, 19, under the heading *Paul's Deeply Emotional Nature.*

---

21 Greet every saint in Christ Jesus. The brothers (who are) with me greet y o u. 22 All the saints greet y o u, especially those of Caesar's household. 23 The grace of the Lord Jesus Christ (be) with y o u r spirit.

4:21-23

IV. *Conclusion*

4:21, 22

A. *Words of Greeting*

21. It is entirely possible that Paul wrote these last three verses with his own hand (see N.T.C. on II Thess. 3:17). To every member of the church of Philippi who by virtue of union with Christ Jesus has been set apart to a life of consecration to the Lord the apostle sends his greeting as a token of brotherly love: **Greet every saint in Christ Jesus.** He adds, **The brothers (who are) with me greet y o u.** Paul's fellow-workers in Rome, having heard that Paul is sending a letter to the Philippians, have asked that their greetings, too, be extended. Some see here a discrepancy or inconsistency. They point to the fact that elsewhere in this same epistle the apostle has spoken disparagingly about this group of colleagues (see on 1:15a, 17; 2:21). So, how can he now convey their kind regards? The following, however, should be noted:

(1) One of the fellow-workers was Timothy. Paul has had nothing but good to say about him (Phil. 1:1; 2:20, 22).

(2) There were also others, with reference to whom Paul had already said that they were "heralding Christ from good will . . . out of love, knowing that I am appointed for the defense of the gospel" (1:15b, 16a).

(3) The so-called contradiction results from a too absolutistic interpretation of Phil. 2:21 (see on that passage).

(4) And if even some of the envious colleagues (who nevertheless, preached soundly!) had joined in asking Paul to convey their greetings, would this have been refused?

22. Paul continues, **All the saints greet y o u.** The circle of greeters widens now so that it includes all believers in Rome. They all tender their regards and good wishes, for

"In Christ there is no East or West,
In him no South or North;

211

But one great fellowship of Love
Throughout the whole, wide earth."
(John Oxenham)

Paul believed very strongly in ecumenicity of the highest type, ecumenicity indeed, but without sacrifice of the truth. Did he not during this same imprisonment devote an epistle to the theme, *The Unity of All Believers in Christ* (Ephesians)? Had he not been the active promoter of a collection for the needy saints in Jerusalem (read II Cor., Chapters 8 and 9)? Was he not the author of I Cor. 12 and 13? How he loved to send to the saints of *Philippi* the greetings from all the saints in *Rome* (cf. John 17:20, 21). Truly, this was not just a merely formal, polite, customary way of ending a letter. These greetings were "from the heart to the heart." The fellowship was functioning (see on Phil. 1:5). Paul adds, **especially those of Caesar's household.**[189] This expression does not as such refer to the emperor's blood-relatives. It refers rather to all persons in the emperor's service, whether slaves or freedmen. Such people who had been given employment in the domestic and administrative establishment of the emperor were found not only in Italy but even in the provinces. Nevertheless, it is rather questionable reasoning to base on this circumstance the conclusion that, therefore, the epistle to the Philippians may have originated outside of Rome, say in Ephesus or Caesarea. No matter how far and wide Caesar's household extended, its heart and center was in Rome and consisted of *servants in and about the emperor's palace.* Besides, Phil. 4:22 does not stand alone. There is, for example, also the reference to "the whole praetorian guard" (Phil. 1:13). Taken together and in connection with similar additional evidence which has been discussed in the Introduction everything points to Rome.

Why did *especially* these members of Caesar's household send their greetings? We simply do not know. The following are among the guesses that have been made. It is impossible to establish which (if any) of these reasons, or which combination of them, furnishes the true answer to the question.

(1) Philippi was a colony; hence, had many servants employed by the government. Because of the work they performed these were acquainted with similar government employees in Rome.

(2) These members of Caesar's household were earlier converts to Christianity. They had become believers before Paul arrived in Rome (see the long list of names in Romans 16); hence, there had been more time for them to establish contact with believers elsewhere, particularly also in Philippi.

(3) It is a known fact that a considerable percentage of those who be-

---

[189] On this see the following: J. B. Lightfoot's *Commentary on St. Paul's Epistle to the Philippians,* pp. 171-178; entry οἰκία in L.N.T. (A. and G.); and the article on this word in Th.W.N.T., Vol. 5, p. 136.

longed to Caesar's household in Rome had come from regions east of Rome. Hence, those — or at least some of those — who were sending these special greetings may have come from Macedonia, and therefore wished to be remembered to their friends and relatives.

Far more important is the fact that Christianity had entered even the circles of these palace-servants. Their position in the midst of a definitely pagan environment in which by many the emperor was worshiped as if he were a god, did not keep them from remaining true to their only Lord and Savior, from spreading the good news to others, and from strengthening the church in Philippi by means of their greetings. Eternity will tell what great blessings must have resulted from lives dedicated to Christ amid such worldly surroundings!

4:23

B. *Benediction*

23. The best textual evidence supports the reading which can be rendered, **The grace of the Lord Jesus Christ (be) with y o u r spirit.**[190] One is reminded immediately of Gal. 6:18 and Philem. 25; but see also I Cor. 16:23; I Thess. 5:28; II Thess. 3:18; and II Tim. 4:22. Picture the situation when this letter, having been delivered by Epaphroditus to the overseers and deacons at Philippi (see on Phil. 1:1), is at their order, read to the Philippian congregation, assembled for worship. Upon them all, thus gathered with God's Spirit in their midst, Paul the apostle, as God's official representative, pronounces God's grace, that is, God's unmerited favor in the Anointed Lord and Savior, based on his merits, conveyed by his Spirit. If this pronouncement is accepted with a believing heart, then from this basic blessing of grace all others flow forth, filling the very spirit, the inner personality viewed as contact-point between God and his child, with the peace of God that surpasses all understanding!

Synthesis of 4:10-23

For this see the Summary at the beginning of this section.

Seed-thoughts of 4:10-23

(1) The Christian is neither too proud nor too thoughtless to say, "Thank you" (verse 10).

(2) Deeds of kindness resemble a tree putting forth fresh shoots (verse 10).

(3) It is easy to find *excuses* to cover *real* neglect on our own part; it re-

---

[190] p[46], Aleph A, the Koine, D most witnesses, Vulgate, and important Syriac translations add Amen, which is wanting in B, G and some other MSS.

quires grace to search out *reasons* for *seeming* neglect on the part of others (verse 10).

(4) One is not *born* with contentment; it must be *learned* (verse 11).

(5) Contentment is a jewel which no amount of gold or silver can buy and which does not depend on outward circumstances (verses 11, 12).

(6) The Author of true contentment is the indwelling, strength-imparting Christ (verse 13).

(7) Sharing your goods with a person in need is good and necessary. Sharing his affliction is even better. The first should be done in the spirit of the second (verse 14).

(8) Kindnesses which others have shown us in the past should be remembered and recalled (verses 15 and 16).

(9) *The fruit* is even more important than *the gift* (verse 17).

(10) The giver enriches two people: the recipient and himself (verse 17).

(11) True gifts are fragrant offerings (verse 18).

(12) When God gives us anything he does so *according to* (and not merely *out of*) his riches (verse 19).

(13) The climax of Christian speech, whether spoken or written, is the doxology. In fact, the Christian breathes doxologies (verse 20).

(14) If among the early Christians there were those who belonged to *Nero's* "household," today's government-employees in far more favorable circumstances will have great difficulty when they try to find an excuse for failing to bear witness for Christ (verse 22).

(15) In the final analysis our entire salvation from start to finish depends on God's sovereign favor in Jesus Christ (verse 23).

SELECT BIBLIOGRAPHY

An attempt has been made to make this list *as small as possible.*

Calvin, John, *Commentarius In Epistolam Pauli Ad Philippenses (Corpus Reformatorum,* vol. LXXX), Brunsvigae, 1895; English translation (in *Calvin's Commentaries*), Grand Rapids, 1948.
Lightfoot, J. B., *St. Paul's Epistle to the Philippians,* reprint Grand Rapids, 1953.
Vincent, M. R., *The Epistles to the Philippians and to Philemon* (in *The International Critical Commentary*), New York, 1906.

GENERAL BIBLIOGRAPHY

Barclay, W., *The Letters to the Philippians, Colossians, and Thessalonians* (in *The Daily Study Bible Series*) , second edition, Philadelphia, 1959.

Barnes, A., *Notes on the New Testament, Ephesians, Philippians and Colossians,* reprint Grand Rapids, 1949.

Barth, K., *Erklärung des Philipperbriefes,* Zürich, 1927.

Beare, F. W., *The Epistle to the Philippians* (in *Harper's New Testament Commentaries*) , New York, 1958.

Braune, K., *The Epistle of Paul to the Philippians* (in *Lange's Commentary on the Holy Scriptures*) , Vol. VII, reprint, Grand Rapids.

Brewer, R. R., "The Meaning of POLITEUESTHE in Philippians 1:27," *JBL* 73, Part II (June, 1954) , 76-83.

Bullfinch, T., *The Age of Fable,* New York, 1942.

Calvin, John, *Commentarius In Epistolam Pauli Ad Philippenses (Corpus Reformatorum,* vol. LXXX) , Brunsvigae, 1895; English translation (in *Calvin's Commentaries*) , Grand Rapids, 1948.

Campbell, J. Y., "Koinonia and its Cognates in the New Testament," *JBL* 51 (1932) , 352-380.

Cobern, C. M., *The New Archaeological Discoveries and Their Bearing upon the New Testament,* seventh edition, New York and London, 1924.

Collart, P., *Philippes, ville de Macédoine depuis ses origines jusqu'à la fin de l'époque romaine,* Paris, 1937.

Conybeare, W. J., and Howson, J. S., *The Life and Epistles of St. Paul,* reprint Grand Rapids, 1949.

Cranfield, C. E. B., "Fellowship, Communion" (in *A Theological Word Book of the Bible,* A. Richardson, editor) , New York, 1952.

Deissmann, A., *Light From the Ancient East* (translated by L. R. M. Strachan) , New York, 1927.

Dibelius, M., *An die Thessalonicher I–II. An die Philipper* (in H. Lietzmann's *Handbuch zum Neuen Testament)* , third edition revised, Tübingen, 1937.

Duncan, G. S., *St. Paul's Ephesian Ministry,* New York, 1930.

Endenburg, P. J. T., *Koinonia bij de Grieken in den klassieken tijd,* 1937.

Erdman, C. R., *The Epistle of Paul to the Philippians,* Philadelphia, 1932.

Ewald, P., *Der Brief des Paulus an die Philipper* (in T. Zahn's *Kommentar zum Neuen Testament,* XI.) , Leipzig and Erlangen, 1923.

Ford, H. W., "The New Testament Conception of Fellowship," *Shane Quarterly* 6 (1945) 188-215.

Greijdanus, S., *Bizondere Canoniek,* Kampen, 1949, two volumes.

Greijdanus, S., *De Brief van den Apostel Paulus aan de Gemeente te Philippi* (in *Kommentaar op het Nieuwe Testament,* Vol. IX, part 2) , Amsterdam, 1937.

Greijdanus, S., *De Brief van den Apostel Paulus aan de Philippenzen* (in *Korte Verklaring der Heilige Schrift)* , Kampen, 1949.

Griffiths, D. R., " Harpagmos and heauton ekenōsen in Phil. 2:6, 7," *Ex.T*69, No. 8 (1958) , 237-239.

PHILIPPIANS

Groenewald, E. P., *Koinonia (gemeenskap) bij Paulus*, doctoral dissertation, Amsterdam, 1932.

Grollenberg, L. H., *Atlas of the Bible*, London and Edinburgh, 1956.

Grosheide, F. W., *De Openbaring Gods in het Nieuwe Testament*, Kampen, 1953.

Harrison, P. N., *Polycarp's Two Letters to the Philippians*, London, 1936.

Hendriksen, W., *Bible Survey*, Grand Rapids, Mich., sixth printing, 1961.

Hendriksen, W., *More Than Conquerors, An Interpretation of the Book of Revelation*, Grand Rapids, eleventh edition, 1961.

Hendriksen, W., *The Bible on the Life Hereafter*, Grand Rapids, 1959.

Heuzey, L., and Daumet, H., *Mission archeologique de la Macedoine*, Paris, 1876.

Jourdon, G. V., "Koinonia in I Cor. 10:16," *JBL* 67 (1938), 111-124.

Keller, W., *The Bible As History*, New York, 1957.

Kennedy, H. A. A., *The Epistle to the Philippians* (in *The Expositor's Greek Testament*, Vol. III), Grand Rapids.

Kraeling, E. G., *Rand McNally Bible Atlas*, New York, 1956.

Laurin, L. R., *Where Life Advances*, Wheaton, Ill., 1954.

Lenski, R. C. H., *The Interpretation of St. Paul's Epistles to the Galatians, to the Ephesians, and to the Philippians*, Columbus, Ohio, 1937.

Lightfoot, J. B., *St. Paul's Epistle to the Philippians*, reprint Grand Rapids, 1953.

Loeb Classical Library, New York (various dates), for The Apostolic Fathers, Josephus, Eusebius, Homer, Herodotus, Plutarch, Strabo, etc.

Lohmeyer, E., *Die Briefe an die Philipper, an die Kolosser und an Philemon* (in Meyer's Kommentar), Göttingen, 1930.

Marsh, F. B., *A History of the Roman World from 146-30 B. C.*, second edition, London, 1953.

Martin, R. P., *The Epistle of Paul to the Philippians* (in *The Tyndale New Testament Commentaries*), Grand Rapids, 1959.

Michael, J. H., *The Epistle of Paul to the Philippians* (in *The Moffat New Testament Commentary*), New York, 1929.

Müller, J. J., *The Epistles of Paul to the Philippians and to Philemon* (in *The New International Commentary on the New Testament*), Grand Rapids, 1955.

Mund, J., *Paul and the Salvation of Mankind*, Richmond, Va., 1959.

National Geographic Magazine, "Lands of the Bible Today" (Dec. 1956); in the same issue, "Jerusalem to Rome in the Path of St. Paul." Also published by National Geographic: *Everyday Life in Ancient Times*, 1953.

Paulus, H. E. G., *Philologisch-kritischer Kommentar über das Neue Testament*, Lübeck, 1800.

Robertson, A. T., *Word Pictures in the New Testament*, New York and London, 1931, Vol. IV.

Rowlingson, D., "Paul's Ephesian Imprisonment, An Evaluation of the Evidence," *Anglican Theological Review* XXXII (1950), 1-7.

Schaff-Herzog Encyclopaedia of Religious Knowledge, The New, thirteen volumes, edition Grand Rapids, 1950. The articles which have been consulted are not listed separately in this Bibliography.

Schmid, J., *Zeit und Ort der Paulinischen Gefangenschafts-briefe*, 1931.

Scott, E. F., *The Epistle to the Philippians* (in *The Interpreter's Bible*, Vol. XI), New York and Nashville.

Shakespeare, W., *Julius Caesar;* also *Antony and Cleopatra*.

Shaw, G. B., *Caesar and Cleopatra*.

Smolders, D., "L'audace de L'apôtre selon saint Paul. Le thème de la parrêsia," *Coll Mech* 43 (Feb. 1958), 117-133.

PHILIPPIANS

Tenney, M. C., *Philippians: The Gospel at Work*, Grand Rapids, 1956.

The Good News, The New Testament with over 500 illustrations and maps, published by the American Bible Society, New York, 1955.

Tucker, T. G., *Life in the Roman World of Nero and St. Paul*, New York, 1922.

Van Til, C., "Karl Barth on Chalcedon," *W.Th.J.* (May, 1960) , 147-166.

Vincent, M. R., *The Epistles to the Philippians and to Philemon* (in *The International Critical Commentary*) , New York, 1906.

Warfield, B. B., *Christology and Criticism*, New York, 1929.

Wells, H. G., *The Outline of History*, Star-edition, Garden City, New York, 1930.

Wright, E., *Biblical Archaeology*, London, 1957.

Wuest K. S., *Philippians in the Greek New Testament*, Grand Rapids, 1942.

Wuest, K. S., *Philippians Through the Revelation, An Expanded Translation*, Grand Rapids, 1959.

NEW TESTAMENT COMMENTARY